FAITH
SPOKEN

Communicating In the
Fourth Dimension

Dr. Leslie Gamble Jr.

PPH Books
Stafford, Virginia USA

Faith Spoken–Communicating in the Fourth Dimension
by Dr. Leslie Gamble, Jr.

Parsons Publishing House
P. O. Box 488, Stafford, VA 22554 USA
www.ParsonsPublishingHouse.com
Info@ParsonsPublishingHouse.com

ISBN -13: 978-1-60273-033-5
ISBN -10: 160273-033-4

Printed in the United States of America.
For World-Wide Distribution.

DEDICATION

To My Dear Sister Jean and Her Husband

It is an honor to dedicate my third book, **Faith Spoken—Communicating in the Fourth Dimension,** to my oldest sister, Sandra "Jean" Gamble Noel. I can truly say while we were children, it was Jean who was our caretaker when mother worked outside the home. Jean was responsible for cleaning the house and baby-sitting all of the children. There were at times up to four to five young children to baby-sit, even though she too was a very young child. As the oldest, she had to learn responsibilities at an early age. She did it well and cared for her young brothers and sisters willingly and cheerfully.

When Jean got old enough to work outside the home, she would take me with her on the public transit bus to the mall, McDonald's, and other places. Mother would often have me waiting for Jean to get off the bus from work on Duvall Street. It was one of the few things I did not mind doing when told. When Jean would step off the bus, she would always greet me by saying, "Hey Bay!"

Jean bought food and groceries for the family and clothes for all her siblings while working. It was a blessing to have additional financial support in the house which Jean provided with love. Jean, this book honors your commitment to family and represents a reflection of how God speaks to you in dreams and visions. God has made exceedingly great and precious promises to you (2 Peter 1:4). Thank you, Jean, for your steadfast love, unyielding faith, persistent prayers, and continued encouragement to me throughout the years. May heaven smile upon you and your family!

Also, I would like to devote this book to Jean's husband, Wilbur "Teddy" Noel, my brother-in-law. Teddy, you have been a tremendous blessing to the Gamble family. From the moment I met you, you have always been a generous, caring, and loving person. God blessed my sister, Jean, with a wonderful husband. After graduating from college and trying to find a career job, I stayed with Jean and Teddy in Memphis, Tennessee. Teddy treated me like one of the family. I never felt isolated or rejected while living with him on Shagbark Court. Teddy, you have been a constant inspiration to me as a career man, father, and husband. May you continue to prosper in your health, mind, and spirit. May God allow you to be the light and catalyst which brings the entire Noel family and clan to know Christ in a very special and intimate way by what God has done supernaturally through you.

It is my prayer for you both, as written by the Apostle Jude which says, "Now unto him that is able to keep you from falling, and to present you faultless before the presence of his glory with exceeding joy, to the only wise God our Saviour, be glory and majesty, dominion and power, both now and ever. Amen (Jude 24)." Wishing you all the best...!

TABLE OF CONTENTS

PREFACE

The third dimension is the physical realm related to Earth and its surroundings. However, the fourth dimension is a higher and more superior dimension than the third dimension. It is the dimension where God operates and functions. The fourth dimension is a supernatural dimension in which God desires for us to dwell [with him] while on planet Earth. Acts 17:28 says, "For in him we live, and move, and have our being."

The fourth dimension and the third dimension can be compared to God's thoughts versus man's thoughts. God said in Isaiah 55:8-9, "For my thoughts are not your thoughts, neither are your ways my ways, saith the Lord, For as the heavens are higher than the earth, So are my ways higher than your ways, And my thoughts than your thoughts."

The fourth dimension is a glorious and godly realm. It represents a greater realm of knowledge, wisdom, and understanding. It is a realm of epic proportions. The fourth dimension is indescribable and inconceivable to the finite mind. Our minds cannot fathom the vast reality and depth of the fourth dimension due to its vicissitude or difference from the finite world.

First Corinthians 2:9 (NLT) says, "No eye has seen, no ear has heard, and no mind has imagined what God has prepared for those who love him." The fourth dimension is so infinitely remote from our third dimensional reality that it is immensely overwhelming and mind boggling.

The Apostle Paul was privileged by God, to experience the fourth dimension which he called the third heaven. Paul said in 2 Corinthians 12:2 that he was caught up into Paradise, the third heaven, and heard inexpressible words, which a man is not permitted to speak. In other words, Paul saw and heard things so astounding in the fourth dimension that no one would believe him even if he told them!

Although the Holy Spirit and the Word of God are our two premier sources of communication to God and from God, there are other devices God uses to commune with His people. In addition to the Holy Spirit and the Word of God, this book highlights other modes of communication in the fourth dimension. Modes of communication are simply portals and passageways God uses to interact with us.

This book, **Faith Spoken–Communicating In The Fourth Dimension** is part three of a ten series collection of books. The first book is called **Faith Driven, A Journey Into The Fourth Dimension**. The second book is called **Faith Proven, The Key To The Fourth Dimension**. As with the other two books, this book opens up with a poem honoring the eternal power and love of the Holy Spirit. Every chapter is introduced by a poem acknowledging the Holy Spirit or the power of faith. Each chapter will allow us to become more familiar with a dimension many know little about called the fourth dimension. We will explore the role angels play as messengers, guardians, and protectors in the fourth dimension.

Moreover, we will discover two special fourth dimensional gifts God has given us, in which the church as a whole has yet to embrace, which are dreams and visions. Dreams and visions are portals or dimensional openings God uses to download instruction, knowledge, and wisdom unavailable in the natural world. The Bible specifically tells us in Job 33:14-15 (NLT), "But God speaks again and again, though people do not recognize it. He speaks in dreams, in visions of the night when deep sleep falls on people as they lie in bed."

God speaks to us more often than we know. Many of us wonder why God does not speak to us as He has done for many others, not comprehending that God May have spoken to us last night in a dream or vision. Oftentimes, we dismiss what we think are silly and foolish dreams never realizing that it is God who is speaking face to face with us.

We will discover that God has systems of communication He uses to transmit messages and pertinent information to us. Other dimensional portals or channels of communication include the heart, prayer, praise, and worship.

Lastly, this book is jammed packed with faith-filled messages concerning God's promised blessings for those who are part of the fourth dimension. God has promised recipients of the fourth dimension a level of prosperity unknown in past generations. Without further delay, let's delve into the realm of the fourth dimension.

Holy Spirit

Holy Spirit, the fourth dimension is known in You,

Holy Spirit, only by faith will God's children see your truth;

Holy Spirit, eyes have not seen neither have ears heard,

Holy Spirit, but if He said it we will believe His holy Word;

Holy Spirit, this supernatural way is God's way,

Holy Spirit, salvation in Christ forever we will stay;

Holy Spirit, the fourth dimension is in Him,

Holy Spirit, His light we take will never grow dim.

CHAPTER 1

The Physics of the Fourth Dimension

Physics is the science that involves the study of matter, time, and space. It attempts to explain the universe and how it behaves. Physics is involved in the fourth dimension, as well as the third dimension. The fourth dimension is a physical reality which involves fourth dimensional space. Fourth dimensional space is the extrinsic variable that holds the fourth dimension and all other dimensions in place.

In fact, the fourth dimension is more real and concrete than our current reality. The Bible says, "So we fix our eyes not on what is seen, but on what is unseen. For what is seen is temporary, but what is unseen is eternal" (2 Corinthians 4:18, NIV). The current reality and dimensions in which we live are only a reflection or a shadow of the real and physical eternal world. The Bible says in Colossians 2:17 (NIV), "These are a shadow of the things that were to come; the reality, however, is found in Christ." The authentic reality, which is in the fourth dimension, is found in Jesus Christ.

Just as our world is made up of third dimensional space which includes length, width, and height, the fourth dimension carries these elements, as well. However, there is another dimension (explained later) which is considered an abstract concept, but supports the rule of three-dimensional space. This additional dimension gives the fourth dimension endless flexibility, maneuverability, and adaptability. Correspondingly, the

1

fourth dimension is able to manipulate, interact, and influence the third dimension.

The fourth dimension has a supernatural element that is distinctive and foreign to anything known on Earth. The fourth dimension represents the "God factor." The "God factor" is the supernatural element of the fourth dimension. In essence, the eternal God is the additional dimension which makes up fourth dimensional space.

The dimensions of the third dimensional world can be altered and transformed by the fourth dimension. The limits and laws of the third dimension can be changed and suspended by the fourth dimension. The third dimension is the dimension in which we live. Our world is a dimension bound by length, width, and height.

Quantum physicists, who study the origin of matter, have theorized that there may be more than eleven dimensions moving linear or in a straight line. The fourth dimension, categorized here, does not move in the same direction or in a straight line as theorized by physicists. The fourth dimension is able to move in all directions, simultaneously, without restrictions or limitations. This dimension can defy the laws of physics and natural laws. Notwithstanding, the fourth dimension is able to move, interact, or coexist with the third dimensional world.

The fourth dimension is trans-dimensional meaning that the fourth dimension can manipulate time, space, and matter at will. The fourth dimension has the ability to transform and influence the third dimensional world. This influence, by the fourth dimension, is known as supernatural occurrences, miracles, wonders, or unexplainable phenomenon. This happens when the fourth dimension intersects or invades the third dimensional realm.

The fourth dimension represents the realm of impossibilities. When the fourth dimension interacts with the third dimension, impossibilities are possible; it is a realm where nothing is impossible. The fourth dimension is a realm which far exceeds the natural boundaries of time, space, and matter. It is a dimension of infinite space perpetuated by the supernatural.

Holy Spirit

Holy Spirit, the sweet aroma of Christ,

Holy Spirit, our only living sacrifice;

Holy Spirit, sweeter than honey dew,

Holy Spirit, precious God made us new;

Holy Spirit, life may have its ups and downs,

Holy Spirit, but it's better when you are around;

Holy Spirit, the sweet aroma of Christ,

Holy Spirit, the presence of God in all His might.

CHAPTER 2

The Latter Rain

There is nothing more refreshing than receiving a cool afternoon rain shower after a hot sweltering summer day. Rain water has the ability to relax and comfort us. All of creation enjoys the bliss of a rain shower after experiencing a blistering summer drought. Birds especially seem to enjoy the exhilarating bath shower that rain provides. They seem to dance and sing as the rain comes down in synchronization, rhythm, and harmony around them.

Personally, I like to take a nap during a rain shower. Rain is therapeutic; it brings restoration and healing. Rain affects everything it touches and brings a soothing change. However, there is another type of rain which is even more life-changing called the latter rain.

We are living in a critical time on the earth in which the promises of the latter rain, that had been foretold centuries ago, are now here. Because the latter rain is here, we must not allow anything to hinder us from God's end-time promises! 2 Corinthians 7:1 (NLT) says, "...Let us cleanse ourselves from everything that can defile our body or spirit. And let us work toward complete purity because we fear God."

God said in Zechariah 10:1, "Ask ye of the Lord rain in the time of the latter rain." In other words, God says to ask what we need and desire during the time of the latter rain. In ancient Palestine, the time of the latter rain was during the harvest/autumn season of the year. Like ancient Israel, God has a set time that He will pour out His Spirit and blessings upon His people. This is known as the time of the latter rain which represents the blessings of God.

Rain symbolizes cleansing, purification, and baptism. God said in Joel 3:21, "For I will cleanse their blood that I have not cleansed." God will pardon every guilt and sin during this set time. In this latter rain season, we must present ourselves pure and holy before God. The latter rain wants to wash you and make you clean. David said in Psalms 51:2, 7, "Wash me thoroughly from mine iniquity, and cleanse me from my sin. Purge me with hyssop and I shall be clean: wash me, and I shall be whiter than snow."

Anything can happen in the season of the latter rain which represents an entirely new season. Maybe your whole life has been one dry and sweltering hot season. Don't be discouraged, I've got good news! Your latter rain has come! The Apostle John records a man who had been lame for thirty-eight years. The Bible says in John 5:5-8,

"And a certain man was there, which had an infirmity thirty and eight years. When Jesus saw him lie, and knew that he had been now a long time in that case, he saith unto him, wilt thou be made whole? The impotent man answered him, sir, I have no man when the water in troubled, to put me into the pool: but while I am coming, another steppeth down before me. Jesus saith unto him, rise take up thy bed, and walk."

The lame man in the above passages of Scripture felt that he was a victim of unfortunate circumstances. He could not get anyone to help him get into the pool of Bethesda when the water was troubled. He was near the pool of healing water, but far from being healed. He was by the water, but due to his condition, he may as well have been miles away in the desert. His physical condition limited his ability to be successful in life.

Notice what Jesus, who represents the latter rain, said to him. Jesus said: Do you want to be made whole (John 5:6)? Listen, it does not matter how long you have been in your situation. You can be made whole! The late Walter Hawkins sang a song saying, "You don't have to stay in the shape that you're in; the Potter wants to put you back together again."[1]

Jesus is now ready and willing to meet your every need. The latter rain has come! Jesus has come as He did for the man who had been lame for thirty-eight years. Like the lame man, there are now no more excuses for why we can't be healed, restored, renewed, revived or be made whole.

Jesus has come into your presence via this book to let you know you no longer need anyone to lift you up (like the lame man thought he did). You now have the power to move, walk, thrive, be fruitful, and prosper. He has given you the power to triumph through any adversity, to conquer every obstacle, and be victorious over any circumstance.

Will you be made whole? God said in Leviticus 26:3-4, "If ye walk in my statues, and keep my commandments, and do them; then I will give you rain in due season, and the land shall yield her increase, and the trees of the field shall yield their fruit." Many of the "water wells" in our lives have been dry and desolate, but God is about to make those "dry wells" gush with fresh flowing spring water.

Have you seen the type of rain-shower which flows steadily and is able to saturate the ground to make the soil fertile and moist? This is what the latter rain has done in the spirit. Are you ready to experience the abundant harvest it provides? The latter rain represents rebirth and new growth. God is taking us to new levels and new dimensions in Him both spiritually, physically, mentally, and financially. We will no longer be confined to the third dimensional box that held us from expansion, growth, and development; we will now burst the seams of the third dimension and begin to enlarge our territory in the fourth dimension.

The Bible declares in Isaiah 54:2-3 (NLT), "Enlarge your house; build an addition. Spread out your home, and spare no expense! For you will soon be bursting at the seams. Your descendants will occupy other nations and resettle the ruined cities." We have experienced a rebirth. The Apostle Paul said in 2 Corinthians 5:17, "Therefore if any man be in Christ, he is a new creature: old things are passed away; behold, all things are become new."

There are seasons of latter rain. Sarah, the wife of Abraham, experienced a latter-rain season in Genesis chapter 18. God asked Sarah in Genesis 18:14, "Is any thing too hard for the Lord? At the time appointed I will return unto thee, according to the time of life, and Sarah shall have a son." The latter rain caused Sarah to conceive, produce fruit, and bring forth life. The latter rain always provides increase, growth, and prosperity.

In Genesis chapter 21, God keeps His promise by returning to visit Sarah and her promised son, Isaac. The Bible says, Genesis 21:1-2, "And the Lord visited Sarah as he had said, and the Lord did unto Sarah as he had spoken. For Sarah conceived, and bare Abraham a son in his old age, at the set time of which God has spoken to him." Sometimes God makes scheduled house calls!

Many of us have lived in the "dry places" of life. We have tasted the dust of the dry barren desert. Some of us have become accustomed to living in desolate surroundings. However, your environment is about to change! Where there was only desert, there shall be rivers of water. What was once a parched place, God will create an oasis for you.

The Word of God said in Isaiah 58:11, "...And thou shalt be like a watered garden, and like a spring of water, whose waters fail not." Furthermore, God said in Isaiah 41:18-19, "I will open rivers in high places, and fountains in the midst of the valleys: I will make the wilderness a pool of water, and the dry land springs of water. I will plant in the wilderness the cedar, the shittah tree, and the myrtle, and the oil tree; I will set in the desert the fir tree, and the pine, and the box tree together:"

The prophet Habakkuk was reminiscent about the latter rain, a time when the fig trees blossomed, fruits were on the vine, fresh olive oil flowed continuously in abundance, and cattle for meat were plenty in the stalls (Habakkuk 3:17). He longed again for the latter rain. However, Israel had not kept the commandments of God. Therefore, the Israelites experienced famine and captivity.

Although many of us have experienced seasons of scalding and scorching temperatures, the heat was never meant to destroy us, but to create vessels of beauty. For instance, if you visit a factory where pottery and glass wares are made, you will enter into a room where the pottery and glass go through a heating process. There you will hear a high pitch sound coming from the glass and pottery. The fine pottery and glass make a high pitch singing sound under the pressure of heat. Like the glass and fine pottery which sing under tremendous heat, can you still sing praises to God while experiencing adverse circumstances? Only the glass and pottery that can sing under pressure will become vessels of beauty!

Unfortunately, as the process continues, some of the pottery and glasses break under the intense heat. Only the pottery and glass that survives the heat are displayed as valuable and priceless works of art. Temperatures of 1200-1300 degrees are used to make fine glass and pottery. After the heating process, there is the cooling off period. This is where the pottery and glassware crystallizes and beautifies into fine glass and pottery.

Rain has the ability to cool down the temperature in the atmosphere. God has sent the latter rain to cool the temperature in your life which will reveal the beauty He has perfected in you. Rejoice for the latter rain has come!

There have been many seeds sown in our lives that never produced a harvest. However, God's latter rain has come to revive the seeds which were sown that failed to produce in its season. Other seeds, in the form of lost and forgotten dreams, which never came into fruition, shall come and spring forth speedily.

The latter rain represents a time of the anointing. The Bible says in Isaiah 61:3 that God will give us beauty for ashes, joy instead of mourning, and the garment of praise instead of despair. Ashes represent burning, heat, destruction, war, and devastation. Many positions of authority in the earth, as it relates to the people of God, have been destroyed, burned, and torn down by the enemies' attacks. God said in Ezekiel 36:10 that He will build up the waste places and the cities shall be rebuilt. During the latter rain, God is going to reestablish our place of authority in the earth.

Mourning represents sorrow, tears, grief, pain, suffering, sickness, and torment. You will not have to cry or mourn anymore! God will replace your mourning with joy unspeakable and full of glory (1 Peter 1:8). Dry your eyes and wipe away your tears! The Word of God says in Psalms 30:5, "...Weeping may endure for a night, but joy cometh in the morning." The joy of the latter rain has come!

In the latter rain, you will throw away the garment of heaviness and despair and replace it with the garment of praise and worship. Praise will be our daily wardrobe covering. Never again will we have to put on sackcloth with ashes. We will wear a royal robe of righteousness and praise.

Don't you think it is about time for you to take off that old garment? The latter rain represents a time of triumph, joy, victory, and praise. The latter rain represents a time of refreshing. It is the end of the dry season and the beginning of the season of replenishment and restoration.

The Bible says in Acts 3:19, "Repent ye therefore, and be converted, that your sins may be blotted out, when the times of refreshing shall come from the presence of the Lord." The latter rain shall send the refreshing of the anointing of God. We must repent of our sins in order to receive the blessing of God's latter rain anointing. The presence of God has come down in the latter rain to execute judgment and justice in the earth.

The famine is over! God will provide fresh manna from heaven. God said in Exodus 16:4, "...Behold, I will rain bread from heaven for you...every day." The latter rain represents the promises of God showering down over the people of God. The Bible says in Psalms 105:41, "He [God] opened the rock and the water gushed out, they ran in the dry places like a river."

This is not the time to give up or throw in the towel. Paul said in Galatians 6:9, "And let us not be weary in well doing: for in due season we shall reap, if we faint not." If you have been believing the Lord for something and it has not come to pass, don't worry, your latter-rain promise is coming!

The latter rain represents the supernatural blessings available in the fourth dimension. The fourth dimension abounds with heavy rain clouds of blessings bursting at the seams. God wants to rain down showers of blessings upon you. God said in Ezekiel 34:26, "And I will make them and the places round about my hill a blessing; and I will cause the shower to come down in his season; there shall be showers of blessing."

God wants to lavish you with His supernatural abundance, healing, power, and glory. In the fourth dimension, we do not have to beg God for what we need and desire, it is available for the asking. Sometimes you can smell rain coming afar off. Can you sense the outpouring of latter rain in the fourth dimension?

Endnotes:

1. McKay, Varn Michael. "The Potter's House." His Eye Music, 1990.

Holy Spirit

Holy Spirit, angels are God's helpers to mankind,

Holy Spirit, He knew with them we would be fine;

Holy Spirit, you know every source,

Holy Spirit, Jehovah is that force;

Holy Spirit, your power is all we need,

Holy Spirit, love, compassion, faith, peace, and holiness in-

deed;

Holy Spirit, having the fourth dimension in sight is a must,

Holy Spirit, speaking, believing, declaring, and decreeing it in

all of us.

CHAPTER 3

The Historical View of Angels

In the past few years, there has been an increased interest and curiosity in the supernatural. One such supernatural creature of interest is angels. The basic questions surrounding angels that many individuals have are as follow: Are angels real? Are they here among us? What are their roles in the affairs of man on Earth? Can we communicate with angels?

Many of the questions can be answered through the ancient Jewish writings called the TANAKH. The writings of the TANAKH began around 1000 BC, ten centuries before the birth of Jesus. Many individuals know the TANAKH as the Hebrew Bible. The TANAKH was composed over a period of roughly 800 years from 1000 to 160 BC. Along with the recording of man and his relationship with the one true God, in the Bible, are angels.

Angels are found in the first book of the Bible called the book of Genesis. The first type of angel we read about in the Bible is cherubs. Cherubs are called cherubim in Hebrew. After God excommunicates or banishes Adam and Eve from the Garden of Eden for disobedience, cherubim are ordered by God to guard the entrance to the Garden of Eden.

The Bible says, "After sending them [Adam and Eve] out, the Lord God stationed mighty cherubim to the east of the Garden of Eden. And he placed a flaming sword that flashed back and forth to guard the way to the tree of life" (Genesis 3:24, NLT).

Cherubim are nothing like they are depicted in pictures or cartoons. Cherubim are not the chubby little cute angels we see on Valentine's Day. Cherubim are the fearsome high-security agents of God. They are tough and fearless both in attitude and appearance. Cherubim are command-driven.

Zachariah, the priest, found out first hand that cherubim mean what they say and say what they mean. Zachariah was struck dumb for his response to Gabriel who is a cherub. The Bible says that the angel said to Zachariah, 'I am Gabriel. I stand in the presence of God, and I have been sent to speak to you and to tell you this good news [Zachariah will have a son named John]. And now you will be silent and not able to speak until the day this happens, because you did not believe my words, which will come true at their appointed time' (Luke 1:19-20).

Cherubim do not play games or play around. These angelic creatures are intimidating and ruthless to say the least. Cherubim are high ranking angelic beings with great authority and power.

Gabriel is the preeminent cherub messenger of God—the official announcer of the Immaculate Conception to Mary. He announced to Mary that she would give birth to the Son of God (Luke 1:26-38).

Another powerful cherub is the archangel Michael. The angel Michael's expertise is in military warfare and conquest. He was created to fight. Gabriel is the angel of revelation whereas Michael is the angel of domination. The archangel Michael will fight at the "drop of a hat." He is the archangel that will fight and ask questions later! He is the archangel with quick temper and muscles. Michael is God's soldier and enforcer angel.

We know of these names of angels from the book of Daniel. We find only in the book of Daniel that angels have names (Daniel 9:21, Daniel 10:13). It is in the book of Daniel that Gabriel and Michael make their official world debut.

In Hebrew, the name "Gabriel" means *by God's strength will save me*. In Hebrew, the name "Michael" means *no one can rival my God and who is like my God*. Notice that the names of the angels are always associated with God. Their names actually give praise and reverence to God rather than to themselves.

Cherubim protect and guard the throne of God. The Bible says in 2 Kings 19:15 (KJ2000) that King Hezekiah prayed before the Lord saying, "O Lord God of Israel, which dwellest between the cherubims, thou art God, even thou alone, of all the kingdoms of the earth; thou hast made heaven and Earth." Here, in this prayer to God, King Hezekiah reveals the role that cherubim provide in heaven: they guard the presence of God.

God provides details of cherubim's role and position, as well. God told Moses to make the Ark of the Covenant as a pattern of what is in heaven. The pattern of the tabernacle, including the Ark of the Covenant was according to a heavenly reality. The cherubim's position around the Ark of the Covenant is a reality of the actual position cherubim's have around God's throne. The Bible declares, "Who serve unto the example and shadow of heavenly things, as Moses was admonished of God when he was about to make the tabernacle: for, See, saith he, that thou make all things according to the pattern shewed to thee in the mount" (Hebrews 8:5). God said to Moses in Exodus 25:18-22 (NASB),

> *You shall make two cherubim of gold, make them of hammered work at the two ends of the mercy seat. Make one cherub at one end and one cherub at the other end; you shall make the cherubim of one piece with the mercy seat at its two ends. The cherubim shall have their wings spread upward, covering the mercy seat with their wings and facing one another; the faces of the cherubim are to be turned toward the mercy seat. You shall put the mercy seat on top of the ark, and in the ark you shall put the testimony which I will give to you. There I will meet with you; and from above the mercy seat, from between the two cherubim which are upon the ark of the testimony; I will speak to you about all that I will give you in commandment for the sons of Israel.*

The Ark of the Covenant was made according to exact dimensions of a scale model around God's throne in heaven. In heaven, cherubim protect the throne of God as the cherubim protect and guard the Ark of the Covenant created by Moses.

Other angels are called seraphim. When the prophet Isaiah had a vision, the Bible says in Isaiah 6:3 that the seraphim worshiped God crying, "Holy, holy, holy." *Seraphim* means burning ones. Seraphim are angels who worship in the manifest presence of God. Seraphs or seraphim are six-winged angels. They are of the highest rank of angelic beings. Seraphim are almost entirely hidden by their wings. Their true bodily form and bodily nature are unknown. Their bodily features and nature are radically beyond what is considered human. Some angels' appearance may even look terrifying to us. The prophet Ezekiel declared,

> As I looked, behold, a storm wind was coming from the north, a great cloud with fire flashing forth continually and a bright light around it, and in its midst something like glowing metal in the midst of the fire. Within it there were figures resembling four living beings. And this was their appearance: they had human form. Each of them had four faces and four wings. Their legs were straight and their feet were like a calf's hoof, and they gleamed like burnished bronze. Under their wings on their four sides were human hands. As for the faces and wings of the four of them, their wings touched one another; their faces did not turn when they moved, each went straight forward. As for the form of their faces, each had the face of a man; all four had the face of a lion on the right and the face of a bull on the left, and all four had the face of an eagle. Such were their faces. Their wings were spread out above; each had two touching another being, and two covering their bodies. And each went straight forward; wherever the spirit was about to go, they would go, without turning as they

> went. In the midst of the living beings there was
> something that looked like burning coals of fire, like
> torches darting back and forth among the living be-
> ings. The fire was bright, and lightning was flashing
> from the fire. And the living beings ran to and fro
> like bolts of lightning (Ezekiel 1:4-14, NASB).

As the chariot of God descended from heaven, Ezekiel saw fire, lightning, and radiant winged creatures with multiple faces. Each of these winged creatures has a human face, a face of an eagle, a lion, and an ox. The living creatures had four faces in all. These are not symbolic creatures, but real physical creatures of God.

How involved are angels in our lives? Listen, man's greatest antagonist is a cherub called satan. *Satan* in Hebrew means *adversary*. Before his fall, satan was a cherub, a high-ranking angelic being. Satan's former name is Lucifer who was called the "anointed cherub." The Bible says in Ezekiel 28:14, 18,

> Thou art the anointed cherub that covereth; and I
> have set thee so: thou wast upon the holy mountain
> of God; thou hast walked up and down in the midst
> of the stones of fire... Thou hast defiled thy sanctu-
> aries by the multitude of thine iniquities, by the in-
> iquity of thy traffick; therefore will I bring forth a
> fire from the midst of thee, it shall devour thee, and
> I will bring thee to ashes upon the earth in the sight
> all them that behold thee.

Although satan has been cast down to the earth, satan still plays a major role in God's redemptive plan of salvation. Satan has the role of a prosecuting attorney who brings evidence before God against man.

The Bible says in Revelation 12:10, "And I heard a loud voice saying in heaven, Now is come salvation, and strength, and the Kingdom of our God, and the power of his Christ: for the accuser of our brethren [satan] is cast down, which accused them before our God day and night."

During scheduled times, satan has been given the opportunity to act as prosecutor or antagonist against man in the heavenly court. The scene of one court appearance can be found in Job 1:6-7. The Bible says,

> Now there was a day when the sons of God [angels] came to present themselves before the Lord, and Satan came also among them. And the Lord said unto Satan, Whence comest thou? Then Satan answered the Lord, and said, from going to and fro in the earth, and from walking up and down in it.

Satan's role is to test and challenge our faith in God. Are there other names of angelic beings in the Bible? In the first century AD, the leading Jewish rabbi's of the time chose the Old Testament books we find in the Bible. They purposely excluded a vast number of Jewish texts largely due to the inconsistency of certain Christian writings, as well as the status angels played in the texts. The works rejected by the rabbis was known as the *Apocrypha*. The literal meaning of *Apocrypha* is "hidden books."

These books were considered dubious or not worthy of being believed or credible. The books listed as Apocrypha consisted of numerous names of angels. Many of the biblical scholars and rabbis feared that there was too much focus and attention on angels, rather than on God and His relationship with man. Therefore, many of the writings or texts about angels and their names were deleted from the Bible as we know it. Some of the hidden books which spoke of angels were called, **The Testimony of the Twelve Patriarchs, The Book of Tobit, The Life of Adam and Eve, The Letter of Jeremiah,** and **The Testimony of Moses.** The best known apocrypha book is called **The Book of Enoch**.

Some early Christian theologians did adopt apocryphal books from Judaism. These books were granted full status as sacred canonical text. One such apocryphal book was the **Book of**

Tobit with the central character the archangel Raphael. The archangel Raphael played the role as protector and guide. However, when the Protestants broke from the church in the 1500's they demoted the **Book of Tobit** to the apocryphal and dropped Raphael from the list of archangels. Today, Raphael and the **Book of Tobit** can only be found in the Catholic version of the Old Testament.

Over the centuries Christian theologians wrote extensively about the nature of angels. Among the most influential of such works was the 6th century text called the **Celestial Hierarchy** which set out in detail nine orders of angels. According to the **Celestial Hierarchy**, the heavens are divided into three levels with each level having three tiers. Each level has a name and type of angel with specific duties. The names were Seraphim, Cherubim, Thrones, Dominations, Virtues, Powers, Principalities, Archangels, and Angels. These names of angels and positions of angels were highly regarded in the Christian church until the 1500's.

Seraphim were the highest rank of angels and nearest to God. Seraphim stand in the presence of Almighty God. The Bible says in Revelation 4:6, 8 (NIV),

> *Also before the throne there was what looked like a sea of glass, clear as crystal. In the center, around the throne, were four living creatures, and they were covered with eyes, in front and in back. Each of the four living creatures had six wings and was covered with eyes all around, even under his wings. Day and night they never stop saying: Holy, holy, holy is the Lord God Almighty, who was, and is, and is to come.*

According to the **Celestial Hierarchy**, those who were close to the material world are of lower rank and are simply called angels. Angels whose positions are close to the earth have close contact with human beings. These angels serve as guardians to individuals rather than angels of higher hierarchy.

Angels of hierarchy such as archangels or chief angels

supervise the lower angels. However, archangels do serve as special guardians to select individuals, such as heads of states and religious leaders. The **Celestial Hierarchy** named seven archangels: Michael, Gabriel, Raphael, Uriel, Chamuel, Jophkile, and Zadkiel; however, the last four names were eliminated from the list because their names appeared in apocryphal works. Apocryphal works are written texts which were considered unorthodox and eccentric-unsuitable for the Holy Bible.

Just because the names of these archangels were deleted from the Bible, does not mean that the names were not genuine or that the archangels did not exist. It does mean, however, that the account of these angels can be misleading to the reader. In other words, angels must always be thought of as agents of God, not as separate entities with unique divine personalities.

One of the main reasons many events and names of angels were left out of the Bible is that angels are not to be worshipped or idolized. Therefore, the books listed above known as apocryphal are not considered divinely inspired because the focus is on the angels instead of God. Angels are simply servants of God, nothing more and nothing less.

Angels stand ready to heed the call and bidding of God. There is a great danger in worshipping angels instead of God. The Apostle Paul went on to say in Galatians 1:8, "But though we, or an angel from heaven, preach any other gospel unto you than that which we have preached unto you, let him be accursed." Although they are impressive and awesome, angels are never to be worshipped or canonized; they are mere servants of the Most High God.

The history of angels dates back before creation. Angels are immortal beings with an eternal existence. Angels are the guardians and the gatekeepers of the fourth dimension. The fourth dimension represents the throne and the Kingdom of God. They have been a major part of world events since the dawn of time. Angels are given a timeless existence; they are interminable beings.

In the question to Job, God lets us know that angels ex-

19

isted long before the inaugural of creation. God asked Job, "Where wast thou when I laid the foundations of the earth? declare, if thou hast understanding. Whereupon are the foundations thereof fastened? or who laid the corner stone thereof; When the morning stars [angels] sang together, all the sons of God shouted for joy?" (Job 38: 4, 6-7) The presence of angels is recorded throughout the Bible from Genesis to Revelation.

Angels are the protectors and defenders of those who are inheritors of the fourth dimension. The fourth dimension represents those who are recipients of eternal salvation. Hebrews 1:14 (NLT) says, "Therefore, angels are only servants–spirits sent to care for people who will inherit salvation." There has been much writing on angelic creatures for thousands of years.

Although angels are infinite, mysterious, powerful, and amazing creatures, they pale in comparison to the Creator who created them. There has been much enthusiasm about angels in recent years; however, they are created beings like man. Angels are never to be worshipped. God alone, who eternally exists in himself, is to be revered, exalted, and worshipped.

Holy Spirit

Holy Spirit, flowers, trees, birds and the bees,

Holy Spirit, from sea to shining sea;

Holy Spirit, the Creator of the universe,

Holy Spirit, God came and blessed man first;

Holy Spirit, our Savior's love deep within,

Holy Spirit, life to Life will never end;

Holy Spirit, you always know what to do,

Holy Spirit, for in you is His loving truth.

Chapter 4

Time As A Constraint

Isn't it rather ironic that when we are in our teen-aged years, we cannot wait to grow older in order to do things we are not allowed as teens and children? We can't wait to be of the age to drive a car, live away from our parents, or to become independent. As a child, we complain that time moves too slow; we want time to move faster. However, as we get into our middle-aged years and older, we want time to slow down. For the most part, we want time to slow down because we would like to accomplish more than what we have presently.

As a child, we saw time as a constraint. When we become older, we see time as a constraint, as well. Furthermore, the older we become, we soon begin to take notice of our fleeing mortality. In other words, we feel that we are running out of time.

The truth of the matter is this: time is a constraint. A constraint is anything that creates limitations, hindrances, and restrictions. Time is always against us whether we are young or old. However, we usually find this truth out later in life, rather than earlier in life. Time can place limitations upon our hopes, dreams, inspirations, and future.

One of the greatest constraints of the third dimensional world [the world we live in] versus the fourth dimensional [the supernatural realm] is time. Time is a major element in the third dimension, but not an element of the fourth dimension. In the fourth dimension, time does not exist. Time is one of the major boundaries that categorize the third dimension.

Although time is an essential element in the third dimension, time was originally never meant to be an impediment or hindrance. Time was made for man, not man for time. In the third dimensional world, time rules over us; it dictates everything that we do. However, this was never God's original intention or plan. Before the fall of man, man had complete dominion in the earth including time. God gave Adam [man] dominion and authority over every dimension of Earth (Genesis 1:26). Time falls under a dimension of Earth. Therefore, time was subject unto Adam.

In the world in which we live, time dictates everything we do. However, no one or no thing dictates to God! God is Lord over time. God said in Isaiah 43:13 (NLT), "From eternity to eternity I am God. No one can oppose what I do. No one can reverse my actions." God has the final word, not time. The chronology of time is not a concern for Him. However, time governs our world. In relation to time, we are like the inner workings of a clock, synchronized in conjunction with the rhythms and motions of time.

God has little value for time. In the fourth dimension, time is not a factor. That's how important God thinks of time! Time was never intended to govern or dominate our lives as it relates to our purpose and destiny in God. I have often heard people say, "My time is about up." They are in essence saying that the ruler called "time" has determined their length of days, years, and future. Notwithstanding, God has the final verdict in our lives, not time.

We must start thinking fourth dimensionally. If you see where time has taken a stronghold over your life as you pursue God's plan in the Kingdom of God, rebuke time. Joshua did! (Joshua 10:12-13). If time says that your three score and ten years (70 years) are over, but your work in the vineyard is not finished, put time on hold until you complete the work God has assigned you. The Bible says in Philippians 1:6, "Being confident of this very thing, that he which hath begun a good work in you will perform it until the day of Jesus Christ." God will complete that which he has purposed in your life.

God made time for man just as God made the Sabbath for man. Jesus said in Mark 2:27, "...The sabbath was made for man, and not man for the sabbath." In other words, as a believer of Christ, you determine your length on the earth, not time. As a matter of fact, when death tells you that your time is up, tell death you will die when you get ready! Tell death God said in Genesis 6:3, that your days "...Shall be an hundred and twenty years." We must abandon our old ways of thinking and shift to a new paradigm of thought, belief, and mind based on the Word of God.

We must view time as God sees time. God sees time as a means to fulfill His will and purpose. When Peter inquired about John, one of Jesus' disciples, Jesus said to Peter, "If it is my will for him [John] to remain until I come back, how does that concern you? You must keep following me!" (John 21:22, ISV). God uses time exclusively for His own plan and purpose.

Do you feel that time is against you? No one knows the debilitating effects of time more than Abraham and Sarah. God promised Abraham a child at the age of 75 and to a barren woman at the age of 65 (Genesis 12:4). Although God has promised Abraham an heir, time was against them at the start due to their age. The promised seed and heir did not come to pass until 25 years later. Time told the elderly Abraham and the barren Sarah it was too late. Each year, time confirmed its position of being correct over the promises of God. However, 25 years later, time was proven a lie. Sarah conceived and delivered her long awaited promise, Isaac. Abraham was 100 years old and Sarah 90 when Isaac was born (Genesis 17:17). Listen, when God makes a promise to you, although much time has elapsed, whose report will you believe, time's report or God's report?

Maybe you have stage four cancer and the oncologists and other medical experts have given you a time–expiration date. If so, you are not reading this book by accident. God's eternal and timeless Word says, "I shall not die, but live, and

24

declare the works of the LORD" (Psalms 118:17).

We must begin to think fourth dimensionally. Life in the fourth dimension represents a new way of thinking, believing, and living. It represents the kind of thinking and belief that if God said it, God's Word will come to pass regardless of the circumstances, situations, or years involved. What is your long awaited prayer? Has time attempted to abort the promises of God in your life? What has time said to you?

The good news is time has no constraints upon those who have received a promise from God. Have you received a promise from God? When God makes you a promise, you can't die until the promise is fulfilled. Simeon, a beloved and devout man of God knows well of the reliability of God's Word. The Bible says:

> At that time there was a man in Jerusalem named Simeon. He was righteous and devout and was eagerly waiting for the Messiah to come and rescue Israel. The Holy Spirit was upon him and had revealed to him that he would not die until he had seen the Lord's Messiah. That day the Spirit led him to the Temple. So when Mary and Joseph came to present the baby Jesus to the Lord as the law required, Simeon was there. He took the child in his arms and praised God, saying, Sovereign Lord, now let your servant die in peace, as you have promised (Luke 2:25-29, NLT).

Simeon, a servant of God, will tell you that time is not a constraint when God has given you a promise. Although time is a true reality on Earth, God's Word is a greater reality. God's Word trumps over the constraints of time in the fourth dimension.

Holy Spirit

Holy Spirit, I thank God the Father for giving me this day,

Holy Spirit, through dreams and visions is a perfected stay;

Holy Spirit, how would we know what belongs to us,

Holy Spirit, stir up our spiritual gifts in the cosmos;

Holy Spirit, grant us your anointed super sight,

Holy Spirit, we are God's children that dwell in the praise of

His all-seeing might;

Holy Spirit, open our spiritual eyes to what we cannot see,

Holy Spirit, even in the fourth dimension through His angels,

He'll show us what we can be.

CHAPTER 5

Launch Out into the Deep

On Saturday afternoons, I love to watch wildlife shows, especially fishing. It is always intriguing to see the fishing experts with their customized boats and large fishing gears far away from the nearest shore. They know that the big game, coveted prize fish, is not near the shore or in the shallow waters, but in the deep open waters. In preparation for the catch, the fishermen would safely strap themselves to the boat in order to compete with the large game fish that would eventually strike their fishing lines. Expert fishermen know that they must launch out into the deep to catch the most valuable and desirable game fish. Jesus gave Simon Peter, an expert fisherman, a similar instruction after fishing all night. The Bible says in Luke 5:4-7,

> Now when he [Jesus] had left speaking, he said unto Simon, Launch out into the deep, and let down your nets for a draught. And Simon answering said unto him, Master, we have toiled all the night, and have taken nothing: nevertheless at thy word I will let down the net. And when they had this done, they inclosed a great multitude of fishes: and their net brake. And they beckoned unto their partners, which were in the other ship, that they should come and help them. And they came and filled both the ships, so that they began to sink.

The Bible records two incidents of Peter and other disciples fishing in the Sea of Galilee. The first recorded incident occurred in the book of Luke and the other in the book of John. The event that occurred in Luke was at the beginning of Jesus' ministry and the event occurring in John was after Jesus' resurrection, the closing of Jesus' earthly ministry. The Bible says in both fishing expeditions that Peter and the other disciples fished all night, but caught nothing. However, on each occasion, Jesus gave Peter an instruction which created a supernatural harvest of fish.

In Luke chapter 5:5-7, Peter and the other disciples had fished all night, but caught nothing. They were tired, weary, frustrated, and discouraged. Isn't it true that you can exert all of your effort and energy on a task and receive little to no benefit from it? All of your efforts seem to be a waste of time and completely in vain.

After Jesus concluded teaching the people on the shore, Peter, who was now washing his nets, is instructed by Jesus to launch out into the deep. Peter tells Jesus that he has toiled or labored all night and caught nothing. Nevertheless, Peter says to Jesus that he will launch out into the deep at His Word.

After doing so, Peter's net is filled with such an abundance of fish that the net began to break under the weight and strain of the enormous catch. Peter then called over to his partners and crew to assist him in transferring the fish from the water to the boats. The Bible says that the weight of the catch of fish filled both ships and both ships began to sink due to the magnitude of fish.

Before the catch, Peter was cleaning his net. In other words, Peter was closing down his business; he was closing shop. Business was slow. There was no money, profit, or revenue to be made. He was feeling the symptoms of a recession.

Jesus instructed Peter to go out into the deep. Sometimes God will ask us to go out beyond our familiar territory, out from our comfort zone. It is important to realize that God will often instruct you to go far from where most people are willing to travel, congregate, [or fish]. Sometimes, God will take us out into the deep waters where we must trust Him.

Peter told Jesus he had toiled all night and caught nothing. To put it plainly, Peter was telling Jesus, "The fish aren't biting. There's nothing to catch. The tide has gone out. Fish don't feed during this time of the day. All the other fishermen have come in to wash their nets. There's nothing out there."

To put it into today's perspective, Peter was telling Jesus that the economy was slow. There are no jobs. Unemployment is at an all-time high. Positions are being cut. People are being laid off and no one is getting raises or bonuses. Foreclosures are at record levels. People are losing their homes and cars.

However, God is telling us to launch out into the deep. He has the power to create jobs and positions. Just as He knows where the fish are, He knows where the jobs are. He knows the areas where new jobs will be created. God can bring the jobs or "fish" right up to your door or "boat." Jesus can bring prosperity in a time of recession, depression, famine, or even when the "fish are not biting." Listen, it's time to go fishing!

What Peter didn't realize was that God has the power to lure fish without bait. He knows where the schools of fish are located. He can command fish to come into the net. If He wishes, He can command fish to jump into your boat!

When God tells you to launch out into the deep for a catch, get ready for an overflow! Peter's net began to break under the tension of the weight of fish. God is saying to us not to be alarmed when we hear the discouraging economic news in the media. Strengthen your nets, strengthen your stakes, enlarge your tents, and enlarge your territory. It is not the time to hold back, but move forward in the faith and power of the Word of God.

Isaiah 54:2-3 says, "Enlarge the place of thy tent, and let them stretch forth the curtains of thine habitations: spare not, lengthen thy cords, and strengthen thy stakes; For thou shalt break forth on the right hand and on the left..." God is about to sink and overflow your ship with the blessings of heaven. God has promised to open up the windows of heaven and pour you out a blessing you won't have room enough to receive it

(Malachi 3:10). God will give you a catch so vast and exorbitant that you may never again have to work for a living!

When Peter received and obeyed the words of Jesus, Peter wasn't fishing alone as before. He had the backing, endorsement, and reinforcement of the Word of God. Peter usually fished under his own ability. However, this time, he had the power and the authority of God with him. God's Word was on his side. When you go in your own strength you will always lose, but when you go in the strength of God you will always triumph. The Bible says in 2 Corinthians 2:14, "Now thanks be unto God, which always causeth us to triumph..."

God says, "Launch out into the deep!" Are you tired of getting the small fish, the minnows, the bait-size fish, the bony fish, and the sardines? Are you tired of scraping the barrel to survive? God says He knows where the "big game fish" are. If you follow Him and launch out into the deep, He will lead you into your Land of Promise.

In Numbers chapter 13 and 14, Israel refused to launch out on the Word of God to receive the harvest of the Promised Land. They would not leave the shore of the desert. God told them to launch out into the deep, but when they saw the "big fish" of giants in Canaan, they ran back to the desert shore.

Peter received a harvest because he obeyed the Word of God. The Children of Israel received a harvest of death because they disobeyed the Word of God. When God gives you a command, do it!

I am reminded of a wedding in Cana in the book of John chapter 2 where Jesus, His disciples, and Mary, the mother of Jesus, attended. Unfortunately, they ran out of wine before the ceremonial festival was completed. Mary told Jesus about the wine depletion. Then she said to the servants at the wedding; whatever He tells you to do, do it.

Maybe God has commanded you to start a business, just do it! May be He has impressed upon you to start a website, just do it! God said in Isaiah 1:19, "If ye be willing and obedient, ye shall eat the good of the Land." Just do it!

Out into the deep is the place where few dare to travel. It is a place known as the fourth dimension. However, the fourth dimension is where the hidden treasures are found. The fourth dimension is where God will give you revelation knowledge and show you things no one has seen before. It is the place God has monies stored in bank vaults, cars at dealerships, and in garages just waiting for you to let down your net.

The fourth dimension is an exclusive hidden dimension only accessible to those who are heirs of salvation. Hidden treasures are found in the unseen realm of the fourth dimension. Hidden treasures include houses in suburban areas, lands with trees and orchards, oceanfront estates overlooking lakes and rivers waiting for you to obtain ownership.

In fact, gold bullion which reside in homes and bank depositories awaits your discovery. Hard to believe? Where is your faith? Launch out into the deep in the fourth dimension!

Holy Spirit

Holy Spirit, He's my Master, Holy Ghost, He's my Savior,

Holy Spirit, in Him is my upright behavior;

Holy Spirit, His heart lives in me,

Holy Spirit, together with God and with thee;

Holy Spirit, my way I no longer seek,

Holy Spirit, His church I will keep;

Holy Spirit, He's my Savior, my Master, and my King,

Holy Spirit, I owe Him everything.

CHAPTER 6

Trans-Dimensional Creatures

Angels are not subject to the limitations of the third dimensional world. Their bodies are trans-dimensional. In other words, the bodies of angels can transform from a spiritual dimension to a natural dimension, or vice versa. Their multi-dimensional bodies can adapt to any given dimension, whether it is third or fourth dimensional.

An example of angels' abilities to transfigure their bodies into different dimensional properties can be found in Judges chapter 13. An angel of the lord visits Manoah and his barren wife to let them know that they will have a son. This son, a Nazarite who would be called Samson, will begin to deliver Israel out of the hands of the Philistines. Judges 13:16, 19, 20 says:

> And the angel of the Lord said unto Manoah, Though thou detain me, I will not eat of thy bread: and if thou wilt offer a burnt offering, thou must offer it unto the Lord. For Manoah knew not that he was an angel of the Lord. So Manoah took a kid with a meat offering, and offered it upon a rock unto the Lord: and the angel did wondrously; and Manoah and his wife looked on. For it came to pass, when the flame went up toward heaven from off the altar, that the angel of the Lord ascended in the flame of the altar.

And Manoah and his wife looked on it, and fell on their faces to the ground.

The "angel of the Lord" carries an awesome anointing and power. This anointing is due to the angel's continually standing in the presence of the Lord. He acts on behalf of God Almighty.

In Judges Chapter 13 above, the angel's body transformed and converged with the fire and smoke from the burnt offering. The angel took on the same dimensional properties as the fire and smoke. As the flame of fire went up toward heaven, so did the angel. In fact, the fire consumed the burnt offering.

Furthermore, angels can pass through solid objects and are not limited to time, matter, and space. The Bible says in the book of Acts 12:7 (NLT),

Suddenly, there was a bright light in the cell, and an angel of the Lord stood before Peter. The angel struck him on the side to awaken him and said, 'Quick! Get up!' And the chains fell off his wrists.

The angel of the Lord was able to breach the dimensions of matter and space. The security of the prison walls and iron bars created no restraint against the angel of the Lord. Solid objects of matter [like wood, steel, iron, or stone] create no limitations or resistance for angels. In regard to physical matter, angels can take on the physical bodily form of man. The Bible in Genesis 6:2, 4:

That the sons of God [angels] saw the daughters of men that they were fair; and they took them wives of all which they chose. There were giants in the earth in those days; and also after that, when the sons of God came in unto the daughters of men, and they bare children to them, the same became mighty men which were of old, men of renown.

Fallen angels during the time of Noah were able to take on physical form as well as mate with human beings. Angels can transform and alter the dimensional makeup of their bodies.

The next person you meet may be an angel from heaven. We must always treat every person we meet and encounter with courtesy, respect, and dignity. Because angels take on human form, we never know with whom we may come in contact. We may be in the presence of God's holy angels! An angel from the Lord may very well be in a position to bless us when we are hospitable, kind, and loving.

The Bible says, "Don't forget to show hospitality to strangers, for some who have done this have entertained angels without realizing it!" (Hebrews 13:2, NLT). In other words, be careful how you treat people, especially strangers–those you don't know. Just because a person looks common, homey, or or-dinary does not mean he is your "average Joe." Looks can be deceiving!

Moreover, angels can move and travel at the speed of thought. Their dimensional bodies have no boundaries. In fact, the Bible says that one angel killed 185,000 men in one night. 2 Kings 19:35 (NIV) says, "That night the angel of the Lord went out and put to death a hundred and eighty-five thousand men in the Assyrian camp. When the people got up the next morning–there were all the dead bodies!"

The angel of the Lord moved so fast that none of the men of war could visually see their opponent. How can you ef-fectively fight, engage, or arm yourself against something you can't see? Angels move at extraordinary speed, momentum, and velocity. They can move in different directions at the same time.

Notwithstanding, angels can move faster than the speed of light. In 2011, a new discovery was found in Geneva, Switzerland. Scientists have discovered a particle that travels faster than the speed of light which has astonished as-tronomers. According to Einstein and the theory of relativity, this is impossible; however, a second test was done to confirm the findings. Angels operate on a far greater dimension than present science.

Science is slowly discovering that the Word of God is factual, valid, reliable, true, and trustworthy. We can always place our faith and trust in God even when we may not be able to fully comprehend or understand [how] on a logical level. Faith can stand alone without the assistance of physical evidence.

Angels constantly travel between physical and supernatural dimensions. However, angels are not the only recipients of supernatural flight. Philip, a disciple of Jesus Christ, was able to experience angelic travel. The Bible says in Acts 8:26-29, 35-40:

> And the angel of the Lord spake unto Philip, saying, Arise, and go toward the south unto the way that goeth down from Jerusalem unto Gaza, which is desert. And he arose and went: and, behold, a man of Ethiopia, an eunuch of great authority under Candace queen of the Ethiopians, who had the charge of all her treasure, and had come to Jerusalem for to worship, Was returning, and sitting in his chariot read Esaias the prophet. Then the Spirit said unto Philip, Go near, and join thyself to this chariot. Then Philip opened his mouth, and began at the same scripture, and preached unto him Jesus. And as they went on their way, they came unto a certain water: and the eunuch said, See, here is water; what doth hinder me to be baptized? And Philip said, If thou believest with all thine heart, thou mayest. And he answered and said, I believe that Jesus Christ is the Son of God. And he commanded the chariot to stand still: and they went down both into the water, both Philip and the eunuch; and he baptized him. And when they were come up out of the water, the Spirit of the Lord caught away Philip, that the eunuch saw him no more: and he went on his way rejoicing. But Philip was found at Azotus: and passing through he preached in all the cities, till he came to Caesarea.

The Bible says in Acts 8:39 that the "Spirit of the Lord caught away Philip, that the eunuch saw him no more..." How could the Ethiopians not see Philip after both of them emerged from the water? Did Philip just disappear? Not hardly!

Philip obeyed the voice of an angel to preach salvation, the gospel of Jesus Christ, to a high-ranking Ethiopian, a eunuch of great authority under Candace Queen of Ethiopia. After receiving salvation and baptism, the angel of the Lord transported Philip from Gaza to Azotus which is approximately 34 miles. In a rugged and mountainous terrain like Palestine, it would take over 10 hours to walk. Just imagine, one moment Philip was in Gaza, the next moment he was in Azotus!

Philip is one of a few who has experienced angelic flight. Philip was able to travel fourth dimensionally through divine [angelic] intervention. Angels are able to perform supernaturally due to their physical make-up.

Angel's physical make-up is diametrically different from humans. The human body or mortal composition is an inferior construction compared to angelic beings. The mortal body is continuously in a process of deterioration and decay. Second Corinthians 4:16 says, "...Though our bodies are dying, our spirits are being renewed every day" (NLT). Every moment we are in this mortal form, we are slowly perishing. The mortal body was never meant to last forever.

There is more than one dimension. The physical dimension or the third dimension is only one dimension. There are other dimensions, as well. The Apostle Paul declared, "There are also celestial [heavenly] bodies, and bodies terrestrial but the glory of the celestial is one, and the glory of the terrestrial is another" (1 Corinthians 15:40).

The same can be said of an angel's bodily composition and man's physical composition. The anatomy of angels versus humans is in an entirely different dimension or category. Paul goes on to say to the church of Corinth that, "...There is a natural [mortal] body, and there is a spiritual [supernatural] body" (1 Corinthians 15:44).

One can only thrive and operate in the dimension he was created for. Angels are multi-dimensional. Therefore, they

37

can operate and function in both the third and fourth dimension. However, we are limited in our own ability to transcend matter, time, and space due to our dimensional, physical, or compositional make-up.

Angels are created out of trans-dimensional light. This is not the same light we receive from the sun which is called electromagnetic radiation. Trans-dimensional light was created from another dimension, a supernatural dimension, called the fourth dimension.

Throughout the Bible, heavenly hosts such as angels are described in association with light. In fact, their appearance is like pure, piercing, and penetrating light, a light far more brilliant and unique than anything known on planet Earth.

Angels' physical make-ups are properties of the fourth dimension, not the third dimension like man. Their bodies do not age, become feeble, or tire. They are products of an eternal dimension which has been in existence before time began. Angels are part of the realm of the Kingdom of heaven in the fourth dimension. The Bible says in Daniel 10:5-6,

> *Then I [Daniel] lifted up mine eyes, and looked, and behold a certain man clothed in linen, whose loins were girded with fine gold of Uphaz. His body also was like the beryl, and his face as the appearance of lightning, and his eyes as lamps of fire, and his arms and his feet like in colour to polished brass...*

This angel's [which many Biblical theologians believe to be Gabriel] physical appearance is associated with light. Where we have blood that helps to create and generate our skin, bones, muscles, sinews, and tissues, angels have light which creates and generates their immortal bodies. Instead of blood running through their veins, like men, angels have immutable light running through their bodies.

The Bible says in Luke 2:9 (GW), "An angel from the Lord suddenly appeared to them. The glory of the Lord filled the area with light, and they were terrified." The Apostle John declared, "After all this I saw another angel come down from heaven with great authority, and the earth grew bright with his splendor" (Revelation 18:1). When angels are described in Scripture, there is usually a depiction of blinding and overwhelming light.

The number of these angelic beings is infinite. The Bible says in Hebrews 12:22, "But ye are come unto mount Sion, and unto the city of the living God, the heavenly Jerusalem, and to an innumerable company of angels."

There are more angels in heaven than all of the people who will ever exist on the earth. The Bible says in Revelation 5:11, "And I beheld, and I heard the voice of many angels round about the throne and the beasts and the elders: and the number of them was ten thousand times ten thousand, and thousands of thousands." Angels are infinite in number, yet God knows the exact number of them as He knows the number of stars in the heavens (Isaiah 40:26).

Angels are intriguing living creatures with physical properties uniquely different from our own. Their bodies can transform between multiple dimensions. Angels are made up of trans-dimensional light. They can travel and move at the speed of thought. Angels can pass through solid matter such as metal, stone, or mortar. They are our intergalactic allies in the fourth dimension.

.

Holy Spirit

Holy Spirit, come, walk with me,

Holy Spirit, so I may live and be free;

Holy Spirit, God said, let us make man,

Holy Spirit, because you know all the plan;

Holy Spirit, keep us as the apple of His eye,

Holy Spirit, giving us His spiritual high;

Holy Spirit, fame and fortune you know,

Holy Spirit, because you are the Holy Ghost.

CHAPTER 7

The Double Portion

Everyone loves things free or free give-a-ways. People drive for miles and rush frantically to stores that advertise, "Get two items for the price of one or buy one get one free." Merchandise sells quickly off the shelves when the products say "20% extra" for the same price or save money by buying a bundle at a reduced rate.

Advertisements are meant to attract buyers and customers. They are created to make customers feel like they have saved a ton of money or acquired a great monetary deal. However, in reality, it is the seller that makes the profit.

God is not like man. He will never make empty promises. God will not make promises, He cannot keep or fulfill. The Bible says in Numbers 23:19, "God is not a man, that he should lie. He is not a human, that he should change his mind. Has he ever spoken and failed to act? Has he ever promised and not carried it through?" (NLT).

Man is not the only one who advertises. God also has created advertisement incentives for those who will obey and take claim of His Word. He has declared unto us a double portion through which He has promised to perform, execute, and bring to pass in our lives.

The prophet Joel declared that God will bestow the promise of a double portion. The prophet Joel writes in Joel 2:23, "Be glad then, ye children of Zion, and rejoice in the Lord your God; for he [God] hath given you the former rain moderately and he will cause to come down for you the rain, the former rain and the latter rain in the first month."

In other words, get ready for what you are about to receive. You are about to experience a two-for-one supernatural blessing. This is not some commercial and advertising gimmick of man. This is God's promise and declaration of a double portion. God is going to shower you down with blessings like the outpouring of a torrential rain storm. The double portion blessing can change your life instantly. What you normally received in a year can be given to you in a month!

Whatever time you are reading this book will be your double portion season. Receive it by faith. Get excited. During this double portion season, not only are we going to gracefully receive the promise of the double portion, God is going to restore back to us what has been lost. God has promised to restore unto us what our harvest should have been as well as an additional harvest. God said in Joel 2:25, "And I will restore to you the years that the locust hath eaten, the cankerworm..." Plainly speaking, God will restore what was lost or stolen from you and include the double portion.

Now, make no mistake, these promises have conditions attached to them. Notice that Joel 2:25 talks about the children of Zion and the Lord their God. God is talking about His people who belong to Him. These promises are not to everybody–only to those who have made Jesus their Lord and Savior.

Listen, before you can receive this double portion from God, you must pre-qualify. If you've been faithful to God, then you prequalify for this double portion, interest free and non-repayable loan! You don't have to repay this loan back. This is simply an appreciation for being a faithful, committed, and devoted child of God.

The bad news is that if you haven't accepted Christ as Lord and Savior, this double portion does not belong to you. The good news is it's not too late; you can still be a part of God's family. The Bible says in Romans 10:9-10, "That if thou shalt confess with thy mouth the Lord Jesus, and shalt believe in thine heart that God hath raised Jesus from the dead, thou shalt be saved. For with the heart man believeth unto righteousness, and with the mouth confession is made unto salvation." You can be a partaker of the benefits God has for His children by accepting Jesus as your Lord and Savior.

The double portion is not a onetime event or a seasonal blessing–it is the anointing of God. The double portion is the Spirit and power of God magnified in your life. In 2 Kings Chapter 2, the prophet Elisha knew of the double portion and wanted to have double the anointing of the prophet Elijah. Notice the conversation, between Elijah and his successor Elisha. The Bible records in 2 Kings 2:9-10,

> *And it came to pass, when they [Elijah and Elisha] were gone over, that Elijah said unto Elisha, Ask what I shall do for thee, before I be taken away from thee, and Elisha said, I pray thee; let a double portion of thy spirit be upon me. And he said, thou hast asked a hard thing, nevertheless, if thou see me when I am taken from thee, it shall be so unto thee; but if not, it shall not be so.*

Elijah was telling Elisha that although he requested a double portion, it is not something that is ordinarily given to anyone. Elisha will have to commit himself in communion and in pursuit of the anointing of Elijah. This passage of Scripture lets us know that a double portion is given only to those who are pursuant of the Spirit and heart of God. Oftentimes, we seek after the things of God instead of His Spirit or anointing. We desire His hand (the things God can give us) instead of His heart. We often want what's in His hand, but not what's in His heart!

There is a selection of men in the Bible who possessed the double portion anointing. One such individual was David. The prophet Samuel told King Saul in 1 Samuel 13:14, "...The Lord hath sought him a man [David] after his own heart..." Do you not think that God gave David a special grace, endowment, and anointing? I would think so! As a matter of fact, Jesus Christ Himself is called the Son of David. The Bible says in Mark 12:35, "...Christ is the Son of David..."

Perhaps David received the double portion because he serenaded God with psalms and music on the backside of the hills and mountains with the sheep. May be it was David's countless written songs, psalms, and hymns that made God's heart melt. Perhaps it was David's constant tugging on the heart of God, saying that he had fallen in love with Him. Perhaps the words and lyrics of the songs moved God so that He decided to promote David from being last in the house of Jesse, his father, to being first. Maybe it was the wonderful melodies and the splendid chords of the harp and lyre that was so inspiring, beautiful, and up-lifting, that it stirred God to make David King of Israel. Perhaps if you magnify God, He will magnify you!

Why not sing God a melody today? Perhaps falling in love with Jesus is the best thing that can happen to us. It is no wonder that the greatest commandment of all is to love the Lord thy God with all your heart, and with all thy soul, and with all thy mind, and with all thy strength (Matthew 22:37-38). Perhaps this is the way to obtain the double portion.

Many people may have perceived the double portion as simply a financial anointing. Even though the double portion anointing may include finances, it is much more. A double portion is an anointed-spirit. A spirit is not limited to finances. A double portion can be defined as an extra endowment of God's favor, anointing, and power. It is a God-given benefit or special grace granted to selective individuals for the sole purpose of fulfilling their God-given assignment and bringing glory to God. Those individuals who possess God's special endowment and favor (double-portion anointing) are living instruments of God and speak on behalf of God.

Let's delve back into the life of Elisha before his request of the double portion from Elijah in order to have a better and deeper understanding of the double portion. In 1 Kings 19:16, God tells the prophet Elijah to anoint Elisha to succeed him as prophet. It is obvious therefore that Elisha loved and served God prior to God anointing him as a prophet. Therefore, it is apparent that God supernaturally anoints those who love Him.

In 1 Kings 19:19, we find that Elisha plowed the field with his 12 yoke of oxen. Elijah placed his mantle upon him.

Elisha left his oxen and ran after Elijah. Elisha then asked Elijah if he could kiss his mother and father good-bye. The double portion does not come without sacrifice.

When Elisha returned home, he took his 12 yoke of oxen and slaughtered them. Cooked the meat and gave it to the people. He then burned his plowing equipment. Afterwards, he followed Elijah and became his attendant. Therefore, we now see that the double portion requires total surrender. Elisha abandoned the things he held dear. He told his mother and father good-bye; he dismantled and liquidated his farming business. Elisha completely destroyed the things he relied upon for his livelihood and future.

One of the great apostles of Jesus Christ, Paul of Tarsus, received a special grace anointing (double portion) by Jesus Christ. Listen to what Jesus says to Ananias concerning Paul in Acts 9:15, "...He [Paul] is a chosen vessel unto me, to bear my name before the Gentiles, and kings, and the children of Israel." The Apostle Paul was not only a prophet but an anointed prophet of Jesus Christ. On one occasion, in Acts 20:9, seated in a window, a young man named Eutychus was sinking into a deep sleep as Paul was long in preaching. He fell from a three-story building and was picked up dead. Paul went down threw himself on the young man and the young man revived.

Paul can echo the same sentiments of sacrifice as Elisha. Paul said in Philippians 3:8, "But the things were gain to me, those I counted loss for Christ...I count all things but loss for the excellency of the knowledge of Christ Jesus...and do count them but dung that I may win Christ." Elisha and Paul gave up everything! Both Elisha and Paul were sold out to God and gave up everything for God. Elisha and Paul qualified for the double portion. Listen, don't bother asking God for the double portion if you are unwilling to deny yourself!

The Apostle Paul will tell you that there is no need to call a coroner, if someone falls out of a three-story building, all you need is the anointing (Acts 20:9). Elijah will tell you that there is no need to possess millions of dollars to sustain yourself during a famine–all you needed is the anointing (1 Kings

17). Elijah and Elisha will tell you there is no need to have a boat to cross the Jordan River–all you need is the anointing (2 Kings 2:8, 14). The widow woman will tell you that there is no need for the creditors to take your two sons to be bondsmen to pay off a debt–all you need is the anointing (2 Kings 4:1). The widow woman of Zarephath will tell you that there is no need to call the funeral home when your son dies–all you need is the anointing (1 Kings 17:8).

You don't need to be a part of the elite, rich, and famous to get ahead–all you need is the anointing. You don't need to sell your body for money–all you need is the anointing. You don't need to sell marijuana and drugs to pay your bills–all you need is the anointing. You don't need to succumb to depression and fear due to unemployment–all you need is the anointing. You don't need to have a million dollars to feel secure, due to a broken and troubled economy–all you need is the anointing.

Are you ready for the double portion? I am! The double portion anointing is what we should aspire for and pray to possess. Just as wisdom is better than rubies, silver, and gold (Proverb 8:11), God's glorious anointing is more precious, valuable, and powerful than anything we can imagine!

The double portion is exclusively for those who are fourth dimensional believers. The double portion is not an anointing that is arbitrarily given to anyone. Only those who are a part of the fourth dimension are eligible. The fourth dimension is not predicated upon the factors surrounding the natural world; it is independent of natural laws. The fourth dimension is a realm of the supernatural anointing. It is a dimension of the highest superiority, immensity, and power. The double portion represents the depth and scope of the fourth dimension.

Holy Spirit

Holy Spirit, travelling from place to place by day and by night,

Holy Spirit, this is the way your spirit gives us vision sight;

Holy Spirit, in the quietness of human space,

Holy Spirit, dreams and visions take their rightful place;

Holy Spirit, angels can see what we cannot see,

Holy Spirit, protecting God's children is their assignment that

must be;

Holy Spirit, the fourth dimension focuses on us,

Holy Spirit, because in everything in God we all trust.

CHAPTER 8

Divine Protectors

Pastor Ron Phillips, Senior Pastor of Abba's House in Chattanooga, Tennessee, told of an encounter he had with an angel in Alabama years ago. Pastor Phillips recalled as a young preacher that he was invited to preach in the rural hills of North Alabama. After preaching that evening, snow and ice had fallen and covered the roads and hills. As he drove home, the car began to skid out of control and stopped near the side of an embankment.

Pastor Phillips began to pray asking God for help. As he prayed, he heard a voice in his spirit say, "Your angel is sitting beside you. Command your angel to help you." Pastor Phillips said, "Angel will you go outside and help me not to skid and get me safely home." Pastor Phillips put the car in drive and proceeded down the mountain road until he came to a road block. The state trooper had closed the mountain and asked him how he made it down the mountain. Pastor Phillips replied that the Lord had helped him.

When the state trooper directed him to proceed down the road, he said, "Y'all be careful now." Pastor Phillips looked to the right on the front passage side of the car and saw a figure of a person sitting beside him. The state trooper had seen the figure of a person [angel], too.

When believers conduct themselves as an heir to the Kingdom of God, angels are sent to serve them. The Bible says in Hebrews 1:14, "Are they [angels] not all ministering spirits, sent out to render service for the sake of those who will inherit salvation?" (NASB). Angels are sent on assignment with those who are willing to go on assignment for God.

After Jesus fasted for 40 days and nights and was tempted of the devil, angels assisted or ministered unto him as He began His 3½ year ministerial assignment. The Bible says in Matthew 4:11, "Then the devil leaveth him [Jesus], and behold, angels came and ministered unto him." The angels cared for the needs of Jesus. They provided nourishment and strength to aid Him on His assignment. As Jesus prepared for His death on the cross, an angel assisted Him in the Garden of Gethsemane. The Bible says in Luke 22:43, "And there appeared an angel unto him [Jesus] from heaven, strengthening him." Angels are available to assist and strengthen those with a purpose and assignment in the Kingdom of God.

Not only do angels provide strength, protection, and guardianship for individuals, angels are highly organized, arranged, and assembled in ranks and hierarchy for certain specified assignments. Angels are strategically organized and ranked in military fashion.

The commander-in-chief of the cherubim angels is Michael, whose name means "who is like God." Michael is the angel warrior; he is the ultimate guardian and protector. He fights demonic principalities and powers on behalf of God and His Kingdom (Daniel 10:13).

Gabriel is another commander-in-chief of angels. He shows up to make announcements and shares the Word of God; he is the chief spokesman for God. Gabriel represents the voice of heaven. Gabriel brought the Word [of the Immaculate Conception] to Mary from the Lord concerning the virgin birth of the Messiah (Luke 1:28).

Gabriel also interprets dreams and answers prayers (Daniel 9:20-27). Divine dreams are messages from God. Gabriel is often sent to interpret and reveal messages, which are often cryptic and mysterious, from God. The angels Michael and Gabriel represent one of the highest ranks of angelic authority.

Moreover, angels are fascinated about salvation and the gospel of Jesus Christ. The Bible says in 1 Peter 1:12 that "It was then disclosed to them that the services they were rendering were not meant for themselves and their period of time, but for you. [It is these very] things which have now already been made known plainly to you by those who preached the good news (the gospel) to you by the [same] Holy Spirit sent from heaven. Into these things [the very] angels long to look!" (AmplifiedAngels have a strong curiosity concerning the power of the gospel and the spiritual lives of believers.

Angels are studious witnesses and active participants eager to assist in the advancement of the Kingdom of God. They rally and celebrate on the side of righteousness and truth. When a sinner comes to Christ, angels rejoice! Jesus said in Luke 15:10, "Likewise, I say unto you, there is joy in the presence of the angels of God over one sinner that repenteth." Angels dance, sing, and shout over a sinner who finds salvation and new life in Christ.

Angels are our invisible protectors and guardians. They defend on the side of righteousness and truth. Christ has not left us defenseless without divine assistance. God has given us His own personal, fourth dimensional, bodyguards to protect us.

Holy Spirit

Holy Spirit, through dreams and visions our purposes are revealed,

Holy Spirit, by God's mighty power our lives He has already lived;

Holy Spirit, you know the way we will take,

Holy Spirit, our guide, blessed Holy Ghost, never makes mistakes;

Holy Spirit, lead by the Master's hand,

Holy Spirit, seeing the future shows us we are under His command;

Holy Spirit, my life is now complete,

Holy Spirit, the fourth dimension is part of heaven's fleet.

CHAPTER 9

The Stronghold of Poverty

As I watch countless people in our community, nation, and abroad, living in slums and disease-infested communities with nothing to eat, I am convinced that there is nothing sacred or sanctimonious about poverty. Poverty is like a communicable disease or curse that will rob you of every aspect of life spiritually, mentally, naturally, and emotionally. Nothing can be worse than trying your best to survive and stay afloat only to sink and spiral deeper in financial destitution, depravity, and degradation.

The children of Israel experienced a time of deep stricken poverty and lack, as well, while in the Promised Land. The Bible says in Haggai 1:6, "Ye have sown much and bring in little; ye eat, but ye have not enough; ye drink, but ye are not filled with drink; ye clothe you, but there is none warm; and he that earneth wages earneth wages to put it into a bag with holes."

Notice here that the children of Israel sowed much, but reaped very little. This cycle began when they took what belonged to God and kept it for themselves. By refusing to obey and give back to God, they received little to nothing. God did not bless their efforts of sowing because they kept what belonged to him. Therefore, we understand that the concept of giving or the lack of giving has direct consequences.

Moreover, your systemic behavior in giving can impact future generations. When a generation fails to give as commanded by God, it can produce strongholds of poverty for the next generation and so on. It is important that we by example teach our children to give in the Kingdom of God. Strongholds are spiritual adhesives that can bond with the next generation, if not broken.

I believe the reason why we see the collapse of financial institutions throughout America and around the world is not just due to poor financial decision-making, but because the financial institutions have not recognized or practiced the Biblical principles of giving.

In other words, businesses have not given God the tithe, 10%, and offerings from their earnings. No person or institution can expect to prosper long without recognizing the God of prosperity, who gives us power to get wealth (Deuteronomy 8:18).

The prophet Haggai declared to the children of Israel that their prosperity had been severed or cut off by a stronghold of poverty, due to their lack of concern for the temple of God in Jerusalem (Haggai 1:6). Notice that the stronghold of poverty replaced their desired objective, prosperity.

Their physical condition of poverty was really an indicator of their spiritual condition. They were not concerned about their obedience to the laws and precepts of God. They were only concerned about their own self centeredness and personal interests. Their spiritual poverty manifested itself in a physical condition of poverty. I wonder how many of us are in physical poverty because of our spiritual condition.

The stronghold of poverty is a spiritual hold or grip that depletes even our basic needs of survival and necessities of life: That is, food, drink, clothes, and shelter. A stronghold is anything that hinders productivity and brings deprivation, desolation, discouragement, lack, and depletion.

Now if you are not in poverty, this message is not for you. However, before you make that assessment that you're not in poverty, let's define poverty in a few statements to see if we can identify with any of the scenarios below. Let's proceed.

If both husband and wife must work and neither one can afford to stop working, chances are we're in poverty. If we live from paycheck to paycheck, chances we're in poverty. If we pay our bills and have nothing left over, chances are we're in poverty. If we claim that we can't pay our tithes and offering because we have to pay our bills, chances are we're in poverty.

If we live in a beautiful house but can't afford to buy furniture because of the mortgage note chances are we're in poverty. If we have to work two and three jobs to make ends meet, chances are we're in poverty. If we have to pay one bill because it's further behind than the others and not pay the other bills, because we are out of money, chances are we're in poverty. If we have to call and make arrangements to pay a bill because we do not have the money on the date it is due, chances are we're in poverty.

If our bank accounts are overdrawn more than when money is in it, chances are we're in poverty. If we get bills in the mail and they are stacked up high on our desk because we have not bothered to open them because we do not have the money, chances are we're in poverty.

If our bills are not due, but past due, chances are we're in poverty. If we are worried about how we are going to pay our utility bills, chances are we're in poverty. If the baby needs a pair of shoes, telephone disconnected, and we're waiting on our next pay check, chances are we're in poverty. If we are always broke before payday, and after payday, chances are we're in poverty!

I once had a dream. There was an image of a man, who looked like my father who was dead in a casket. I prayed for the interpretation and understanding of the dream. I was a bit disturbed about the dream because I felt a sense of inner peace and not grief or sorrow. I asked myself, "Why would I feel at peace after dreaming about the death of my father?"

I consulted the Holy Spirit for the understanding of the dream. This is what the Spirit of God shared with me. He said, "The dead man that resembled your father was not your father, but the image of the generational stronghold of poverty, which God had destroyed. The image of your father was a representation of past generations. The death in the dream represented the death of the stronghold that had held the family back from wealth and prosperity for generations."

Imagine, if you will, a pond which is backed up and no fresh water or oxygen can flow freely in or out of the pond. This, of course, will produce and create problems for fish and other wildlife recipients in the pond. Most of the life in the pond would come to a slow crawl and eventually die. This is the effect of poverty. Poverty drains the life out of individuals, until they are unable to thrive and produce the way God intended.

This book is for every family member that can believe the Word of God by faith and declare in the Name of Jesus that this is the last day you will ever be broke for the rest of your life!

The Holy Spirit said no longer will you have to nickel and dime your way through life. The stronghold of poverty is over! No longer will you struggle with bouts of depression, oppression, anxiety, frustration, fear, and doubts because of the lack of financial resources. God has killed the stronghold of poverty in our lives.

The stronghold of poverty cannot be released or eliminated by receiving a million dollars. The stronghold of poverty has spiritual significance. Poverty is not only a generational stronghold but it is also tied to our spiritual genetics and spiritual DNA. You can't cure the stronghold of poverty by working seven days a week or working 16 hours a day!

The stronghold of poverty has to be released and eliminated by the power of God. Although giving is an important element in releasing the stronghold of poverty in our lives, giving is only half the battle. Have you ever noticed that when you give God blesses you, but as time goes on, you find yourself back in the same state you were before?

Giving with a stronghold of poverty only eliminates the symptoms. It's just like a person with a cold or the flu. You can eliminate many of the symptoms associated with a cold-like coughing, sneezing, congestion, and fever by taking cold medicines, but that does not cure the cold. It just makes you feel better.

If there is a stronghold of poverty in your life, it must be destroyed. The only thing that can destroy the stronghold of poverty is the anointing of God. Isaiah 10:27 says, "And it shall come to pass in that day, that his burden shall be taken away from off thy shoulder, and his yoke from off thy neck, and the yoke shall be destroyed because of the anointing." What Isaiah is saying here is that the spiritual yoke that binds, hinders, and prevents us from progressing must be destroyed. How are strongholds released or destroyed? By the anointing and the power of God!

Poverty is more spiritual than most people think. The spirit of poverty is a stronghold established for the purpose of keeping us from walking in the fullness and the victory gained for us at the cross. In other words, poverty attempts to keeps us from our blessed inheritance in Christ.

What better way for satan to stop the advancement of the Kingdom of God than to impede upon our financial resources? The first church was established by individuals bringing money to the apostles in support of the ministry.

The Bible says, "Neither was there any among them that lacked: for as many as were possessors of lands or houses sold them, and brought the prices of the things that were sold, And laid them down at the apostles' feet: and distribution was made unto every man according as he had need" (Acts 4:34-35).

Therefore, if it took financial resources to establish the first church, it will continue to take financial resources in spreading the gospel of Jesus Christ.

Satan understands and knows the Word of God. He knows that if you don't have anything to give, you will not receive. God established the law of sowing and reaping in the beginning. In Genesis 8:22, the Bible says "While the earth remaineth, seedtime and harvest... shall not cease."

Even the poor widow in Mark 12:42-44 understood this law and principle. The Bible says:

> And there came a certain poor widow, and she
> threw in two mites, which make a farthing; And he
> [Jesus] called unto him his disciples and saith unto

56

them, Verily I say unto you, That this poor widow hath cast more in, than they which have cast into the treasury; for all they did cast in of their abundance; but she of her want did cast in all that she had, even all her living.

Notice here that she gave because she wanted to, not based on her need, but based upon her desire.

Yes, she only gave two mites (which is equivalent to a penny), but she gave something. Jesus never recognized those who did not give, but wanted to, or had a desire to give. He only recognized those who wanted to and gave. Listen, you have got to give something. The Bible says in 2 Corinthians 9:7, "...For God loveth a cheerful giver." In other words, God loves those who want to give and have a desire to give—and gives.

There's a story of a woman who would always tell her pastor that she had a mind to give, but she just didn't have the money. Have you ever heard people say, "I got the mind to give, but don't have the money?" Well, she was one who would say it often. Then one day, she inherited a great sum of money. After some time passed, the pastor asked her about giving and about blessing the church with an offering. She stated she has the money, but now she didn't have the mind! Therefore, having the mind to give is not enough; you must give something.

Strongholds can be subtle and difficult to detect. Why do we pray for salvation and healing for the body, but never for the release of the stronghold of poverty? It is because we never see poverty as a stronghold. We accept the idea of poverty as our fate in life. Just because you were not born in a wealthy family does not mean you have to die poor. The devil is a liar!

When we start accepting the fact that poverty is a curse that can be released, as well as sin, we will begin to see life in a whole different light. The Bible says in 2 Corinthians 8:9, "For ye know the grace of our Lord Jesus Christ, that, though he was rich, yet for your sakes he became poor, that ye through his poverty might be rich." In other words, for poverty, God has given us wealth; for sickness, God has given us health; and for death God has given us eternal life.

57

Life is all about the choices and decisions we make. We will be judged and evaluated based on the decisions and choices that we make. Our choices and decisions drive our lives and the actions we perform. You can choose to believe God or not. However, I want to caution you that the Bible says in Romans 14:23 "...for whatsoever is not of faith is sin." What do you choose?

In the book of Joshua 24:15, Joshua tells the people of Israel "And if it seem evil unto you, to serve the Lord, choose you this day, whom ye will serve...but as for me and my house, we will serve the Lord." Many have chosen to accept poverty, and yes, you can go to heaven poor. Lazarus did. Remember, Lazarus? In the book of Luke 16:20, the real meaning of Lazarus and the rich man had little or nothing to do with God favoring the poor, over the rich. The rich man did not go to hell because he was rich, neither did Lazarus go to heaven because he was poor. The real meaning of the rich man and the poor man is that one decided to make Jesus Lord and the other decided to make his money Lord.

Listen, there will be as many poor people in hell as there are rich people, and there will be as many rich people in heaven as there are poor people. Lazarus' only failure on Earth was not that he was lazy or refused to work, but his failure was that he depended on man for provision instead of God.

Why is it true that we can believe God for salvation and healing, but not for the blessings of prosperity? Often times, we believe our prosperity and provision will come from man. However, the Bible makes it clear in Deuteronomy 8:18 "But thou shalt remember the Lord thy God: for it is he, that giveth thee power to get wealth..."

The rich man's failure was not that he was rich, but that he believed that his prosperity was enough to gain salvation. Do you know that many believe and think their works alone will gain them eternal life, without having a heart and love for God?

You can also go to heaven sick if you choose. However, I believe God can heal both financially and physically. I choose to believe Isaiah 53:5 for financial healing as well as physical healing. The Bible says in Isaiah 53:5, "But he was wounded for our transgression, he was bruised for our iniquities: the chastisement of our peace was upon him; and with his stripes we are healed." God promises include healing in every area of our lives, including our pocketbook!

I have chosen to live life the way Christ intended, more abundantly. Jesus said in John 10:10, "...I am come that they might have life, and that they might have it more abundantly." This abundant life starts now, not when you die.

In fact, even in death, we can have abundant life in Christ. Death in Christ is not a means to an end; it is rather a means to a greater dimension. Death is not a state of no longer existing, but rather a transfer of one state or place to another. Therefore, we shall never die. Eternity is ours right now!

Saints of God may leave their earthly body, but they will never die. Paul said in 2 Corinthians 5:6 that to be absent from the body is to be present with the Lord. So death in Christ is just going from an inferior dimension to a greater and glorious dimension. As a believer of Jesus Christ, we are living eternally with Christ right now

You can choose to be bound by curses or you can choose to be set free. However, the Word of God is crystal clear that, "If the Son therefore shall make you free, ye shall be free indeed" (John 8:36).

In Deuteronomy 30:19, Moses said unto the children of Israel, "I call heaven and earth to record this day against you that I have set before you life and death, blessing and cursing, therefore choose life that both thou and thy seed may live." The choices we make today will determine our earthly future and eternal destiny.

Some choices result in blessings while others result in curses. The Bible says in Galatians 3:13 that "Christ hath redeemed us from the curse of the law being made a curse for us..." We are redeemed from every curse and every stronghold of the enemy.

By the authority of the Holy Spirit, we must no longer allow or tolerate any strongholds which hinder the working of the power of God. A fourth dimensional believer is one who is free from the strongholds of the enemy. We must rebuke every stronghold in our lives by the name of Jesus.

In the fourth dimension, there is total freedom and liberty in the author and finisher of our faith. Hebrews 12:2 says, "Looking unto Jesus the author and finisher of our faith; who for the joy that was set before him endured the cross, despising the shame, and is set down at the right hand of the throne of God."

God has given us an overflow of His riches and abundance in the fourth dimension. We will no longer be servants of poverty. You are now released from the stronghold of poverty in the fourth dimension.

Holy Spirit

Holy Spirit, write the Spirit's way in our hearts,

Holy Spirit, in the night we will receive our parts;

Holy Spirit, through dreams and visions our calling comes forth,

Holy Spirit, the fourth dimension is that driving force;

Holy Spirit, the invisible you can see,

Holy Spirit, all that heaven has for me;

Holy Spirit, everything will be revealed,

Holy Spirit, when we stay close to you in God's will.

CHAPTER 10

Prayer and Angels

Do you desire angels to minister to you and work on your behalf like they did for Christ while He was on the earth? There are certain actions or behaviors that cause angelic hosts to become more involved in our lives. One such action is prayer.

Angels are attracted to prayer. Anytime fervent prayer and supplication to God are known and present, so are angels. Philippians 4:6 says, "...but in every thing by prayer and supplication with thanksgiving let your requests be made known unto God." When we pray angels are drawn to our words. Angels come to watch over our words of prayer and ensure that our prayers are not hindered.

Angels are sent to safeguard our prayers. The angel said unto Daniel, "...Fear not, Daniel: for from the first day that thou didst set thine heart to understand, and to chasten thyself before thy God, thy words were heard, and I am come for thy words" (Daniel 10:12). Notice that the angel came for the words that Daniel spoke in prayer. Daniel had a consistent and committed prayer life.

If we want angelic hosts continuously around us, we must develop a daily routine of praying throughout the day. The Bible commands us not only to pray, but to pray without ceasing (1 Thessalonians 5:17). The Apostle Paul, the writer of Thessalonians, knew that continuous prayer creates an increase in supernatural results and brings continuous angelic support.

In fact, prayers are sacred to God and angels. Prayer, worship, and praise are the three elements which make up the atmosphere of heaven (Revelation 4:8). Although innumerable angels are stationed on Earth, just as military soldiers are stationed in foreign countries, our prayer, worship, and praise to God reminds them of their home in heaven.

The more we pray, worship, and praise God the more angelic beings revolve around us. Who would not like for heavenly angels with protection and blessings to hang around them?

Angels know of the spiritual power and value of prayer. We are the ones who fail to understand the spiritual and supernatural significance of it.

Moreover, angels are the ones who carry our prayers to the throne room of God. They know that God is pleased with them, and with us, when they bring our prayers to Him. Prayers are the gifts that God receives from angels.

Angels watch over the prayers of the saints of God like cherished and precious treasures. Angels keep the prayers, which are not answered, in the presence of God. The Bible says in Revelation 8:4, "And the smoke of the incense, which came with the prayers of the saints, ascended up before God out of the angel's hand."

No prayer ever prayed is forgotten. Have you prayed today? Have you given God a gift through prayer? Your angel is waiting to receive your prayer gift and present it to the Lord!

Prayers are illustrated as "golden vials" of incense. The Bible says, "And when he had taken the book, the four beasts and four and twenty elders fell down before the Lamb, having every one of them harps, and golden vials full of odours, which are the prayers of saints" (Revelation 5:8). Every angel desires to have a golden vial of believer's prayer incense in their hands in the presence of God.

Golden vials, which are the prayers of the saints, represent the requests of the sons and daughters of the King of Kings and the Lord of Lords. Angels present our prayers as sweet–smelling incense before the throne of God. Prayers are adored in heaven and are in the care of worshipping angels. No prayers ever go unnoticed. Angels collect all of our prayers and they are offered to God as a holy sacrifice.

If you want an angel near you, just start praying! When we pray, angels are immediately drawn to our prayers. Angels nurture our prayers and provide answers to our prayers. There is an account in Luke chapter 8 which bears record. The Bible says in Luke 1:8-12 that while Zacharias was serving as the priest an angel appeared to him. An angel would always come down to receive the prayers from the altar of incense at the hour of incense in Jerusalem. As the crowd gathered outside to worship God in prayer, Zacharias burned incense in the temple of the Lord.

On this occasion, the angel Gabriel, who was usually invisible, became visible. Not only was the angel there to receive the prayers from the altar of incense, but also to tell Zacharias that he and his wife Elizabeth would have a son. Their prayers of having a child would be granted, although he and his wife were well over the child-bearing years.

The answer to Zacharias and Elizabeth's long awaited prayer was so incomprehensible that Zacharias did not believe the announcement from the angel Gabriel. Because of Zacharias' doubt and unbelief, he was instantly struck mute so that he would not confess a single word of unbelief during Elizabeth's entire pregnancy. The angel Gabriel knew that the words of doubt and unbelief would abort the Word of God from coming to pass, including the birth of John the Baptist.

This event in the life of Zacharias and Elizabeth lets us know that it does not matter how long it takes, God will answer prayer. Our prayers are never a waste of time nor are they ever wasted. Angels are always present to collect our prayers. Although our prayers may not be answered immediately, wait on God; He will come through!

When we pray, angels are there to give us urgent aid and support during times of struggle and affliction. Because of the Apostle Paul's prayers, 276 people were saved while ship wrecked for 14 days on the sea (Acts 27:27-37). Paul speaks to the ship's crew and passengers on board the ship saying,

> *And now I exhort you to be of good cheer: for there shall be no loss of any man's life among you, but of the ship. For there stood by me this night the angel of God, whose I am, and whom I serve, Saying, Fear not, Paul; thou must be brought before Caesar: and, lo, God hath given thee all them that sail with thee. Wherefore, sirs, be of good cheer: for I believe God, that it shall be even as it was told me"* (Acts 27:22-25).

The Apostle Paul was committed to prayer and supplication throughout his ministry.

Paul continued saying to the centurion and to the soldiers, "Except these abide in the ship, ye cannot be saved. Wherefore I pray you to take some meat, for this is for your health: for there shall not an hair fall from the head of any of you" (Acts 27:31, 34).

Without the faithful and persistent prayers of Paul, no one would have survived the hurricane-fierce winds that impacted their journey on the sea. Although the journey was hazardous and arduous, the power of prayer saved everyone on board.

Prayer is a fourth dimensional mode or medium that reaches heaven. It is a portal by which we can ascend into the throne room of God for immediate assistance. Listen, if you prayed today, your name and prayers were mentioned in the presence of Almighty God. If you have not prayed today, it's not too late; your prayers can still make it to heaven on time. Do it today! No prayer to God in the matchless name of Jesus is a waste of time.

Holy Spirit

Holy Spirit, our eyes have not seen,

Holy Spirit, what dreams and visions can bring;

Holy Spirit, carrying us in this blessed flight,

Holy Spirit, giving us your spiritual sight;

Holy Spirit, in that place our future will know,

Holy Spirit, spoken by God long ago;

Holy Spirit, you promised to show us things to come,

Holy Spirit, in the fourth dimension it's already done.

CHAPTER 11

The Power of Humility

Oftentimes, when people hear the word "humble" or "humility" they immediately think of a person who is quiet and easy-going. Others may see a person of humility as a push-over, weak, soft, timid, and with no backbone. However, this is far from the truth and erroneous thinking. Humility has nothing to do with being walked over like a door mat. Humility is strength and power under control. True humility can be seen as one having the ability or power to execute [or wield judgment], but chooses not to do so.

Jesus said in Matthew 23:12, "And whosoever shall exalt himself shall be abased and he that shall humble himself shall be exalted." Notice here that Jesus says that one may choose to live and walk humbly or not. Humility is a choice in response to the way we think–not a shy, bashful, or timid personality trait. This one verse of Scripture spoken by Jesus is one of the most significant verses in the entire Bible – the power of humility. What many do not understand is that humility has its roots in authority.

Humility is not the absence of power, but the recognition that the power given to you originates from a greater source. Our power and ability is based on the authority of another. Jesus, who is the prototype of humility, said, "I can of mine own self do nothing...because I seek not mine own will, but the will of the Father which hath sent me" (John 5:30).

In essence, Jesus is saying that all power and authority comes from God. This truth is revealed in Psalms 62:11 which says, "God hath spoken once; twice have I heard this; that power belongeth unto God."

Jesus is our greatest example of humility. Christ, the epitome of all-power, might, and strength, took on the form of perfect humility. The Bible says in Philippians 2:5-8:

> *Who [Jesus Christ], being in the form of God, thought it not robbery to be equal with God: But made himself of no reputation, and took upon him the form of a servant, and was made in the likeness of men: and being found in fashion as a man, he [Jesus] humbled himself, and became obedient unto death, even the death of the cross.*

Jesus humbled himself to the will of His Father that we may receive salvation through His death. Humility is always based on the benefit and good of one other than self. It represents selflessness in its purest form.

Those in positions of power and authority in the nations of the world get their dominion from God. Pontius Pilate, Roman Governor of Judaea, thought he had the power to impose the death sentence or set Jesus free. However, Jesus told Pilate that what he was given to perform execution and impose judgment came from God. The Bible says in John 19:10, "Then saith Pilate unto him [Jesus], Speakest thou not unto me? Knowest thou not that I have power to crucify thee, and have power to release thee? Jesus answered, Thou couldest have no power at all against me, except it were given thee from above..." Jesus was telling Pilate that he was not some lowly, weak, insignificant Jew under Roman rule. Jesus could quite well defend Himself if He wanted. The authority that Pilate had to execute judgment was given to him by God the Father who is the giver of all authority and power. The Bible is clear where power resides. Power originates and rest with God (Psalms 62:11).

After Jesus' betrayal and arrest in the Garden of Gethsemane, Jesus assured those who came to arrest him that He had the vested authority to immediately call down more than twelve legions of angels [72,000] to defend Him if He desired. Jesus said in Matthew 26:53-54, "Thinkest thou that I cannot now pray to my Father, and he shall presently give me more than twelve legions of angels. But how then shall the scriptures be fulfilled, that thus it must be?"

Jesus not only had the power to resist arrest, but He could call down 12 legions of angels to fight and defend Him at a moment's notice. Yet, Jesus humbled Himself. Humility is the ability to rely on a higher power than your own. It is the desire to succumb to the will of another and the understanding to know that your ability is insufficient of itself.

To humble yourself is to give yourself to another. The power of humility comes into fruition when you place yourself in the hands of an omnipotent, all-powerful God. When you submit to God's authority, He will use you in the most powerful, glorious, and awesome ways. You will defeat every enemy and bring glory to the Name of Jesus

When you have humbled yourself to God, you are in essence surrendering your life to Christ. But if you choose to rely upon your own self, as if you are all sufficient, you will lose your life. Jesus said in Matthew 16:25, "...Whosoever will save his life shall lose it, and whosoever will lose his life for my sake shall find it."

The opposite of humility is pride. A prideful person is one who thinks he is self sufficient and self reliant. There is an imminent danger in exalting oneself. The originator of pride is satan. Before the beginning of creation, we find satan lifted up in pride, exalting himself, thinking that he should have the position of Almighty God. Isaiah 14:13 says, "For thou [satan] hast said in thine heart, I will ascend into heaven I will exalt my throne above the stars of God, I will sit also upon the mount of the congregation, in the sides of the north."

Listen to satan's thoughts, not only did he believe he was self sufficient, he believed he should be greater than God. I want you to know that satan didn't just wake up and say I should be God. The pride in him grew so that he became obsessed with himself and that obsession led to sin.

In the book of Ezekiel 28:15, the Word of God says "Thou [satan] wast perfect in thy ways, from the day that thou wast created, till iniquity was found in thee." What started out as the pride ended up as sin. The moment you think you are all-sufficient and all-encompassing, you are in danger of failing. The Bible says in Proverb 16:18, "Pride cometh before destruction and a haughty spirit before a fall."

The moral lesson here is when you exalt yourself you are taking what belongs to God. Don't take what belongs to Him; God alone is to be exalted. He alone is worthy of all the glory and the honor. God said in Isaiah 42:8, "I am the lord that is my name and my glory will I not give to another, neither my praise to graven images." Listen, if you are in the business of promoting and exalting yourself, you are acting just like the devil. If you want to be promoted, get humility not pride. Humility will lift you up when everything else is falling down.

Jesus said in Mark 10:43-44, "But so shall it not be among you, but whosoever will be great among you, shall be your minister; and whosoever of you will be the chiefest shall be servant of all." What Jesus is saying is if you want to be great, you must humble yourself. In other words, if you want to go up, you must first come down.

In the book of Job, I've often wondered what is the reason God is, seemingly, forever silent with Job. I soon discover that Job struggled with pride. In the book of Job, Job is forever defending himself. Why does God not help this man? The answer is because Job has not yet come to the place where he is willing to let go of himself and surrender. As long as people are defending themselves, God will not defend them.

There is a continual theme that runs throughout the Bible: as long as you justify yourself, God will never justify you. As long as Job thought he was some self-righteous ground on which to stand, God's silence remained. This is true in our lives, as well.

As long as we think we have justification in our own righteous, we cannot receive the Christ's perfect justification of righteousness. 1 Corinthians 2:30 says, "But of him are ye in Christ Jesus, who of God is made unto us wisdom, and righteousness, and sanctification, and redemption."

Jesus began His first sermon, called the Sermon on the Mount, saying, "Blesseth are the poor in spirit for theirs is the Kingdom of heaven" (Matthew 5:3). Those who are bankrupt in themselves, who have come to the end of themselves, and rely on God, shall inherit the Kingdom of heaven. When we stop defending and justifying ourselves, God will rise to take up our cause.

This is one of the important lessons in the book of Job. God taught Job a lesson on humility. We must remember it was God who brought satan in remembrance of Job. Satan wasn't even thinking about Job at that time. God taught Job that he must have a spirit of humility, regardless of whether he felt that he did anything wrong. The Bible says in Isaiah 64:6 "But we are all as an unclean thing and all our righteousness is as filthy rags..."

When the book of Job opens up, we see that there is a challenge between God and the devil; but this is not just about a challenge between God and the devil regarding Job's allegiance and faithfulness to God. God used satan to teach the preacher (Job) a lesson on humility.

God is so awesome. When satan thinks he is getting the upper hand on God's people, God is using satan to elevate us and bring glory to His name. God always has an ace up His sleeve! Remember this: when you are going through changes, stay humble; God is setting you up for elevation and supernatural breakthrough!

What satan does not understand is that he is being used by God! When he messes with God's children it causes promotion to come to us and demotion to come to satan. He still has not figured out that no created being (man or angel) can defeat a non-created, self existing, and eternal God. Satan is just as stupid as he was when he tried to take over heaven (Isaiah

14:13-14). Satan couldn't defeat God then, and he can't defeat him now, nor can he defeat God's children.

One thing we must give satan credit for is his persistence. If we were half as persistent as the devil, we would be a force to be reckoned with in Christ! We would not be so quick to give up. Nothing could just blow us over.

It was only when Job humbled himself (Job 42:6) that God exalted him (Job 42:12). The Bible says "Humble yourselves under the mighty hand of God that he may exalt you in due time (1 Peter 5:6). Notice that the Bible says "humble yourselves" under the mighty hand of God. In other words, you must submit to the Word and authority of God, recognizing that we are nothing without Him. Your attitude should be one of submission and meekness. Job was in error because he thought God was unjust. Therefore, his attitude toward God was self righteous, putting God on trial. Job thought he was right and God was wrong (Job 13).

Again, the Bible says: humble yourself under the mighty hand of God. It does **not** say, humble yourself under the mighty hand of the devil! Listen, when it comes to satan you must stand straight, square your shoulders, look the devil straight in the eye, and let him know that you are under the authority of Jesus Christ. Command and rebuke him with the power and dominion that you have in the Holy Ghost because the only thing he respects is the power of God! To put it plainly, humility is power under cover.

The idea of humility reminds me of the mild-mannered fictitious character Clark Kent. He is the humble and meek gentleman working as a news reporter for the Daily Planet. However, when trouble comes he takes off his shirt and reveals who he really is–a force to reckon with. When he takes off his shirt there's a big "S" on his chest which stands for Superman. The same way Clark Kent behaves, we should too. Clark Kent doesn't roll over when there's enemies to fight. He just pulls his shirt off and reveals the power under the cover – the power of humility.

In a way, we are like the DC Comics™ character, Superman, who can leap over tall buildings with a single bound, stronger than a locomotive, and faster than a speeding bullet. God has given us power to tread on serpents and scorpions, cast out devils, and lay hands on the sick. He has given us power over all the power of the enemy and nothing shall by any means hurt us (Mark 16:17-18; Luke 10:19).

The difference between Superman and the children of God is that Superman has a weakness and is vulnerable to the radioactive element kryptonite. We, who are in Christ, have no weakness or vulnerability because our God has no weaknesses.

We must always be strong in the Lord and the power of His might (Ephesians 6:10). There's a song that says, "God don't need no coward soldiers." You see, you can't have a cowardice attitude when you are facing the devil; he smells and senses fear and unbelief. The devil cannot defeat you if you are standing under the authority of the Lord, Jesus Christ. The Bible says in 1 John 4:4, "Ye are of God, little children and have overcome them, because greater is he, that is in you, than he, that is in the world." Don't run from the devil, he is supposed to flee from you because of the God in you!

God gives favor and dispenses power to those who are willing to submit to His authority. The Bible says in James 4:6, "But he giveth more grace, wherefore he saith, God resisteth the proud, but giveth grace unto the humble." This means that God blesses those who honor and give glory to Him instead of themselves.

All God is looking for is for someone to give Him praise and worship. God deserves our praise. The Psalmist said in Psalms 113:3, "From the rising of the sun unto the going down of the same the Lord's name is to be praised." Humility is the recognition that without God we can do nothing.

The power of humility changes lives and affects the lives of those it encounters. If you want power and authority, seek humility. There are hidden treasures in the strength of humility. The Apostle Paul said in 1 Corinthians 2:9, "But as it is written, Eye hath not seen nor ear heard neither have entered into the heart of man, the things which God hath prepared for them that love him."

Imagine finding a book that reveals hidden treasures that have been lost for centuries and you alone have discovered its hidden mysteries. This is the revelation of the power of humility. This precious and life-changing characteristic still eludes many Christians. Thus, the power of humility remains a hidden treasure.

God has already given us power over sickness, power to open the blinded eyes, power to unstop the deaf ears, power to command the lame to walk, power to command the dumb to talk, power to break the bonds of poverty, power to heal all manner of sickness and diseases, power to cast out devils, power to raise the dead, and power to deliver and set free.

If you only knew what was in store for you and all you had to do was humble yourself, you wouldn't hesitate to submit your will to God's will. In the book of John 4:10, Jesus tells the woman of Samaria, "If thou knewest the gift of God and who it is that saith to thee, Give me to drink, thou wouldest have asked of him, and he would have given thee living water." Jesus was saying to the woman of Samaria that she didn't have a clue to whom she was talking. If she only knew, she would be asking Him about life that flows through Him—a life that gives power, authority, and dominion just for the asking!

However, just like many today, this woman was trying to fix her own problems by looking to man and entering one relationship after another. Every time she tried, her situation and troubles grew worse. But when she humbled herself and turned it over to Jesus, the problem-solver, He delivered her and set her free.

God won't work on your behalf until you stop trying to work it out. Humble yourself and realize that Jesus is the only One who can handle your situation. Stop trying to work your problems out, give them to Jesus.

Humility is a foundational infrastructure of the fourth dimension. Unfortunately, humility has no value or significance in the natural world. Humility represents the personification and character of Jesus Christ.

When you humble yourself, based on the work of Christ on the cross you become like Christ. The power and authority of humility is available to all believers in the fourth dimension. Fourth dimensional beings are those who have humbled themselves before the mighty hand of God. Humility is not weakness, but power under control. You can possess the unlimited power and authority of humility in the fourth dimension.

Holy Spirit

Holy Spirit, you are wrapped in the three-in-one,

Holy Spirit, you bring in the blessed presence of the Father and the

Son;

Holy Spirit, we are talking about the fourth dimension here,

Holy Spirit, there is no space you have not filled, you were already

there;

Holy Spirit, because of Christ, mysteries will all be revealed someday

I know,

Holy Spirit, the Trinity, God the Father, God the Son, and God the

Holy Ghost;

Holy Spirit, now I am wrapped up in the One,

Holy Spirit, Jesus is my Messiah, God's only Son.

CHAPTER 12

Faith and Angels

Faith is more than believing in God. According to the Word of God, faith is a fruit of the Spirit. Galatians 5:22 says, "But the fruit of the Spirit is love, joy, peace, longsuffering, gentleness, goodness, faith..."

Faith is the magnetic form that draws the third dimensional and fourth dimensional realms together. Hebrews 11:6 says, "But without faith it is impossible to please him: for he that cometh to God must believe that he is, and that he is a rewarder of them that diligently seek him." Faith is the spiritual magnet that draws us to God and God to us.

Faith is the heart and soul of the Christian experience. Faith is not only the hallmark of our relationship with God, it governs the supernatural world. Nothing can be accomplished in the supernatural world of the fourth dimension without faith. The Bible says, "...Even God, who quickeneth the dead, and calleth those things which be not as though they were" (Romans 4:17). If God utilizes or practices the act of faith in all that He does, then faith is the single most attribute we must all possess and utilize.

Just as God does not change, faith is unchanging and eternal. It works the same in our world as it does in heaven. Every being in heaven is filled with faith. It is the one thing that every believer of Jesus Christ has in common in both heaven and Earth. Faith is the element which bridges the connection between human beings and heavenly beings.

The word "angels" come from the Greek word *aggelos* meaning herald or messenger. God uses angels to communicate with the third dimensional world. Angels transport messages and communicate to Earth the instructions of God. Angels are disciplined, orderly, and obedient beings; they do not deviate from the laws of the Kingdom and Word of God.

Angels only respond to and are activated by the Word of God to those who have faith. The Bible says in Psalms 103:20-21, "Bless the Lord, ye his angels, That excel in strength, that do his commandments, Hearkening unto the voice of his word. Bless ye the Lord, all ye his hosts; Ye ministers of his, that do his pleasure."

When believers of Christ speak the Word of God by faith out of their mouths, angels see the Word as "marching orders". The Word of God is marching orders to angels. Angels quickly stand at attention and move out in formation when the Word is spoken by faith. When you confess the Word of God, angels move instantly to manifest or bring to pass what was spoken. Angels reverence and duly respect the Word of God.

Just as people like to be around others who share commonalities or similar interests, angels are driven and allured to people of faith. Faith is a spirit, just as angels are ministering spirits. Spirits attract other spirits. The Bible says, "What are all the angels? They are spirits sent to serve those who are going to receive salvation" (Hebrews 1:14, GW).

Since faith is a fruit of the Spirit (Galatians 5:22), faith acts as a magnetic attraction with other spiritual beings. What people of faith believe about the Word of God, angels already know. Therefore, angels align themselves with faith-filled believers.

Jesus said in Matthew 18:19-20, "...If two of you shall agree on earth as touching any thing that they shall ask, it shall be done for them of my Father which is in heaven. For where two or three are gathered together in my name, there am I in the midst of them." Even if you are standing alone in believing what the Word of God says, you have angels [on Earth] who agree with you. You are never alone in faith when it pertains to the Word of God.

The opposite of faith is fear which is also a spirit. Fear is the same spiritual force as faith, but in reverse order. Faith is produced by hearing the Word of God (Romans 10:17). Fear comes by hearing and believing things which are not the Word of God.

Fear is the belief in the enemy's ability to harm you. Imagine faith and fear in terms of the drive and reverse gears in an automobile. When faith is released the car is in drive. When fear is released the car goes into reverse. You cannot move a car forward and in reverse at the same time. The same with faith, you cannot operate in faith and fear simultaneously.

As believers of Christ, we must always be driven by faith instead of fear. Fear attracts spirits as faith attracts spirits. The Bible says in 2 Timothy 1:7, "For God hath not given us the spirit of fear; but of power, and of love, and of a sound mind."

Angels assist faith-filled believers consistently more often than those who operate in fear, doubt, and unbelief. Abraham, the father of faith, received support from several encounters with angels. On one occasion, three angels visited Abraham. In chapter 18 of Genesis, three angels came to bring Abraham a prophetic word concerning the birth of his promised son, Isaac (Genesis 18:1-14).

Faith-filled believers are surrounded by angelic beings. Once a believer sets out on a new frontier of faith, angels stand ready to undergird them with support and spiritual strength in the fourth dimension.

Holy Spirit

Holy Spirit, when He came to set me free,

Holy Spirit, all that is God is now in me;

Holy Spirit, my life is now complete,

Holy Spirit, because you are the Spirit I seek;

Holy Spirit, your breath is my living source,

Holy Spirit, sealed by the power of the Trinity's force;

Holy Spirit, now there's in the fourth dimension no boundaries,

Holy Spirit, because He reigns and rules throughout all countries.

CHAPTER 13

The Anointed Seed of Prosperity

Everything begins with a seed! It is amazing to me how the seed of a tiny acorn can turn into a mighty oak tree. Oak trees grow as much as 100 feet high and four feet in diameter. Oak trees can live to be 600 years or older. Amazingly, the potential of an awesome tree is stored in a tiny and seemingly insignificant seed called an acorn.

I have often wondered what is so special about a seed. Seeds are special because they are supernatural. They come from God. God is the creator of the seed. He is the seed producer and manufacturer. Every seed came from God. Man is not a seed-creator; he is not the creator of seed. God is!

The Bible says in Genesis 1:11-12, "And God said, let the earth bring forth grass, the herb yielding seed and the fruit tree yielding seed, after its kind, whose seed was in itself upon the earth and it was so."

Therefore, we see that seeds were created by the spoken wWord of God. Moreover, God spoke and life was created in the seed! Seed has the innate ability to produce and multiply due to the invisible instruction written in it by the Word of God at the dawn of creation. The seed has no choice but to multiply!

Not only is God the Creator of seed, God Himself became a seed. The greatest seed ever given to us was in the person of Jesus Christ. God gave Abraham a promise saying, "And in thy seed shall all the nations of the earth be blessed; because thou hast obeyed my voice" (Genesis 22:18). The seed God is referring to, through Abraham, is the person of Jesus Christ. Jesus would be born under the Jewish nation. His birth would bring complete deliverance and eternal salvation to all the nations of the world.

Notice the first four words of Genesis 22:18 (above), "And in thy seed..." The word "seed" is singular *meaning that of a person*. The Apostle Paul explains this idea of a single "seed" further in Galatians 3:16 saying, "Now to Abraham and his seed were the promises made. He saith not, and to seeds, as of many; but as of one, and to thy seed, which is Christ."

Paul makes it clear that the seed that God is referring to in Genesis is Jesus Christ. Therefore, when God tells Abraham "in thy seed shall all the nations of the earth be blessed," He was saying: in Jesus Christ will all the nations of the earth be blessed. Our eternal harvest and prosperity begins in the anointed seed of Jesus Christ. Without Jesus, true prosperity is unobtainable and unachievable.

God's eternal plan of salvation for man was hidden in a seed, Jesus Christ. Naturally, the secret to an apple or an apple orchard is hidden in the seed; the seed produces the harvest. The secret to godly prosperity is hidden in a seed!

Notice in Genesis 1:11 (above), that the seed can only reproduce after its kind. In other words, the seed that you sow is the fruit that it will yield or produce.

A seed represents a beginning. Everything on Earth has a beginning. Even your prosperity must have a beginning. Let's define prosperity in its simplest form. Prosperity simply means, "no debt and no loss." In essence, everything you acquire or obtain is increase. It has nothing to do with the amount of Italian or European cars you own or how many condos and high-rise apartments and town houses you possess.

Let's go to an often preached, but often misunderstood, chapter on sowing and reaping, in Genesis chapter 26. The Bible says in Genesis 26:12, "Then Isaac sowed in that land, and received in the same year an hundredfold, and the lord blessed him."

The first word in verse 12 is "Then" which denotes something happening before Isaac had sowed. What happened before he sowed? In the preceding verses starting with verse 7, Isaac lied about his relationship with his wife in fear of being killed by the Philistines. Because Rebekah, his wife was beautiful, Isaac lied and said that she was his sister. Listen to what Isaac said in verse 7 of Genesis 26, "...She is my sister, for he [Isaac] feared to say, she is my wife; lest said he, the men of the place should kill me for Rebekah; because she was fair to look upon."

Isaac lying about his wife was absolutely wrong. He messed up! However, this event in the life of Isaac lets us know that even when we mess up, God is still faithful. Isaac made a bad decision by trying to save and protect himself instead of trusting God for his survival.

What caused Isaac to lie? Fear. Even we, as believers, make bad and poor decisions in fear of what could happen to us, not willing to rely and trust in God for our needs and protection. Listen, when God gives you a promise, as He did Isaac, the enemy will always try to stop the promises of God in your life by creating fear.

You cannot operate in faith with a fearful spirit and fearful mentality. Often times, we too go into self-preservation mode due to fear. We don't fully realize that God is our life preserver, and we cannot save ourselves. We cannot preserve our selves. Just like his father, Abraham, when Isaac saw the Philistines he immediately panicked. When we hear and see the economic news about our world, do we go into self-preservation mode or do we rely on God?

Self-preservation mode is all about self. Self does not think about God, His Word, or the things of God. In other words, self or flesh does not believe the Word of God. When you trust the Bible more than you trust self, you will begin to live and prosper.

In Genesis 26:12, we find that Isaac learned a valuable lesson about trusting God. Because in verse 12, we see Isaac trusting God by sowing seed from what he had preserved for himself and saved for his own survival. Let's read verse 12 again, "Then Isaac sowed in that land, and received in the same year an hundredfold; and the Lord blessed him."

Instead of relying on the mode of self-preservation, Isaac began to trust God for his survival and needs. If you want to prosper with God, fear must leave. You must be of good courage; you cannot be in fear and prosper because fear always brings doubt.

Doubt is a sign of instability. The Bible says in James 1:6-8, "But let him ask in faith, nothing wavering. For he that wavereth is like a wave of the sea driven with the wind and tossed. For let not that man think that he shall receive anything of the Lord. A double minded man is unstable in all his ways."

The Bible says in Proverb 3:5, "Trust in the Lord with all thine heart; and lean not unto thine own understanding..." Isaac thought if he lied about his wife, his life would be spared. Not fully understanding that if he trusted God with his life, God would protect and preserve him. The consequences of lying could have been detrimental because when he lied, he put his wife in a very precarious situation. Rebekah could have been placed in an adulterous situation because of Isaac's lie!

What Isaac did was not the will of God. Not fully realizing that when he lied about his relationship with his wife, Rebekah, he created another problem. How many times do we try in our own power to solve a problem only to create a bigger problem? The idea of lying could have resulted in Isaac and his wife, both, being put to death by King Abimelech!

Yet, we see the faithfulness of a forgiving God. The prophet Jeremiah said in Lamentations 3:22-23, "It is of the lord's mercies that we are not consumed, because his compassions fail not; They are new every morning; great is thy faithfulness."

After Isaac undoubtedly repents of his sins, he sows. Did God tell Isaac to sow? It does not say. But God did say to Isaac that the land where he resided (Gerar) was his. Therefore, Isaac sowed based on the promises of God. Listen, when God promises blessings, it means that He has already given the blessings to you. All you have to do is sow into the promise through faith!

Balaam told Balak in Numbers 23:19, "God is not a man that he should lie; neither the son of man, that he should repent: hath he said, and shall he not do it? or hath he spoken, and shall he not make it good?"

You may have made some poor financial decisions in your life, but you can still sow into the promises of God. We see in the life of Isaac that he did not receive the promises of God in verse 4 of Genesis 26 until he sowed in verse 12.

In verse 4, God said to Isaac "And I will make thy seed to multiply as the stars of heaven, and will give unto thy seed all these countries; and in thy seed shall all the nations of the earth be blessed..." God promised Isaac a harvest if he would only sow in obedience to His Word.

Are you in doubt of the Word of God? If Jesus can take two fish and five loaves of bread, feed 15,000-20,000 people, and have 12 baskets of fish and bread left over (Mark 6:40-44), why is it so hard to believe that He can multiply your seed? As Christ did with the two fish and five loaves of bread, He can take the limited seed in your hand and create your harvest.

When the woman of Zarephath in 1 Kings 17, sowed her oil and meal into the life of the prophet Elijah, she received a perpetual harvest of oil and meal. In other words, whatever you want, that's what you must sow. You cannot reap something you have not sowed. You cannot yield a harvest when you have not planted.

The Bible says "[Isaac received] possession of flocks, and possession of herds, and great store of servants: and the Philistines envied him" (Genesis 26:14). What was the difference between Isaac's sowing and the Philistine's sowing? The difference between Isaac's seed sowing and the Philistine's seed sowing was that Isaac's sowing was based on the promises of God.

In fact, Isaac's promised blessing and sowing came from a different dimension. The dimension of the Kingdom of God always overrides the dimension of Earth and its laws. The Philistines did not have a promise from God, Isaac did. Do you have a promise?

What made Isaac's crops thrive and the Philistine's crops die during the famine? As a believer of Christ, what you will be able to do with a seed, based on the promises of God, will not work for the unbeliever.

The seed of the Philistines could not produce a harvest. If you looked at the conditions of the earth and ground in the land of Gerar, Isaac's dirt and ground was just as hard, dry, and parched as the Philistines. The atmospheric weather conditions where Isaac lived were the same as the Philistines. It wasn't that it rained on Isaac's crops and not on the Philistine's crops! What then made Isaac's seeds grow and produce? It wasn't that Isaac's seeds looked any different than the Philistines. Your financial seed or money does not look any different than the unbeliever's. It's the same seed or money.

The difference is found with whom the seed belongs. Isaac had a promise and a relationship with the One who is not bound by time, matter, and space. It is about who you know! Believe it or not, Isaac did not plant all of his seeds by himself; he had servants, maidens, and handmaidens who assisted him with his planting. It's not about who puts the seed in the ground, it's about who the seed belongs to! The seed belongs to the One who is anointed; in this case, the seed belonged to Isaac. You see, Isaac's seeds possessed the anointing!

In other words, the anointed seed had everything it needed to grow, produce, and prosper. Isaac's seed did not need the rain or fertilizer to produce. All that was needed was the anointing. The anointing has within it, all the vitamins and nutrients, not only to produce, but to produce a hundred fold!

If you want your seed to multiply you don't need synthetic, man-made, fertilizer that you buy in the garden stores disguised as Miracle-Gro®. You need the anointing that produces "miracle growth!" The synthetic fertilizer, Miracle Gro®, doesn't have anything on the anointing! You don't need synthetic and natural conditions to be just right in order to prosper when you have the anointing.

As a matter of fact, you don't have to be gifted in grammar and verbal articulation; all you need is the anointing.

You don't need to be educated at the most prestigious schools in America and around the world; all you need is the anointing. You don't need to be able to quote 10,000 Biblical passages from the Old and New Testaments; all you need is the anointing. You don't need to be born in a family possessing wealth and riches; all you need is the anointing. The anointing makes up a hundred-fold what you lack and don't have. Just like Isaac, you can prosper in desperate economic times with the anointed seed of prosperity. Wall Street and the stock market don't have to have gains in order for you to experience prosperity.

On the surface, the seed of Isaac looked the same as the Philistines. The anointing of favor and power of God cannot always be seen physically with the eye, but you can always see the manifestation and the harvest.

The Bible says in 2 Corinthians 4:18, "While we look not at the things which are seen, but at the things which are not seen: for the things which are seen are temporal; but the things which are not seen are eternal." What the natural eyes cannot see is that the anointing of God causes you to prosper.

When Isaac's seed hit the ground under the anointing, everything that was a hindrance to the seed was destroyed. The smoldering heat and dry desert ground choked the life and substance out of the tender plants of the Philistines. Therefore, the plants of the Philistines died. But the conditions in the earth had no affect on Isaac's seeds. Isaac's seed, under the anointing from a different dimension, produces better in the worst of atmospheric and climatic conditions. When things are famished and desolated is when the anointing works best.

You see, the anointing makes up what we lack naturally and equips us supernaturally. As a matter of fact, not only did Isaac's crops grow, they produced and multiplied exponentially. When the world says there is no capital growth due to the economy, you can still experience prosperity under the anointing.

Do you have the anointing? You see, the anointing is not just the empowerment of God's power. It also has another role.

It acts as a defensive weapon. It protects against any attacks which are not the will of God. It is not enough to be prosperous without protection. The anointing acts as a powerful weapon that destroys burdens, yokes, and strongholds! Don't you know that the anointing can set you free from any stronghold in your life right now?

Those who are anointed by God, in the fourth dimension, will experience supernatural increase when the world is experiencing an economic collapse! The Bible says in Isaiah 10:27, "And it shall come to pass in that day, that his burden shall be taken away from off thy shoulder, and his yoke from off thy neck, and the yoke shall be destroyed because of the anointing." What caused the burden and the yoke to be destroyed in the life of a believer? The anointing.

Furthermore, you can't stay under the anointing and not be blessed. If you stay under the anointing long enough, the anointing will rub off on you. In the book of Exodus 34:29-30, Moses' face shined because he was in the presence of the anointed Jehovah. You can't be in God's presence and not experience the anointing of God.

You don't need a six or seven figure income to prosper; all you need is the anointing. The anointed seeds of Isaac had all the water and fertilizer they needed to produce a hundredfold. If you are a giver, your financial seed has all the money, abundance, and wealth in it for you to receive a prosperous harvest! When you sow your financial seed under the anointing, it doesn't matter about the climatic conditions of Wall Street, Fortune 500 companies, and financial institutions. It doesn't matter about the financial forecast that the world says you will experience.

You don't have to experience a recession, a depression, or a famine under the anointing. Just like Isaac, your anointed seed has nothing to do with the ground or the condition of the world. Your anointed seed has nothing to do with your background, the state of the economy, your education, your credit score, or your net worth, but it all has to do with the God, who specializes in being more than enough!

God has the power to favor you, establish you, and set you on high. The anointing is all you need. The anointing makes up for the lack of job security, the lack of education, and the lack of financial stability that exists in the world. In the book of Job 1:9-10, notice what satan says to God regarding Job,

> *Then Satan answered the Lord, and said, Doth Job fear (honor, reverence) for nought (nothing)? Hast not thou made an hedge about him, and about his house, and about all that he hath on every side? thou hast blessed the work of his hands, and his sub-stance is increased in the land. But put forth thine hand now, and touch all that he hath, and he will curse thee to thy face.*

In essence, satan said to God that he has anointed Job to prosper, but if God would remove the anointing which kept him protected and financial secure, Job would curse God to His face. The anointing has the power to protect.

It was the anointing that protected the seed from being destroyed by the parched ground where Isaac sowed. It was the anointing that produced the hundred-fold return on the seed. There's nothing you have experienced or have gone through that the anointing of God can't increase or destroy. The yoke shall be destroyed because of the anointing!

There was a TV commercial that talked about the American Express® Card. The phrase said, "Don't leave home without it!" But I say unto you, it's the anointing that you should never leave home without!

When you step into the fourth dimension, you will begin to experience seasons of prosperity. When you plant seeds, whether it is your money, time, energy, and resources, in the anointed ground of the fourth dimension, your seeds will become anointed.

An anointed seed has no choice but to multiply. The laws of the fourth dimension are reciprocal. What you sow in the fourth dimension will be returned to you magnified. The Apostle Paul said in Galatians 6:7, "Be not deceived; God is not mocked: for whatsoever a man soweth, that shall he also reap."

For example, if you sow a financial seed in the fourth dimension, the Kingdom of God, you will reap a supernatural financial harvest season. A season of prosperity is not three months in a year; a season of prosperity in the fourth dimension is a lifetime on Earth.

A season in the natural world signifies only three to four months, however, a season in the fourth dimension is an eternity. David said in Psalms 30:6, "And in my prosperity I said, I shall never be moved."

The seasons of prosperity in the fourth dimension never changes due to the finished work of Christ on the cross. Jesus Christ is the seed of salvation and eternal prosperity. Everything begins with a seed.

Holy Spirit

Holy Spirit, just the mention of His name,

Holy Spirit, heaven and Earth have never been the same;

Holy Spirit, He is our Redeemer and King,

Holy Spirit, now satan hears His name ring;

Holy Spirit, the handwriting on the wall,

Holy Spirit, reclaimed me for His call;

Holy Spirit, just the mention of His name,

Holy Spirit, now heaven and Earth will proclaim.

CHAPTER 14

The Fallen Cherub

Eons ago before time, space, and matter existed, there was a time when only goodness and righteousness reigned. The only world in existence was the perfect and holy Kingdom of God which was void of darkness, evil, and wickedness. However, this perfect world would not last forever. In a scene unfamiliar in heaven, angels are seen fighting each other with flaming swords. The Bible says:

> And there was war in heaven. Michael and his angels fought against the dragon, and the dragon and his angels fought back. But he was not strong enough, and they lost their place in heaven. The great dragon was hurled down–that ancient serpent called the devil, or Satan, who leads the whole world astray. He was hurled to the earth and his angels with him (Revelation 12:7-9).

Trouble looms in paradise [heaven]. Before the angelic war commenced, there had been many secret closed-door discussions about who has the power and the ability to rule heaven and the universe. Many of the angels in heaven were convinced that the leadership of heaven should be usurped and overthrown. Many of the angels became persuaded that one of their own had the power to defeat God Almighty. As a result, a coup d'état, a heavenly governmental takeover, would be attempted by one of God's most trusted and anointed cherubs–Lucifer.

Like the angels Michael and Gabriel, Lucifer, known now as satan, was the chief cherub of praise and worship. God created satan as the perfect songster, musician, and composer (Ezekiel 28:13). He could sing any note or arrangement on any musical scale: bass, baritone, tenor, alto, and soprano. Satan could make you shout, scream, and dance with joy like nobody else!

Satan was one whom all the other angels looked up to and aspired to be like. Satan represents the earliest of all creation. It has been said that satan was the first created [angelic] being; he was there in heaven when it all began.

When it came to music, satan had no rivals. Satan was heaven's director and minister of music. Not only was he talented, he was the most beautiful angel in heaven. No other angel is described as "beautiful" other than satan. The Bible says, "Thine [satan's] heart was lifted up because of thy beauty, thou hast corrupted thy wisdom by reason of thy brightness..." (Ezekiel 28:17). Unfortunately, in spite of all the gifts and talents God gave satan, he turned against God.

Satan became God's number one adversary. As children of God, we too have only one enemy. Although it may appear we have many enemies on Earth, we really have only one. Our enemy is not our boss, our next door neighbor, or those who do not like us; satan is our enemy.

The Apostle Peter makes it clear who our adversary is in no uncertain terms. The Bible says in 1 Peter 5:8, "Be sober, be vigilant because your adversary the devil as a roaring lion walketh about seeking whom he may devour." Our enemy is not flesh and blood, but spirit. The Bible says that we wrestle not against flesh and blood but against the devil and his angels (Ephesians 6:12). The devil is a spiritual being who operates and manipulates the world in order to gain control and dominate the lives of individuals.

The Apostle Paul lets us know that as saints of God, we should know our adversary, the devil. Paul said in 2 Corinthians 2:11, "Lest Satan should get an advantage over us for we are not ignorant of his devices." We must know who satan is, how he acts, how he responds, what his tactics are, and what strategies he implements so that he does not gain an advantage over us or defeats us. We must understand that we have been set free by God to do battle, fight, and to become the channel by which others are set free.

Satan primarily appears to man in two ways:

1. An angel of light: satan has the ability to deceive and appear in a godly character and form. 2 Corinthians 11:14 says, "And no marvel, for satan himself is transformed into an angel of light." One of satan's main strategies is to appear as someone good, someone attractive, or someone who is credible and trust worthy. Satan's powers lie in his ability to deceive.

2. Secondly, the devil can appear as a roaring lion. 1 Peter 5:8 says, "Be sober, be vigilant because your adversary the devil as a roaring lion walketh about seeking whom he may devour." This means he can create tragedy, sickness, devastation, and evil, as he did in the life of Job. When he appears as a lion, he can strike fear into the hearts of man.

Because of Adam's disobedience, the dominion that was given to Adam, by God, was forfeited to satan. Satan is described, by the Apostle Paul, as the prince of the power of the air. Ephesians 2:2 says, "Wherein in time past ye walked according to the course of this world according to the prince of the power of the air, the spirit that now worketh in the children of disobedience."

Moreover, satan is described as the god of this world. Again Paul eludes in 2 Corinthians 4:4 saying, "In whom the god of this world hath blinded the minds of them which believe not, lest the light of the glorious gospel of Christ who is the image of God, should shine unto them."

Why is satan called a prince and a god? Because through trickery and deception he has received power and authority in the earth (See Genesis chapter 3). Many individuals in the world have fallen prey under the control of satanic forces.

When you look around at the success of evil in history, especially in our day, you can see that the enemy has obtained and accumulated great power and authority.

Think of our world and what's going on in terms of the agony, struggles, evil, violence, terrorism, and mass confusion abounding on every side. When we think of the killings, hatred, murders, and death which characterize our world, we can see the magnitude and the extent of the power of the enemy. A writer once said, "Our race had a hopeful beginning but man spoiled his chances by sinning. We hope that the story will end in God's glory, but at present the other side seems to be winning."

Who is this mystical diabolical creature called satan? Satan was once an anointed cherub. His innate expertise was in the realm of worship and praise to God. Satan would cause heaven to ring with the resounding sound of his angelic voice. When satan sings, he doesn't need music as a back up to accompany his singing. When he opens his mouth the sound of harps, organs, clarinets, flutes, violins, oboes, piccolos, trumpets, trombones, French horns, saxophones, violas, cellos, bassoons–woodwinds, brass, string, and percussion instruments fill the air.

A symphony from his own voice accompanies him. Ezekiel 28:13 says "...Thy workmanship of thy tabrets [a percussion like tambourine with a covering like a drum] and of thy pipes [sounds of the woodwind, brass, and string instruments] was prepared in thee in the day that thou wast created."

Although heaven has a heavenly orchestra, satan didn't need a woodwind, brass, string, or percussion section which accompanies an orchestra. An orchestra was built inside of him! Satan didn't need a choir; he was a choir all by himself. You couldn't out sing him, out worship, or out praise him. He was created and perfected to praise God! The Bible says in Ezekiel 28:15, "Thou wast perfect in thy ways from the day that thou wast created..."

Lucifer means *the son of the morning or the morning star, for when you saw him light illuminated from him.* Isaiah 14:12 says, "How art thou fallen from heaven, O Lucifer, son of the morning..." In fact, Jesus Christ and Lucifer are two names which mean "morning star." Moreover, Lucifer in the Hebrew language means *hallelial* from which we get the word hallelujah meaning, "Praise God". His name means "praise God."

However, after his fall from heaven, God changed his name to satan. In the oldest book of the Bible, the book of Job, God addresses Lucifer as satan in Job chapter 2. Satan is not someone who does not have knowledge of man. He knows how and when man was created; he was on the scene of creation before time began. You can hear satan singing at the opening of creation in Job chapter 37.

The Bible says, "...The morning stars sang together and all the sons of God shouted for joy" (Job 37:7). This is a scene of Lucifer singing and praising God, at the dawn of creation, with all the heavenly hosts before his downfall.

Later, we find Lucifer in Eden, the garden of God. The Bible says in Ezekiel 28: 13, "...Thou hast been in Eden the garden of God..." Many biblical scholars believe that prior to satan's fall; satan was given rulership to oversee Eden.

However something catastrophic happened between Genesis 1:1 and Genesis 1:2 that made the earth "without form and void" (Genesis 1:2). In Isaiah 45:12, Isaiah declared that God did not make the earth "without form and void." It has been assumed that the old earth was destroyed when Lucifer fell from heaven.

The Bible says in Isaiah 14:12, "How you are fallen from heaven, O Lucifer, son of the morning." When satan fell from heaven, the old earth was destroyed as if an enormous asteroid or meteor hit it. All this occurred because of satan's covetous desired to have God's position of preeminence and power.

After the fall of satan, we see him in Eden, the garden of God, after God recreated the earth. Genesis 3:1 says, "Now the serpent [satan] was more subtil than any beast of the field which the Lord had made..."

In Hebrew the word for *serpent* is "shinning." What Adam and Eve may have seen before them was not a serpent or snake that we think of today, but a shinning figure as "an angel of light" (2 Corinthians 11:14).

Satan used and manipulated the serpent beast in the garden. Because of this, God cursed the serpent for allowing the devil to use it. Genesis 3:14 reads, "And the lord said unto the serpent because thou has done this thou art cursed above all cattle and above every beast of the field upon thy belly shalt thou go and dust shall thou eat all the days of thy life."

In Genesis 3:14, we see God changes the appearance and form of the serpent saying, "...upon thy belly shalt thou go and dust shall thou eat all the days of thy life." No other animal in Scripture does God change in this manner. Why? Perhaps the serpent's appearance may have been deceptive and deceitful because it had the appearance of light and truth.

Because of satan's deception, he is eternally depicted as the serpent. In Revelations 20:2, he is called "That old serpent which is the devil and satan..." Do you think satan would have come to Adam and Eve any other way than as an appearance of light? Probably not! What better way to deceive someone by appearing credible and trustworthy?

Satan was the anointed cherub. There was no angel created like him. In heaven before his downfall, satan ascends unto the mountain of God [in Eden]. Satan's garment was decked with precious stones of sapphires, emeralds, jaspers, diamonds, gold, and other precious gems. Light illuminated from him from all directions! Satan walked in and out of the presence of God in which only the Son and the Holy Spirit were privileged to do. The Bible says in Ezekiel 28:14 that satan walked up and down in the midst of the stones of fire.

Satan's God-given, ability was to praise Him. Satan would cause heaven to ring with the sound of his angelic voice. However, now he only creates flattery and lies in the ears and hearts of those who listen to his voice.

Flattery is the highest form of deception, which is, insincere praise. Everything that satan once was is now distorted, corrupted, twisted, and perverted, the opposite of the beauty of holiness, righteousness, truth, and godliness. Satan delights in mangling, smashing, twisting, destroying, and blasting everything that pertains to God.

The Bible says in John 8:44, "... he [satan] is a murderer from the beginning and abode not in the truth, when he speaketh a lie; he speaketh of his own for he is a liar and the father of it." Where praise once stood, now stands flattery. Flattery is a way of praising an individual in deception with hidden motives to self promote or for personal gain.

As satan once lifted up the name of God, he now attempts to lift up himself by deceiving all mankind for his own gain and glory. Remember what satan told Adam and Eve in Genesis 3:5 saying, "Ye shall be as gods." It was satan who wanted to be God; he did not want that for Adam and Eve. We must not allow satan to fool us!

What makes satan powerful and a force to reckon with is the magnitude of forces working on his behalf (sin in the world). He is called the god of this world and the prince of the air. Satan likes to sit high as if he is God.

In Isaiah 14:13-14, satan said "I will ascend into heaven, I will exalt my throne above the stars of God: I will sit also upon the mount of the congregation, in the sides of the north: I will ascend above the heights of the clouds; I will be like the most High."

In verses 13 and 14 (above), there are five references to "I." The letter "I" happens to be the center of attention or the main emphasis in those two verses. "I" is also the center letter in the word "sin" and in the word "pride." King Solomon said in Proverb 16:18, "Pride goeth before destruction and a haughty spirit before a fall."

Satan's lustful and deceitful desires caused him to take his focus off God and place the attention on himself. Satan is the great deceiver. The worst kind of deception is not deceiving others, but self deception. In other words, satan convinced himself that he should be God and that he could defeat God Almighty!

Satan was anointed to praise God, not be God. When we step out of our calling or anointing of what God has designed for us, and covet after what someone else has or does; we are in danger of being destroyed.

Proud people or individuals filled with excess pride are never content with what God has done or created them to be or do. They always lust for more and are never satisfied or thankful. The Bible says in James 1:15, "Then when lust hath conceived, it bringeth forth sin: and sin, when it is finished, bringeth forth death."

When satan sinned and fell, God created man (in His image) to praise him in satan's place. God created Adam (man) as the king and ruler of the earth in the place of satan. The reason satan came to Adam and deceived Eve in the garden was to take what God had given man – rulership in the earth. Satan came to usurp man's position. The thing that now puzzles satan is why does God place so much emphasis on man, even when man had sinned against him, like he did?

The answer can be found in Psalms 8:4-6 which says, "What is man, that thou art mindful of him, and the son of man that thou visitest him? For thou hast made him a little lower than the angels and hast crowned him with glory and honor, thou madest him to have dominion over the works of thy hands thou hast put all things under his feet."

Unlike angels, God made man to have a unique relationship with Him. Man was made to be God's child, His sons and daughters. Man has the very breath of God. Man has God's DNA! Man is higher in hierarchy and position than any angelic being, including satan's position before his fall.

The Bible says in 1 Corinthians chapter 6 that we shall judge angels. Listen to what Paul says in 1 Corinthians 6:2-3, "Do ye not know that the saints shall judge the world...And know not that we shall judge angels?"

You want to know your position in the hierarchy of the Kingdom of God? Two thousand years ago, Jesus came to teach and to be a model for man, which is God's ultimate creation, as well as what it is to be a son of God.

Jesus, the God-Man, was sent from heaven to demonstrate God's original plan and design for man, that is, to be the expressed image and character of God. The Bible says in 2 Corinthians 4:4, "...Christ, who is the image of God..."

Remember before Adam sinned, we were created in God's image. The Bible says in Genesis 1:27, "So God created man in his own image, in the image of God created he him, male and female created he them."

Notice that Jesus did not come as an angelic being or as His glorified self, but wrapped Himself in flesh as man. In fact, it was God who wrapped Himself in a fleshly tabernacle (as man) in order to dwell among us.

The Word of God says in Romans 8:3, "For what the law could not do, in that it was weak through the flesh, God sending his own Son in the likeness of sinful flesh, and for sin, condemned sin in the flesh." God demonstrated His intimate relationship with us and our position with him by becoming us (a man)!

As born-again believers possessing the righteousness of God in Christ, we are the only created creature like unto God. The Bible says in 1 John 3:2, "Beloved now are we the sons of God, and it doeth not yet appear, what we shall be; but we know that when he shall appear, we shall be like him; for we shall see him as he is."

To be crowned with glory, honor and dominion, according to Psalms 8:4-6, are attributes that Satan wanted bestowed about him, not man! Satan hates humanity (especially the men and women of God) because God placed upon man what satan wanted for himself!

Satan wants to be God. If he can't have heaven, he will take the next best thing – Earth. Since man had legally defaulted on the commandments of God, by disobeying Him, satan feels that Earth including man, by virtue of default, should legally be his. However, Christ put a major obstacle in the plan of satan by becoming man.

The Bible says in 1 Corinthians 2:7-8, "But we speak the wisdom of God in a mystery, even the hidden wisdom, which God ordained before the world unto our glory: which none of the princes of this world knew; for had they known it, they would not have crucified the Lord of glory."

Satan had no idea concerning the mystery of the plan of salvation. Like it or not, God is not going to tell everything concerning His plans. Now the rights, authority, power, and dominion has been reverted back to man, provided that he who puts his faith and trust in Jesus Christ. This is an important statement because many believers do not understand or exercise their rights and privileges under the authority of Jesus Christ.

It was satan who caused Adam and Eve to default on the commandment of God. By default, we pledged our allegiance to the devil. Adam obeyed the devil; therefore, the devil became his lord. Adam lost all rights, authority, power, and dominion in the earth. All that God had given him was now deferred to satan.

The Bible says in Romans 6:16, "Know ye not that to whom ye yield yourselves servants to obey, his servants ye are to whom ye obey; whether of sin unto death or of obedience unto righteousness?"

But because of Christ, we now have power over the enemy. However, oftentime we do not believe it–far less practice it. Why? Because the devil is a deceiver. The devil continuously tries to minimize and destroy our faith by planting doubt and unbelief in our minds. He is the master of illusion. He continuously attempts to paint an erroneous perception of truth, of the Word of God, in our minds. He does not want you to believe and stand on the Word of the Living God!

He is the stealer of the Word of God. According to Mark 4:15, the Bible says, "But when they heard the word of God, Satan cometh immediately and taketh away the word that was sown in their hearts." Notice, satan comes immediately because he does not want the Word of God to take root and grow. Why? Because the sown Word in the heart yields and produces an abundant harvest of faith and righteousness.

Another reason why the devil comes immediately to steal the Word from the hearers of the Word of God is because he knows, what many do not fully understand, that faith cometh by hearing and hearing the Word of God. The Bible says in Romans 10:17, "So then faith cometh by hearing, and hearing by the Word of God."

Faith comes by hearing God's Word. You cannot obtain the faith of God outside the Word of God. We are not talking about positive self thinking, positive self image or mental assertiveness; we are talking about the faith of God!

Satan's primary mission and objectives are given in John 10:10 which declares that, "The thief [satan] cometh not but for to steal and kill and to destroy." Unfortunately, Satan is able to do this systemically and with great success through deception.

If we allow satan to diminish the Word of God, by stealing it from our heart and mind, he will defeat us every time! You are no greater than your thoughts. The Bible, in Proverb 23:7, says, "For as a man thinketh in his heart so is he." Know this: satan will destroy us with destructive and erroneous thoughts if we succumb to his wicked devices!

The Word of God sown in our hearts generates life. You see the Word is living and alive. The Bible says in Hebrews 4:12, "For the word of God is quick [alive] and powerful and sharper than any two-edged sword piercing even to the dividing asunder of soul and spirit and of the joints and marrow and is a discerner of the thoughts and intents of the heart."

In fact, the Word of God can stimulate and bring to life those things which are dead. Paul said in Romans 4:17, "...Even God who quickeneth the dead and calleth those things which be not as though they were." What Paul is simply saying is those things that we desire, but are unobtainable in the natural realm, are revealed and manifested supernaturally through God's Word.

Because the Word of God is alive, it brings those things that are dead or impossible in the natural realm to life. The thing that brought Sarah's aged and barren womb to life was God's Word. In Genesis 18:14, before God was able to bring life into the womb of Sarah, God spoke life into her heart by saying to her, "Is anything too hard for the lord? At the time appointed I will return unto thee according to the time of life and Sarah shall have a son."

Therefore, the faith of God is demonstrated when we hear the Word, believe the Word, and take heed to the Word of

God. Why wouldn't the enemy attempt to take away one of the most powerful weapons of the Kingdom of God, which is our faith? Satan is the enemy of our souls!

Satan has become proficient at stealing the Word of God from us. You see, satan knows us and is also a studier of the God's Word. The devil knows what the Word of God says and he believes it. We are the ones who do not know or believe the God's Word. The Bible says in James 2:19, "...The devils also believe and tremble." We must become zealous and studious of the living Word of God.

Unbeknownst to many is the fact that the more often individuals practice sin, the more authority, permission, power, and dominion they give satan. This is why he is called the prince and god of this world because the world has given satan authority, power, and dominion to be so!

By virtue of sin, we give satan territorial and earthly dominion. In the book of Daniel, we see an angel sent to give Daniel a message from God that his prayer had been heard and tells him what was about to come to pass for Israel but the Prince of Persia (a high principality demonic spiritual being) withstood the angel for 21 days (Daniel 10:13).

The reason why the Prince of Persia, the demonic being, fought and prevailed against the angel of God was because Persia was his legal territory. He had every right to be there. To the Prince of Persia, it was the angel of the Lord who was in violation of trespassing.

However when we pray to God as believers and as Daniel prayed, we exercise our God-given rights as possessors of Earth and give the angelic hosts of heaven permission to work on our behalf. This is the reason satan fights us so much in prayer because the more we pray, the more we exercise the authority, power, and dominion God has given us. When we pray, we set heaven in motion to loose and bind strongholds in our lives. Notice in the book of Daniel 10:13 that the spiritual battle raged on for 21 days. However Daniel received the answer and victory because he did not cease from praying. Had he stopped praying before his breakthrough, he may not have received his answer. It was his continual prayer that allowed the angels of the Lord to continue to fight with legal territorial authority on behalf of Daniel. Never stop praying, help is on the way!

I have shared with you who satan is, how he acts, how he responds, and what his strategies are, and the power that he seems to have in this world. But, I only gave you half of the story. Now I want you to know satan's position in relationship to what Christ has done.

In the book of Colossians 2:15, the Bible says "And having spoiled principalities and power, he [Jesus], made a shew of them openly triumphing over them in it." Jesus disarmed the principalities and powers of darkness and made a bold open display and public example of them. Jesus stripped satan and the forces of darkness of their power, authority, and dominion.

The first Adam was stripped by the devil of his innocence, stripped of his power, stripped of his glory, stripped of his honor, stripped of his authority, stripped of his dominion, stripped of his godliness, stripped of his righteousness, and stripped of his holiness. Adam and Eve were stripped to the point where the Bible says in Genesis 4:7 that Adam and Eve knew that they were naked!

Before Adam and Eve sinned, they were clothed in holiness and righteousness; after they had sinned they were stripped of all their authority, all of their power, and all of their dominion given by God. The last Adam, Jesus Christ, went down to the grave, defeated death and hell, and stripped the powers of darkness of their authority. Jesus said in Revelation 1:18, "I am he that liveth and was dead and behold I am alive for evermore and have the keys of hell and of death."

Jesus took the sting out of death by coming back from the dead, and He took the victory from the grave by rising from the grave. The Apostle Paul said in 1 Corinthians 15:55-57, "O death where is thy sting, O grave where is thy victory? The sting of death is sin; and the strength of sin is the law. But thanks be to God which giveth us the victory through our Lord Jesus Christ."

When we understand this truth that the enemy has no power over us, we can then look at satan as he really is. He is stripped of power, stripped of authority, and stripped of any dominion. When we can look at him as a defeated foe–a defeated cherub–who thought he could be God, we then have a true assessment of satan. We must look at him with a new revelation and understanding and say what the prophet Isaiah said about satan. Isaiah said," Is this the man that made the earth to tremble, that did shake kingdoms" (Isaiah 14:16)?

Like Isaiah we must say, "What was I thinking? You mean I was afraid of that? Why did I allow satan to defeat me?" When we realize that satan has no power over those who are in Christ Jesus, we will never be defeated by him again!

Believers of the fourth dimension know who they are and whose they are. Know that satan is defeated and you have complete victory in the fourth dimension.

The Holy Spirit

Holy Spirit, heaven rejoices over me,

Holy Spirit, the day I gave my life to Christ and now I am free;

Holy Spirit, the party keeps going on and on,

Holy Spirit, because you gain more daughters and sons;

Holy Spirit, in this Book of Life you can read,

Holy Spirit, all the names of God's children indeed;

Holy Spirit, heaven rejoices over me,

Holy Spirit, I am sealed in the fourth dimension by the love of

the Trinity.

CHAPTER 15

Speak Those Things

Have you ever met people who talk so much, but have very little to say? They spend hours on the cell phone gossiping and spreading rumors which accomplish absolutely nothing. There is no significant value or worth to their conversations.

The Apostle Paul admonishes us in Philippians 1:27 saying, "Only let your conversation be as it becometh the gospel of Christ..." In other words, when we speak, our conversation should be in accordance with the Word of God. We need to make sure that the words which we speak are filled with life, healing, and inspiration. Why? It is because words have the power to create.

We are not the only beings in the universe that speak. God has been speaking from eternity past until now. However, when God speaks He does not use vain and meaningless words because God knows when He speaks, things happen.

The Apostle Paul said in Romans 4:17, "...Even God who quickeneth the dead and calleth those things which be not as though they were." Paul lets us know that the Words of God gives life to dead things. God continuously speaks things that are not as though they were. In essence, God speaks things which may not exist, but when he finishes speaking, the things that do not exist must come to pass. We, as children of God, are admonished to emulate our Father God by the words that we speak.

Jesus who is our primary example said in John 8:28, "I do nothing of myself as my Father hath taught me, I speak these things..." Jesus said that He only speaks what he has heard the Father say. It is imperative that we speak in kind as the Father does. Therefore, we too can speak to dead things and they must come to life. Just as the Father and the Son, Jesus Christ, we too can speak those things that do not exist and bring them into existence.

Like God, our words have creative power. Before making man, God said in Genesis 1:26, "Let us make man in our image and after our likeness." Before God created man, He first spoke man into existence. Listen, before you can have it, you must speak it. The Bible says in Proverbs 18:21, "Death and life are in the power of the tongue: And they that love it shall eat the fruit thereof." Our words, which we speak, can create life or death.

Do you want to know what you are going to be like five years from now? Just listen to what you are currently saying about yourself. Are you saying that you are sick? Are you saying that you are broke and cannot make ends meet? What you are currently speaking concerning yourself is what you are prophesying for your future.

Too many of us go around saying, "I'll never get well. I'll never get out of debt. This marriage is never going to work. It doesn't look like we are going to make it." Depending on what you say, you can call in God's favor and increase in your life. When you speak words out, your words have the power to "call in" defeat or "call in" victory based on what you have called out. What have you been "calling out" of your mouth? Because what you are "calling out" will determine what will be "called in." What have you been speaking over your family, over your children, over your health, or over your finances?

Your mouth must align itself with what you believe. Isn't it strange that we talk one way at church, talk another way at home, and talk another way on our jobs? You can't do that and expect to receive from God. The Apostle James said in James 3:11, "Doth a fountain send forth at the same place sweet and bitter water?" You can't speak death, gloom, and doom and expect life, blessing, and restoration. The Bible says also in James 1:6-7, "But let him ask [or speak] in faith nothing wavering, for he that wavereth is like a wave of the sea, driven with the wind and tossed; for let not that man, think that he shall receive anything from the Lord." We must learn to speak the words of life constantly everywhere we go regardless of where we are and who we are with!

We breathe life into our faith when we speak what we believe. We must speak with faith. Our faith becomes alive when we speak and act according to God's Word. You must come into agreement with God by using His words and promises for your life. If you are on the Lord's side, you must come into agreement with Him. Jesus said if you are not for me, you are against me (Matthew 12:30).

Words act as a boomerang. God said in Isaiah 55:11, "So shall my words be that goeth out of my mouth it shall not return unto me void but it shall accomplish what I sent it out to do." Our spoken words work the same way. Because we are created in the image of God, our words will eventually return unto us. Paul said in Galatians 6:7, "Be not deceived God is not mocked, whatsoever a man soweth that shall he also reap."

All some people talk about is how bad their situation is. They continuously speak words of defeat, doubt, uncertainty, and unbelief. If you are not speaking what the Word of God says, you are not in agreement with God. God is in agreement with His Word.

In fact, many people love to have a pity party and talk for hours at a time about what terrible shape they are in. They invite other people by phone, and in person, to the party to hear their sad and pitiful story. Have you ever noticed who is never invited to a pity party? Jesus! Why? If Jesus was invited to the pity party, the party would turn into a praise party. I heard a song which says, "When I think of the goodness of Jesus all he has done for me, my soul cries out hallelujah thank God for saving me." Instead of a pity party, the party would turn into a praise party. When was the last time you had a praise party? It's easy to turn a pity party into a praise party. You don't need to bring in any drinks, hors d'oeuvres, or appetizers to the party. Just your mouth filled with praise. When was the last time you hung out at a party and the only person at the party was you filled with words of worship and praise to God?

But oftentimes, we focus only on ourselves. There's a saying that says, "Misery loves company." Not only do we invite people to our pity party, sometimes we pay individuals top dollars to hear our sad stories. Some people pay as much as $150-$300 per hour to see a psychoanalyst or a psychiatrist. Just for someone to listen and take notes concerning their mishaps and misfortunes instead of telling Doctor Jesus.

We tell the psychologist and psychiatrist our problems just to hear them say, "Well what do you think you need to do?" Now, why would you pay someone for advice to have them turn around and ask you for advice? Most of the time these certified and licensed practitioners cannot give you sound advice or wisdom because they too have broken and shattered lives. If they knew the answer they would have fixed and repaired their own broken lives.

Listen, don't talk about the way you are, talk about the way you're going to be. The Scripture says in Psalms 107:2, "Let the redeemed of the Lord say so, whom he hath redeemed from the hand of the enemy." Notice what the Word of God says, "Let the redeemed of the Lord say so..."

You have got to say so! If you are going to the next level, you have got to say so. If you are going to overcome that addiction, you have got to say so. If you are going to have a blessed and prosperous year, you have got to say so. If you are going to get out of debt, you have got to say so. If you are going to accomplish and fulfill your dreams, you have got to say so. If you are going to start that business, you have got to say so. Nothing happens until you speak it out!

Notice what Psalms 107:2 does not say. It does not say, let the redeemed of the Lord think so or believe so. It says, let the redeemed of the Lord, "say so." In other words, something supernatural happens when you say so or speak it out. Therefore, if you get a bad report from the doctor and he tells you that you are going to die, what are you going to say in response to such a decree? Well, I would respond by saying what the psalmist said in Psalms 118:17, "I shall not die but live and declare the works of the Lord." In other words, I am going to say what God says.

Words are spirit. Jesus said in John 6:63, "...The words that I speak are spirit and they are life." When you speak, your words invoke the spirit and unseen realm. The spirit or the unseen world responds to words. The origin of all things was created by words – the Word of God. John 1:1-3 clearly states, "In the beginning was the Word, and the Word was with God, and the Word was God. The same was in the beginning with God. All things was made by him; and without him was not any thing made that was made."

Your words can command the supernatural world. Jesus said in Matthew 18:18, "Verily I say into you, whatsoever, ye bind on earth shall be bound in heaven and whatsoever ye loose on earth shall be loose in heaven." Therefore, we have the power through our words to bind and loose.

Oftentimes, we start off speaking the right things, but as time goes by we start speaking defeat. We cancel out the promises of God that we have spoken with negative, doubtful, and unbelieving words. Listen, you can't speak defeat and expect victory. You can't speak sickness and expect healing and health. You can't talk lack and poverty, and expect to live an abundant life.

The devil doesn't have to defeat us, most of the time; we defeat ourselves when we speak doubt and unbelief. God said in Hosea 4:6, "My people are destroyed for a lack of knowledge..." However, when we speak faith, we are in agreement with God. When you speak defeat you are in agreement with the enemy. Our words that we speak cause spirits to repel or attract.

The fourth dimensional, supernatural, world is the "real world" behind the curtain of carnality or the visible world. The words you speak, which are spirits, attract spirits. In other words, God-talk brings God on the scene. Negative and evil-talk bring the enemy on the scene. There is a strong correlation or relationship between what we say and what God does.

Psalms 91:2-3 says, "I will say of the Lord, He is my refuge and my fortress: my God; in him will I trust. Surely he shall deliver thee from the snare of the fowler, and from the noisome pestilence." Notice the correlation, "I will say of the lord... and God shall." This tells us that if we are not "saying of the Lord," God will not do what we want Him to do.

Find the promises of God in Scripture and start "saying of the Lord." Scriptures like 3 John 2, "Behold I wish above all things that thou mayest prosper and be in health even as thy soul prospereth." Psalms 118:17, "I shall not die, but live, and declare the works of the Lord."

If we are not saying anything, we are not releasing or activating our faith. We must get in agreement with God and His Word. Joel 3:10 says, "...Let the weak say I am strong." Start saying what you want to be. If you are weak, start saying, I am strong. If we keep saying the right things, speaking victory, speaking favor and prosperity, we shall have whatsoever we say (Mark 11:23)!

Speaking God's Word out of our mouths is the greatest power we will ever experience. Words are the most powerful force in the universe. The fourth dimension responds to words. You invoke the fourth dimension, the unseen realm, by the words that you speak. Your words have the power to open and close the doors of the fourth dimension.

Holy Spirit

Holy Spirit, come and fill the emptiness in me,

Holy Spirit, it's your divine pleasure I seek;

Holy Spirit, fill me with the Holy Ghost,

Holy Spirit, you know what we need the most;

Holy Spirit, I surrender my very own,

Holy Spirit, to teach that the fourth dimension must be

known;

Holy Spirit, my inner indwelling savior within,

Holy Spirit, now living the life free from all sin.

CHAPTER 16

Praise and Worship

As mentioned in chapter 10, there are three elements which make up the atmosphere of heaven: prayer, worship, and praise to God. These three elements should be a vital part of our everyday lives. If we are not comfortable with constantly praying, worshipping, and praising God on Earth, we will not be comfortable in heaven. The Bible says "...They are in front of the throne of God and worship him night and day in his temple. The one who sits on the throne will shelter them. (Revelation 7:15, ISV). Prayer, worship, and praise to God must be our daily and most fervent desire.

Like prayer, angels are drawn to praise and worship of God. Not only do they appear whenever praise to God occurs, angels join in with the praise. The Apostle John said,

> Then I looked and heard the voice of many angels, numbering thousands upon thousands, and ten thousand times ten thousand. They encircled the throne and the living creatures and the elders. In a loud voice they sang: Worthy is the Lamb, who was slain, to receive power and wealth and wisdom and strength and honor and glory and praise (Revelation 5:11-12).

Angels will not stand in the awesome presence of God without praising God.

In fact, angels crave the presence of God. Even when we praise God alone, we are never alone; angels join in welcoming the presence of God. The Bible says in Psalms 22:3 that God inhabits the praises of His people. When you praise God, angels assist in creating an atmosphere whereby God will inhabit. They assist in making the atmosphere conducive and suitable for God. Angels facilitate in charging and electrifying the atmosphere. When you praise God in your home, car, on your job, or at the store thousands of angels are in worship and praise with you!

In fact, when we praise and worship God the atmosphere shifts from third dimensional to fourth dimensional allowing God and angels to commune and dwell among us. Praise and worship always creates a shift in the atmosphere, which can radically alter our present and future circumstances. It was the praise and worship of Paul and Silas that caused a dramatic change in the prison which held them captive.

The Bible says in Acts 16:23-26:

> And when they [the multitude] had laid many stripes on them [Paul and Silas], they threw them into prison, commanding the jailer to keep them securely. Having received such a charge, he put them into the inner prison and fastened their feet in the stocks. But at midnight Paul and Silas were praying and singing hymns to God, and the prisoners were listening to them. Suddenly there was a great earthquake, so that the foundations of the prison were shaken; and immediately all the doors were opened and everyone's chains were loosed.

Who or what loosed or released the locks and chains from the doors of the prison and the prisoners? Angels!

Praise and worship bring angelic beings on the scene. Angels' favorite "hangout" spots are places of worship such as churches and homes where there is praise and worship occurring. However, they are not limited to places of worship. Acts

chapter 16 lets us know that they will show up in the most un-
likely places even in a prison!

Nothing pleasures angels more than giving praise and
worship to God. The Bible says in Revelation 4:8 (NLT), "Each
of these living beings [angels] had six wings, and their wings
were covered with eyes, inside and out. Day after day and night
after night they keep saying, Holy, holy, holy is the Lord God
Almighty–the one who always was, who is, and who is to come."

As we move toward the end of the age, angelic appearances will become more frequent. The book of Revelation reveals the ongoing actions and performances of angels during the
end times. The activities of angels are on every page from
chapter 1 through chapter 22 in the book of Revelation.

As we approach the time of the rapture and the second
coming of Jesus Christ, the Holy Spirit will reveal a greater revelation of the Kingdom of God called the fourth dimension. The
Bible says in Joel 2:28-29:

> *And it shall come to pass afterward, that I will pour*
> *out my spirit upon all flesh; and your sons and your*
> *daughters shall prophecy, your old men shall dream*
> *dreams, your young men shall see visions: And also*
> *upon the servants and upon the handmaids in those*
> *days will I pour out my spirit.*

In the end times, praise and worship of God will increase
exponentially throughout the body of Christ and the world.
Dreams and visions will become more common, clear, vivid,
and prominent as we progress toward the prophetic end times.

There is no greater time to be alive than this present
time. We are in the time of what the Apostle Peter called "the
times of refreshing." Peter said in Acts 3:19, "Repent ye therefore, and be converted, that your sins may be blotted out, when
the times of refreshing shall come from the presence of the
Lord."

The outpouring of the Holy Spirit represents the times of
refreshing which is the climactic stage in the era of the Holy
Spirit. The Holy Spirit will reveal himself through the workings

of miracles, supernatural manifestations, and demonstration in all arenas of life including our health. God has promised that even our health will spring forth speedily due to the out pouring of the Holy Spirit. The Bible says in Isaiah 58:8,

> *Then shall your light break forth like the morning, and your healing (your restoration and the power of a new life) shall spring forth speedily; your right-eousness (your rightness, your justice, and your right relationship with God) shall go before you [conducting you to peace and prosperity], and the glory of the Lord shall be your rear guard" (AMP).*

All things, including our health, must be restored unto us before Christ returns.

The Apostle Peter continued in Acts chapter 3 saying, "For he [Jesus] must remain in heaven until the time for the final restoration of all things, as God promised long ago through His prophets (Acts 3:21, NLT)." In other words, Jesus cannot come back until the things which we have lost have been restored to us.

Many would agree that one of the main areas the enemy has stolen from believers of Christ is in the area of finances. God said in Exodus 22:1-5, 9 (NIV):

> *If a man steals an ox or a sheep and slaughters it or sells it, he must pay back five head of cattle for the ox and four sheep for a sheep. If a thief is caught breaking in and is struck so that he dies, the defender is not guilty of bloodshed; but if it happen after sun-rise, he is guilty of bloodshed. A thief must certainly make restitution...If the theft be certainly found in his hand alive, whether it be ox, or ass, or sheep; he shall restore double. If the stolen animal is found alive in his possession–whether ox or donkey or sheep–he must pay back double. If a man grazes his livestock in a field or vineyard and lets them stray and they graze in another man's field, he must make restitution from*

the best of his own field or vineyard. In all cases of il-
legal possession of an ox, or donkey, a sheep, a gar-
ment, or any other lost property about which
somebody says, 'this is mine,' both parties are to bring
their cases before the judges. The one whom the
judges declare guilty must pay back double to his
neighbor.

The above verses of Exodus 22:1-5, 9 represent financial loss. God has created a system of rewards for the things which are lost or stolen from us. The lowest level of restoration is double. God has promised that we will receive double for our trouble. God has promised in His Word that the things which had been stolen from us must be restored before Christ returns.

God has commanded you in the book of Isaiah 54:2-3 (NLT) to "Enlarge your house; build an addition; spread out your home, and spare no expense! For you will soon be bursting at the seams. Your descendants will occupy other nations resettle the ruined cities."

Instead of lack, barrenness, and emptiness, the outpouring of the Holy Spirit in the end times will replace what the devil has stolen with abundance, fruitfulness, and fullness. This anointing of prosperity will rest upon you, your children, and descendants.

The role of the angels will assist in making sure we are restored with interest all that has been lost to us. Never in the history of mankind will you see such awesome supernatural power in the earth. The Day of Pentecost will pale in comparison to "the times of refreshing." Angels will be key players in aiding and reinforcing this monumental "end time" release of the supernatural.

This blessed message alone should prompt us to praise and worship God. Angels know the gratification, benefits, and joy of praise and worship. Nehemiah 8:10 says, "...For this day is holy unto our Lord: neither be ye sorry; for the joy of the Lord is your strength."

There are untold benefits in praising and worshipping God. Angels receive strength, restoration, and power from praising and worship God. As a recipient of salvation, let's not allow the angels to out praise and worship us as the children of the Most High God in the fourth dimension.

Holy Spirit

Holy Spirit, embracing God's master plan,

Holy Spirit, in this we will always stand;

Holy Spirit, His mercy we will seek,

Holy Spirit, because you hold life's peak;

Holy Spirit, our dwelling place forevermore,

Holy Spirit, the promise of Jehovah's fourth dimension door;

Holy Spirit, our spiritual sight is what You see,

Holy Spirit, my past, my present, and my future, my Trinity.

CHAPTER 17

The Prescription from Heaven

Many of us are familiar with prescribed medications. Prescribed medication is intended only for the person whose name appears on the prescription label. A prescribed drug is written by a doctor who has examined a patient at the hospital or doctor's office.

If the doctor discovered that the patient contracted an infirmity or abnormality, they write a prescription for the patient. This prescription is intended to relieve the symptoms associated with the disease and hopefully, in time, the patient would get better and become whole again.

This is similar to what God did for us. Mankind had contracted a deadly disease called sin which contaminated every human being. The disease of sin flowed through our bloodline like an infectious virus which affected all humanity. However, God sent us a prescription from heaven in the person of Jesus Christ.

Before a person can develop immunity to a virus, he must be given a dose of the virus. Jesus became sin for us so that we can become immune to the effects of sin. John the apostle, said in 1 John 3:9, "Whosoever is born of God doth not commit sin; for his [God] seed remaineth in him: and he cannot sin, because he is born of God." A person who is born of God is immune to sin.

However, this does not mean he is perfect or sinless. It means that this person has been made the righteousness of God in Christ. The Bible says in 2 Corinthians 5:21, "For he [God] hath made him [Jesus] to be sin for us, who knew no sin; that we might be made the righteousness of God in him." In other words, sin will not be able to infect or destroy a believer of Christ. The Bible says in Romans 6:23, "For the wages [or consequence] of sin is death: but the gift of God is eternal life through Jesus Christ our Lord."

Sin is the worst virus known to man. It has killed more people than the black plague, polio, smallpox, malaria, cholera, ebola, bubonic plague, Spanish flu, influenza, and AIDS combined. It had no cure until the prescription called Jehovah Rapha [the God that heals] came from heaven.

The price of sin requires the payment of death based on the law of God. The Bible says in 1 Corinthians 15:56-57, "The sting of death is sin; and the strength of sin is the law. But thanks be to God, which giveth us the victory through our Lord Jesus Christ." Jesus, who had no sin, took on the virus of sin so that we can receive the antidote or vaccine from death.

Jesus made the announcement of His arrival, as the one who is the answer to all of mankind, at the commencement of His ministry. The Bible says in Luke 4:17-21,

> *And there was delivered unto him the book of the prophet Esaias. And when he [Jesus] had opened the book, he found the place where it was written, the spirit of the Lord is upon me, because he hath anointed me to preach the gospel to the poor; he hath sent me to heal the brokenhearted, to preach deliverance to the captives, and recovering of sight to the blind, to set at liberty them that are bruised, to preach the acceptable year of the Lord. And he closed the book and he gave it again to the minister, and sat down. And the eyes of all them that were in the synagogue were fastened on him. And he began to say unto them, this day is this scripture fulfilled in your ears.*

Jesus arrived at His home church, in the synagogue of Nazareth, as it was accustomed or traditional to do on the Sabbath. Jesus proceeded to read from the scroll of the prophet Isaiah, chapter 61 in our Bible. After unrolling the scroll of Isaiah, he read Isaiah chapter 61:1-2 and graciously rolled the scroll up and gave it back to the attendant.

Now there was nothing wrong with reading from the scroll of the prophet Isaiah. Many priests, prophets, scribes, and Pharisees, alike, have read aloud the words of the prophet Isaiah. What stirred up the controversy in the temple wasn't what Jesus read but what he said after quoting the words of the prophet Isaiah.

Jesus sat down and said, "This day is this scripture fulfilled in your ears!" (Luke 4:21). Everyone knew that the words of Isaiah chapter 61 spoke of the coming Messiah, the Anointed One of God. In other words, Jesus said, I am the one of which all of the prophets of antiquity spoke and wrote about. I am the "prescribed" word written aforetime by the ancient prophets.

Jesus was saying that He was the one who was prophesied to come. He was the anointed one of God. Isaiah was anointed to preach to the people of Israel, but Jesus was the one who anointed Isaiah. Jesus was saying He is the One who will save Israel and the nations of the earth.

The blessings of salvation, through Jesus Christ, are what Isaiah wrote centuries before Christ came to Earth. In Luke 4:17-18, Jesus summed up all natural and spiritual conditions that affected mankind:

- Good news to the poor
- Healing to the broken
- Freedom from captivity
- Recovery of sight to the blind
- Release from oppression

All of the above conditions are both natural and spiritual. Jesus is saying, as He said 2000 years ago, that He is the prescribed Word of God. He is the one spoken of before the foundation of the world.

The Bible says in John 1:1-2, 14, "In the beginning was the Word and the Word was with God and the Word was God. The same was in the beginning with God. And the Word was made flesh, and dwelt among us, (and we beheld his glory, the glory as of the only begotten of the Father,) full of grace and truth."

Not only is Jesus the "prescribed" or foretold Word of God, Jesus is the "prescription" for all natural conditions and spiritual ailments. There is no ill–whether it is physical, social, mental, emotional, situation, or conditional–that He cannot heal.

What is a medical prescription? Medically speaking, a prescription can be defined as a written formula, drug, remedy, medicine, or dosage administered by a certified expert to alter the effect of a given disease or condition.

The Bible says in Malachi 4:2 (NLT) "...The Sun of Righteousness [Jesus] will rise with healing in his wings." Jesus is the only cure for sickness both physically and spiritually.

Scripture says in Matthew 9:12, "But when Jesus heard that, he said unto them, they that be whole need not a physician, but they that are sick." Jesus realized that no man is immune from the effects of sin; therefore, He has come to provide the cure. Jesus healed all who wanted to be made whole.

Jesus came to heal. He is the Great Physician. Whatever satan and sin has mustered up throughout the centuries, Jesus can cure it. Notwithstanding, Jesus has your prescription! This is what Jesus meant in Luke 4:18 (above). He is the Good News. He is healing. He is freedom. He is restoration and recovery. He is the release from oppression.

If you're broken, Jesus has the prescription to put you back together. If you are sick and in need of medicine, Jesus is your medical prescription. If you're poor and in need of money, Jesus is your financial "bailout" from poverty. The Bible says in Deuteronomy 8:18, "But thou shalt remember the Lord thy God, for it is he that giveth thee power to get wealth..."

If you're hungry, Jesus said in John 6:41, "...I am the bread which came down from heaven." If you're thirsty, Jesus said in John 4:10, I am the living water. If you are in prison or jail, Jesus is your court attorney (legal advocate) from captivity. If you are oppressed and suffering in the mind, Jesus is your psychiatric prescription from depression and oppression. If life has robbed you of many of its abundant pleasures, Jesus said in John 10:10, "...I am come that you might have life and that you might have it more abundantly."

Perhaps you have seen the TV commercial for the iPhone® from Apple™, which says, "There is an app for that." Jesus says there is an "app" for whatever ails you. Jesus has the "app", prescription, and the cure. Jesus said in Luke 4:18 that He came all the way down from heaven to give you your medicine and your prescription.

Moreover, Jesus can properly diagnose your condition without using a CAT scan or MRI. In fact, Jesus never took a CAT scan or MRI of the woman with the issue of blood to determine the cause of her hemorrhaging in Mark chapter 5. The woman with the issue of blood had an incurable disease. In fact, Jesus had no plans to heal her. She was not on His agenda or itinerary. Yet, the woman with the issue of blood knew that Jesus was her prescription from heaven.

In Mark 5:25-34, Jesus was headed to Jairus' house to heal his daughter who was at the point of death. In verses 28-29 of Mark chapter 5, the Bible says "For she [the woman with the issue of blood] said, if I may touch but his clothes I shall be whole. And straightway the fountain of her blood dried up and she felt in her body that she was healed of that plague." The healing power or prescription of Jesus just didn't relieve the symptoms or make her feel better. The healing power of Jesus always brings a cure. There is no disease Christ can't cure.

You may have a medical condition or problem that the doctors can't cure. However, your prescription from heaven has come! May be your condition is not sickness, may be you are held captive and bound by the enemy through addictions, alcoholism, drugs, bad habits, and other debilitating situations. Jesus can set you free today. The Bible says in John 8:36, "If the Son therefore shall make you free, ye shall be free indeed."

If you have any sickness and disease, please follow these prescription directions from the Great Physician: take two scriptural doses of God's Word every 24 hours. These medications can be taken internally or orally by opening your mouth. Take the capsule, Isaiah 53:5, which says, "But he was wounded for my transgression, he was bruised for my iniquities, the chastisement of my peace was upon him, and with his stripes I am healed." Take the second capsule, 3 John 2, which says, "Beloved, I wish above all things that thou mayest prosper and be in health even, as thy souls prospereth."

These two high-dose medications are best taken when mixed with faith. Swallow each capsule with the water of the Word. Psalms 107:20 says, "He sent his word and healed them and delivered them from their destructions."

In other words, please "use as directed." There are no OTC (over the counter) medicine substitutes for this prescription. Side effects? There are none. Allergic to anything? No allergic reactions will result.

All believers of the fourth dimension have been inoculated from the disease of sin and have been promised healing for the body. Fourth dimensional believers do not have to suffer from any medical affliction or infirmity. Jesus bore all of our sicknesses and diseases on the cross.

The Bible says in 1 Peter 2:24, "Who his own self bare our sins in his own body on the tree, that we, being dead to sins, should live unto righteousness: by whose stripes, ye were healed." If Christ has borne our sickness then why are we bearing it? The prescription from Heaven is available to all believers in the fourth dimension.

Holy Spirit

Holy Spirit, from now through eternity,

Holy Spirit, thou art the Trinity;

Holy Spirit, the Godhead three-in-one,

Holy Spirit, all powerful is the Son;

Holy Spirit, now the fourth dimension we enter in,

Holy Spirit, washed, cleansed, sanctified, and free from sin;

Holy Spirit, one day at a time,

Holy Spirit, only in You our lives will be fine.

CHAPTER 18

The Real World

In 1999, a popular science fiction-action movie written and directed by Larry and Andy Wachowski, starring Keanu Reeves and Laurence Fishburne hit the big screen called **The Matrix**. The movie depicted a time in the future in which reality, as perceived by most humans, was actually a computer-generated fantasy. However, Morpheus (Laurence Fishburne) awakens Neo (Keanu Reeves) to the real world behind the artificial computer-generated reality known as the Matrix.

After learning about the truth of the artificial reality that he thought was real, Neo enters back into the matrix to witness to those caught in its stronghold and to share the truth to all mankind who would listen. In other words, Neo went back into the world to save others. We have been commanded and commissioned by Jesus to do the same. Jesus said unto His disciples "...Go ye into all the world, and preach the gospel to every creature (Mark 16:15).

Neo fought against the machine rebels and the tyranny of evil in the Matrix. He and the forces of Zion fought against the resistance who wanted to keep humanity in the dark and from a greater reality known as the city of Zion. The Bible declares, "For we are not fighting against flesh-and-blood enemies, but against evil rulers and authorities of the unseen world, against mighty powers in this dark world, and against evil spirits in the heavenly places" (Ephesians 6:12, NLT).

This movie really caused me to think about what is truly real and what is not. The film revealed that the majority of the human population lives in a dream world from which many never awake from their sleep. The Bible says, "The hour has come for you to wake up from your slumber, because our salvation is nearer now than when we first believed" (Romans 13:11, NIV).

In the movie, most of the people who were plugged into the Matrix lived a lie. What they thought all their lives to be reality was an illusion from the enemy. This is truth of the individuals in our world. The Bible admonishes us to set our affection or minds on the true reality which is heaven. Colossians 3:1 (NLT) says, "Since you have been raised to new life with Christ, set your sights on the realities of heaven, where Christ sits in the place of honor at God's right hand."

When we received the gift of salvation through Christ, we were "unplugged" from the world's system. We are in the world but not of the world. In the movie Matrix, Morpheus and Neo had the ability to come and go between the real world and the dream world. We, as believers of Christ, are able to operate and function in the third dimension (natural world) and the fourth dimension of the Kingdom of God (eternal world).

Although we are in the world, the Word of God commands us to not be conformed to this world. Once we have been "unplugged" we must reeducate and transform our minds to conform to the will of God. The Bible says, "Don't copy the behavior and customs of this world, but let God transform you into a new person by changing the way you think. Then you will learn to know God's will for you, which is good and pleasing and perfect" (Romans 12:2, NLT). Throughout **The Matrix** movie, Neo had to retrain his mind and discard who he thought he was and learn to accept his true identity and calling. The Bible says, "Therefore if any man be in Christ, he is a new creature: old things are passed away; behold, all things are become new" (2 Corinthians 5:17).

Many individuals truly believe that this world is all there is. They have committed and devoted all of their energy, time, and effort in a temporal world with no thought of an eternal world. In the movie, the machines represented the kingdom of darkness and Zion represented the kingdom of light. The kingdom of darkness and the kingdom of light are constantly in a struggle for control and rulership. The Kingdom of heaven, which represents the kingdom of light, is in constant warfare. The Bible declares that the Kingdom of heaven suffereth violence, and the violent take it by force. The movie, Matrix, is a classic example of good versus evil.

The real world is the absolute eternal world of the fourth dimension. Saints of God must know that this is not the real world. As in the movie Matrix, we must look past the neurons of the five senses of the brain and embrace the truth of another dimension. Our limited physical and neurological senses are not a true acid test of what is reality. This is why the Bible declares that we must walk by faith and not by sight (2 Corinthians 5:7). Faith transcends the world of the senses [temporal world] into the realm of the unseen and infinite.

The Apostle Paul said in 2 Corinthians 4:16-18, "...We do not look at the things which are seen, but at the things which are not seen. For the things which are seen are temporary, but the things which are not seen are eternal." The world in which we currently live in is temporary at best. We can transcend the evil [matrix] world in which we live and enter into the fourth dimension [Zion].

Jesus displayed the reality of the fourth dimension while on Earth with three of His most trusted disciples. The Bible says in the book of Matthew 17:1-2 that on a high mountain, Jesus was transfigured before Peter, James, and John. His face shined as the sun and His raiment was white as the light. Jesus showed His disciples another dimension, a state of eternal being, and a realm of reality in which He existed before coming to Earth. Jesus transformed His third dimensional body into His fourth dimensional glorified body.

There are realms of reality and life in the fourth dimension beyond human reasoning. God lives outside the limits of the third dimensional world. Time, space, and matter are products of our world. God lives beyond the limits of time, space, matter, and human history in a world called the fourth dimension.

Holy Spirit

Holy Spirit, this love I have for You so,

Holy Spirit, Jesus, my Christ He really knows;

Holy Spirit, God's promise from up above,

Holy Spirit, saturated and dipped with God's love;

Holy Spirit, You live within the fourth dimension of my heart,

Holy Spirit, only because of the Creator's human part;

Holy Spirit, You are forever walking and talking with me,

Holy Spirit, God the Father, Christ the Son, and the Holy

Ghost, the Trinity.

CHAPTER 19

The Blessings of Abiding in God

Have you ever asked yourself what are the advantages of being in fellowship with God or what special privileges are there in being in harmony with God? I am here to announce that there are more blessings than we can ever imagine in God. There are countless multitudes and manifold advantages, privileges, and blessings in God. Are you ready to receive the blessings of God? Let's read what Jesus, the Living Word of God, says. Jesus said in John 15:4-7,

> *Abide in me and I in you, as the branch cannot bear fruit of itself, except it abide in the vine, no more can ye, except ye abide in me; I am the vine, ye are the branches; he that abideth in me, and I in him, the same bringeth forth much fruit, for without me, ye can do nothing; if a man abide not in me, he is cast forth as a branch, and is withered; and men gather them, and cast them into the fire, and they are burned; if ye abide in me, and my words abide in you, ye shall ask what ye will, and it shall be done unto you.*

To "abide" means *to live or dwell.* Jesus said in John 15:4-17, that we must abide or be a part of the body of Jesus Christ in order to experience the fullness of life. The Apostle Paul said in Romans 12:5, "So we, being many, are one body in

Christ..." When you become a part of the body of Christ, you become a part of God's family.

Your desires and concerns are important to God. Because you are abiding in him, your desires affect the decisions that God makes. As one who abides in Christ, your thoughts count to God. Listen, what concerns you concerns Him. When you become a branch connected to the vine, you become one with God in Christ Jesus.

In John 10:30, Jesus said, "I and my father are one." Just as Christ is one with the Father, we have become one in Christ and with the Father through faith. Therefore, when you ask anything according to the Word of God as one who is connected to the vine, God will grant any desire and fulfill every petition.

God cannot deny you when you abide in Him; to do so is to deny Himself. Why can't God deny you when you abide in Him? When you speak the Word of God that abides in you, God has to honor His Word because He is His Word. The Bible says in John 1:1, "In the beginning was the word and the word was with God and the word was God." When you abide in God, none of God's Words that you speak will fail.

What does it mean to truly abide in God? Let's start by saying what abiding is not. If your will has not aligned itself with the Word of God, you are not abiding in God. Those who are abiding in God are subject to the will of God and to His Word. To abide in the fullness of God is to experience what He feels, to see what He sees, to love what He loves, and to honor the things that honor Him.

Oftentimes, we view God in relationship to Him abiding in us. While this is true and scripturally correct, John, the apostle of Jesus Christ, wants us to look at a different point of view as well which is, you abiding in Him. Imagine yourself dwelling and abiding in God, as well as Him abiding in you. To dwell or abide in God means that the enemy has to face God to get to you.

To abide in God is to have intimate communion with Him. God's Spirit becomes your own. Your Spirit becomes His.

You and God become inseparable. In order for the enemy to destroy you, he must first destroy God, and you know that's not going to happen! No wonder God is called a mighty fortress, a strong tower, a mighty deliverer, and our dwelling place.

When we abide in God, (according to John 10:29), "...No one is able to pluck us out of God's hands." To abide in God is to dwell in the secret place. David said in Psalms 91:1. "He that dwelleth in the secret place of the most high shall abide under the shadow of the Almighty." Imagine if you will, the devil coming to destroy you because you have become a great witness for Christ. But because you abide under the shadow of the Almighty, as a son and daughter of the Most High God, your fight becomes God's fight.

I remember as a little boy in grade school a big bully named Rochelle. Rochelle was supposed to have been in middle school, but he wasn't due to failing numerous times. One day, he beat me up something awful; I went away battered and crying. When my oldest sister saw me coming down the street crying, she asked me what was wrong. I told her a big boy down the road had beaten me up. Instead of saying, "I'll get him when I see him or he'd better not ever put his hands on you again", she said, "Let's go find him!" She took me back down the road to find the big bully, Rochelle. I said, "There he is!"

My oldest sister approached him with tears in her eyes, picked up an empty glass bottle, broke it, and with the jiggered and ragged edges of the bottle in the big boy's face. She said, "If you ever put your hands on my brother again, I'll kill you."

Rochelle, with all his big muscles and great stature, didn't have the nerve to even open his mouth! At any moment, it seemed that my sister was going to thrust the glass into his face and kill him. Never again did Rochelle touch me or even say anything to me! When we are in trouble, just like my big sister, God takes it personally! Your fight becomes God's fight.

God said to the children of Israel, through His servant Moses, in Exodus chapter 23 that if they would obey and abide in Him, He would be an enemy to their enemies. Exodus 23:22 says, "But if thou shalt obey his voice, and do all that I speak, then I will be an enemy unto thine enemies and an adversary unto thine adversaries."

Just like my oldest sister, you don't have to fight your battles alone when Jesus is your big brother! Satan is careful about whom he picks on. Why do you think demons were so fearful in the presence of Jesus? It was because Jesus was God in the flesh. Devils know that you don't pick on God!

In Luke Chapter 4, the demons cried out saying to Jesus saying "...Let us alone; what have we to do with thee, thou Jesus of Nazareth? art thou come to destroy us? I know thee who thou art; the Holy One of God" (Luke 4:34). Devils know who they can pick a fight with and who they can't!

When you abide in God, you are protected. Furthermore, the fact that you dwell and abide in God denotes the power of agreement. When you are in agreement with God there is no spiritual difference between you speaking and God speaking. Why? You and God are speaking as one, with the same voice.

In the book of Matthew chapter 8, a storm arose as Jesus and the disciples were going to the other side of the Sea of Galilee. In verse 26, the Bible says, "Jesus arose and rebuked the wind and said unto the sea, peace be still. And the wind ceased and there was a great calm" (Matthew 8:26). The wind and the sea did not hear and obey the voice of a man, but what the sea and the wind heard was the voice of the Creator, God.

That's why the disciples said after He calmed the storm, in Matthew 8:27, "What manner of man is this, that even the winds and the sea, obey him?" Know this; when you abide in God and the troubles of life are hindering you from passing over to the other side, you can speak to your troubles and they must obey. Why? When you abide in God the voice that your troubles hear is not your voice, but the voice of Jehovah God.

Abiding in God means that you become infused with God, as a branch is infused in the vine. It can be difficult to determine where a vine stops and where the branch begins when a branch is connected to a vine. When you abide in him you take on the image of God.

Moses understood the concept of abiding in God. Exodus 34:29 says, "And it came to pass when Moses came down from

Mount Sinai, with the two tables of testimony, in Moses hand, when he came down from the mount, that Moses wist not that the skin of his face shone, while he talked with God; and when Aaron and the children of Israel saw Moses, behold the skin of his face shone; and they were afraid to come nigh him."

Because Moses abided with God on the mount, Moses began to take on the character, image, attributes, glory, and the anointing of God. Remember this, those who dwell with the anointed, become the anointed!

Because Moses was in constant communion and agreement with God, Moses began to take on the image of God. Moses is called a friend of God (Exodus 33:11). Friends often share in many things and have many things in common. When you abide in God, God calls you His friend. In fact, when you abide in God, you can affect the decisions of God, even to the point that God will change His mind based on what you say!

Let's go to Exodus 32:9-12, 14 where God is about to destroy the children of Israel because of the sin of idolatry. God said:

> *...I have seen this people and behold it is a stiff-necked people, now therefore let me alone [Moses] that my wrath may wax hot against them and that I may consume them and I will make of thee a great nation; and Moses besought the Lord his God and said Lord why doth thy wrath wax hot against thy people which thou hast brought forth out of the land of Egypt with great power and with a mighty hand? Wherefore should the Egyptians speak, and say, For mischief, did he [God] bring them out to slay them in the mountains and to consume them from the face of the earth? Turn from thy fierce wrath and repent of this evil against thy people. And the Lord repented of the evil which he thought to do unto the people.*

Imagine Moses telling God, Jehovah, to repent! Man repents, God doesn't. Yet, when we abide in God, we can calm

God's anger and change the mind of God. Imagine Moses using simple psychology on God! Moses was saying, "God, what would the neighbors think if you would slay the very ones You delivered with a mighty hand in the wilderness? They would think You were a "bad God" to devise such an evil scheme against Your own people. Think and consider Your reputation as a mighty deliverer, You would give yourself a bad name, if You do this!"

What do you think would have happened if Moses had not spoken up in defense of the nation of Israel? The children of Israel would have been destroyed! When you abide in God your will and desire can affect the decisions of God. That's the power of abiding in God.

When you abide in God, you can ask God for anything! When you cry and call out to Him, His eyes and ears perk up; His attention will be focused directly on you. Psalms 34:15 says, "The eyes of the Lord are upon the righteous and his ears are open unto their cry."

The prophet Amos says in Amos 3:3, "Can two walk together except they be agreed? Jesus adds by saying in Matthew 18:19, "Again I say unto you, that if two of you, shall agree on earth, as touching anything, that they shall ask, it shall be done for them, of my father, which is in heaven."

Yes, there are special privileges, advantages, and blessings when abiding in Christ. Vines naturally provide a flow of nourishment to the branches. Nourishment found in the vine provides healing and restoration for the branches. Jesus is the vine. He is the One which connects divinity to humanity and through His death, we have life. For Jesus said in John 10:10, "I am come that ye might have life and have it more abundantly." Jesus took on sickness and iniquity so that we could take off infirmity and every weight of sin.

When you abide in God whatever Christ has inherited becomes your inheritance and prosperity. Jesus said in Matthew 28:18, "...All power is given into me in heaven and in earth." All power includes the power to receive healing and wealth. When you abide in God your inheritance is connected to the wealth and abundance of the fourth dimension.

When you abide in the vine you don't have to spend your life trying to get connected with the elitists of this world. The psalmist says in Psalms 75:6, "For promotion cometh neither from the east, nor from the west, nor from the south, but God is the judge, he putteth down one and setteth up another." When you abide in God God exerts His holy influence upon you and gives you His favor.

Right now, God is releasing favor, restoration, deliverance, and healing into your life. Don't believe the "never-lies" of the devil: that is, you'll "never" get out of debt; you'll "never" get well; you'll "never" get the house you desire; you'll "never" get out of the situation that you are in. When you abide in the vine you are blessed and safe in the loving arms of Jesus.

When you abide in God, you can ask for what you want and God will do it. When you abide in God, God will give you the desires of your heart (Psalms 34:7). Jesus goes further saying, "And whatsoever ye shall ask in my name that will I do, that the Father may be glorified in the Son; if ye shall ask anything in my name, I will do it" (John 14:13-14).

There are countless blessings when we abide in the God of the fourth dimension. Luke 12:32 says, "Fear not little flock for it is your father's good pleasure to give you the kingdom." The Kingdom of God is the Kingdom of the fourth dimension. Come and possess the manifold blessings of God when you abide in the fourth dimension.

Holy Spirit

Holy Spirit, the Pentecost You know,

Holy Spirit, You came to anoint us years ago;

Holy Spirit, please give us Your sound,

Holy Spirit, that rushing mighty wind all around;

Holy Spirit, our Savior sits at the right hand of God,

Holy Spirit, now the problem of sin has permanently been solved;

Holy Spirit, our counselor, teacher, and friend,

Holy Spirit, because you came our Christ lives within.

CHAPTER 20

The Word of God

The Bible is an ethical book. Ethics are moral rules or laws that govern a the behavior of a person or group. Rules and laws are central to everything we do say and do. Our world is inundated with laws and rules.

Laws and rules are everywhere. When we drive we see signs posting speed limits, traffic lights indicating stop or go, and painted lines in the streets revealing proper lanes and turns. When we go to work most employers have rules, laws, and employee manuals governing the workplace.

Even churches have bylaws, constitutions, ordinances, beliefs, and creeds. Others are unwritten traditions concerning fellowship and worship in the church.

The Word of God is no exception. The Word of God is the law of God. The Word of God is one of the two main dimensional portals in which God has given us to know him in the fourth dimension. The other main dimensional portal is the Holy Spirit about whom we will discuss in a later chapter.

A dimensional portal represents a doorway into another dimension. Through the Word of God, we can travel from the third dimension of time, space, and matter to a fourth dimension, an eternal dimension of the Kingdom of God.

The Word of God gives life. The Bible says in Psalms 119:93 (NLT), "I will never forget your commandments, for by them you give me life." Peter said to Jesus in John 6:68, "...To whom shall we go? thou hast the words of eternal life."

Adherence or obedience to the law of God opens up a portal to an infinite and supernatural life in another dimension, the fourth dimension. In this spiritual and supernatural dimension, that which we hold dear, value, and treasure comes to us and that which we abhor and devalue moves away from us.

Because God values and loves us, He draws us to Him. Jesus said in John 6:44, "No man can come to me, except the Father which hath sent me draw him..." Conversely, when we value and love God, God draws near to us. James 4:8 (NASB) says, "Draw near to God and He will draw near to you..."

Furthermore, Jesus has extended an official invitation to all who would come to him. Jesus said in Revelation 3:20, "Behold I stand at the door, and knock: if any man hear my voice, and open the door, I will come in to him, and will sup with him, and he with me."

A spiritual dimensional portal immediately opens up when you open your heart to Christ. Having fellowship with Jesus opens up a whole new dimensional world.

We must desire and thirst after the law of God in our hearts before the Kingdom of God opens to us. Psalms 119:10-11 says, "With my whole heart have I sought thee: O let me not wander from thy commandments. Thy word have I hid in mine heart, that I might not sin against thee."

The Word or the law of God activates or releases the fourth dimensional portal which leads to the Kingdom of God. As you commit and devote your life to the words and commandments of Christ, you move further along into the portal of the fourth dimension.

The Word of God and the fourth dimension are inseparable; they are one in the same. The foundation of the fourth dimension is the eternal Word of God. Isaiah 40:8 says, "The grass withers, the flower fades: but the Word of our God shall stand forever" (KJ2000).

The fourth dimension is the compilation of all the promises and blessings spoken and written of God. It is the realm where all the promises of God are no longer spiritual, but tangible and available to you at your disposal.

The Word of God is preeminent above all things. It takes precedent over all thoughts, ideas, philosophies, opinions, and experiences. Paul said in 2 Corinthians 10:5, "Casting down imaginations, and every high thing that exalteth itself against the knowledge of God, and bringing into captivity every thought to the obedience of Christ."

Nothing takes precedent over the Word of God. No doctrine, religion, or new-age philosophy has authority over the Word of God. Regardless of how wonderful or life-changing it appears, no one or thing has jurisdiction over the matchless and unadulterated Word of God.

God has placed His Word above His holy name. The Bible says in Psalms 138:2, "...For thou hast magnified thy word above all thy name." God's name is holy. His name alone calms raging storms, heals infirmities, delivers, and saves. Yet, God has placed His Word above His name. In other words, God's Word is absolute, guaranteed, unchanging, irrefutable, and eternal.

Reading and obeying the Word of God opens up the portal to the fourth dimension. God wants you to experience life in a different dimension than the one you currently reside. It is time to move your residence from the third dimension which brings loss, sorrow, and defeat to a dimension of prosperity, joy, and victory waiting for you only in the fourth dimension.

Holy Spirit

Holy Spirit, Jesus is mine,

Holy Spirit, He died to make us His kind;

Holy Spirit, we are sitting in heavenly fourth dimension places,

Holy Spirit, with God there are no races;

Holy Spirit, come and let us sing songs of praise,

Holy Spirit, for in Christ all dead are raised;

Holy Spirit, our spiritual, earthly, compassion of Light,

Holy Spirit, you bring the tree of life in sight.

Chapter 21

What Time is It?

In our world, there are many time zones. There are the U.S. time zones, Canadian time zones, American time zones, and international time zones. In other words, there is no correct or standard time. Time is relative depending on where you are.

Everywhere we go in the world, we must be aware of the governing laws of time. Time in one place is not the same as time in another. The concept of time rules over all things and everyone except one–God. In fact, when God shows up, time is subject to Him. God is never late or too early; He is always on time. In Mark chapter 11, Jesus teaches us a powerful lesson about time and His sovereignty and supremacy over time. The Bible says in Mark 11:12-14, 20,

> *And on the morrow, when they were come from Bethany he was hungry: And seeing a fig tree afar off having leaves, he came, if haply he might find any thing thereon: and when he came to it, he found nothing but leaves; for the time of figs was not yet. And Jesus answered and said unto it, No man eat fruit of thee hereafter for ever. And His disciples heard it. And in the morning, as they passed by, they saw the fig tree dried up from the roots.*

On this particular event in the life of Christ on Earth, Jesus anticipates receiving figs from a fig tree as He traveled from Bethany. Far away, the fig tree looked fruitful, abundant, and full of life, but up close and personal, it bore nothing; there was not a fig on it. We find that one thing Jesus detests greatly are things that appear good, pious, righteous, and holy, but within it is full of darkness, emptiness, and wickedness (Matthew 23:27).

Throughout Jesus' ministry, He spoke out against hypocrisy. Jesus stated in the book of Revelation 3:15-16 (NLT), "I know all the things you do, that you are neither hot nor cold. I wish that you were one or the other. But since you are lukewarm water, neither hot nor cold, I will spit you out of my mouth!" It does no good to wear a robe of righteousness, resembling holiness, when your heart is filthy and unclean.

The Bible says in the latter part of Mark 11:13 that the time of figs was not yet. Have you ever wanted something, but the time or season to obtain it was not evident or conducive? Just like Jesus, you may have been anticipating and waiting to receive a blessing or harvest. Perhaps you have been waiting a long time for your deliverance, but it seems the more you believe, by building up your faith, the more moments of disappointments you receive.

Before leaving the fig tree, Jesus does something remarkable; He talks to it. Both the fig tree and Jesus conversed together in verses 13 and 14 of Mark chapter 11. Notice that there is a conversation going on between Jesus and the fig tree.

Mark 11:13-14 says, "And seeing a fig tree afar off having leaves, he came, if haply he might find any thing thereon: and when he came to it, he found nothing but leaves; for the time of figs was not yet. And Jesus answered and said unto it..."

Now it may appear that there is nothing wrong with the state of the fig tree because the Bible says that it was not yet time for the fig tree to bear fruit (Mark 11:13). All this may be true however, when Jesus shows up things must change!

When Jesus stood in the presence of the fig tree, the fig tree refused to believe that it was now time to bear fruit. In essence, it was telling Jesus, the One who created it, "I am sorry, but it is not time for me to produce or bear fruit."

Jesus' expectation for receiving figs revealed that now was the time for the fig tree to bear fruit. However, the fig tree was essentially saying that it was not ready, nor was it the right time. However, what the fig tree failed to realize was that when Jesus shows up, it's always the right time!

In the life of the disciples, they had seen withered arms and legs become whole in their sights by the Words of Jesus. Now they would see Jesus demonstrate another kind of miracle. Instead of witnessing a miracle of creation, abundance, and prosperity, Jesus taught the disciples another lesson that we too can perform: we have the power to rebuke anything that does not yield to the authority of God.

A miracle of yielding fruit was about to take place right before the disciples' eyes, in the life of this fig tree, but the fig tree refused to believe and cooperate with its Creator. Listen, regardless of where you are, how long you've been in it, or what season you're in; when Jesus shows up, it's always the right season. The mere fact that Jesus expected to find fruit is evident that a miracle was about to happen.

What are you expecting? Are you expecting to experience a miracle today? The expectation of the fig tree should have aligned itself up to the Creator's expectations. Are you ready to experience a harvest when Jesus' presence is known? The tree shared with Jesus excuses of why it could not produce such as it's not time or I need a few more weeks and months, instead of making itself available for the Master's use. Are you making excuses for why you are not available to be used by Christ today?

Notice that the tree spoke to Jesus for the Bible says that Jesus answered back to it. The Bible says in Mark 11:14, "And Jesus answered and said unto it, No man eat fruit of thee hereafter for ever."

What are you saying to Jesus? Are you saying it's not time to serve Him? Are you saying it's not time to bear fruit? Are you saying it is not time for God to bring deliverance and prosperity into your life? Please understand this: Jesus can hear you (just like He heard the fig tree) without you saying a word.

Does Jesus hear your unbelief? The difference between seasons is God's presence. Jesus is saying He can cause you to bear fruit even in the wintry months of life, in times of economic fallouts, in the midst of stock market crashes, when the dollar is at an all-time low, and when gas and food are no longer affordable. All you have to understand is that when you invite Jesus' presence into your life, His presence brings abundance and prosperity. If you desire to have a continuous harvest, seek after the presence of God.

Natural conditions and circumstances of life have no power over Christ. The fig tree was telling Jesus that in order for it to produce fruit, the condition and the time must be right. The fig tree did not realize that its source of life and strength was not in itself, nor in the soil, nor the time of season, but it was in Jesus Christ, the Creator. Sometimes we think our strength, power, and abilities come from ourselves. However, David said in Psalms 121:1-2, "I will lift up mine eyes, unto the hills, from whence cometh my help. My help cometh from the Lord, which made heaven and earth."

The fig tree thought that it was self-existing and self-sustaining governed only by the forces of nature. But, what the fig tree did not realize was that there was One greater than the forces of nature in its presence. The Bible says in Isaiah 40:12 that God holds the oceans in His hand and measured off the heavens with His fingers.

When Jesus comes, as He did in the presence of the fig tree, He always expects something to happen. Here was a wonderful opportunity for the disciples to see the Creator of all life cause an unseasonal fig tree to blossom with fresh ripe fruit ready for the picking. But the fig tree refused to yield to the miracle working power of God. How can you come into the presence of God and not yield yourself to His will and desire for your life?

The fig tree refused to yield its fruit because it was not the right season, but when Jesus is present it is always the right season. The moral of the lesson is this: Jesus will never ask of us anything that He has not already given us the power to do. If He asks us, He has already given us the power to perform it, regardless of what time it is. What time is it in your life? The fig tree refused to do what Jesus had given it the power to do. Are you yielding your fruit to God? What time is it? When Jesus comes it is the right time!

Notice again Mark 11:14, Jesus answered and said unto it, "No man eat fruit of thee, hereafter, for ever..." Here we see Jesus making a powerful declaration. He declared a thing. Notice the words "for ever." For ever is an indication, measure, or unit of time. You also have the power to command time. Just like Jesus, we too, can call in time at our command.

It's time to speak words which will last forever. The Bible is a book of words that will last forever. Start speaking what the Word of God says. Jesus said in Mark 13:31, "Heaven and earth shall pass away; but my words shall not pass away." Isaiah 40:8 says, "The grass withereth, the flower fadeth, but the word of our God shall stand for ever."

Situations and circumstances do not determine your time or your season. Your faith and speaking the Word of God determine the seasons you choose to live in. Your season of prosperity is released the moment you choose to believe and speak the Word of God. It's time to speak words like Psalms 112:3, "Wealth and riches shall be in his [my] house..." It's time to speak words like, Psalms 30:6, "...In my prosperity, I shall never be moved", and words like Psalms 1:3 "...and whatsoever he [I] doeth shall prosper."

What time is it? It's time to start declaring a thing. The Bible says in Job 22:28, "Thou shalt also decree a thing, and it shall be established unto thee..." In other words, you have the power to create and establish your world based upon your faith and the words you speak. You have the power, in the name of Jesus, to speak eternal words that will out last time.

The power of eternity is in your mouth. We see in Mark 11:14, the words of Jesus saying, "No man shall eat of thee, hereafter, for ever." Therefore, we see that the power of our words can and will last for all eternity. What time is it? It's time to start talking like God by speaking God's Word. Start talking to your problems, talking to your mountains, talking to your trials, and talking to the things that hold you back from your divine destiny.

The story of the fig tree lets us know that just as we have the power to bless with our words, we have the power to curse with our words. Jesus cursed the fig three. There's nothing wrong with cursing the things that do not bring glory to God. There's nothing wrong with cursing the things that do not provide health, healing, and prosperity in our lives. Curse that addiction. Curse that taste for drugs and alcohol. Curse that sickness. Curse that disease. Curse that hindering spirit. Curse that stronghold. Curse that curse!

What time is it for that sickness to leave your life? Give it the same timeline that Jesus gave the fig tree. Jesus gave the fig tree a timeline. Just as Jesus commanded the fig tree and gave it a timeline, tell that spirit of infirmity to leave your body and do not return, forever. What time is it for poverty and lack in your life? Give it the same timeline, Jesus gave the fig tree.

Because we are a spirit, we can talk to spirits (Romans 8:16, NLT). Say, "Spirit of poverty, leave my life and family and do not return forever in the name of Jesus!" You don't have to be broke another day in your life. Speak the Word of God over yourself!

What time is it for your prosperity? Give it a timeline, and say: "Tomorrow about this time, God's anointing of prosperity shall be a part of my life" (2 Kings 7:1-20).

The Holy Spirit is speaking to fourth dimensional believers who believe the Word of God. He is saying that we will be blessed regardless of the cost of food, gas, and clothes. It will be like paying a penny for what other people are paying top dollar. In other words, because of our prosperity, we will not feel the effects and impact of the recession or famine that others will experience.

For so long, we have listened to the advice of this world for our health, healing, prosperity, and deliverance instead of the Word of God. We must take God at His Word. In fact, tomorrow about this time, all of your debt can be cancelled. By this time tomorrow, sickness and disease that ravished your body can be gone.

One of the greatest offenses that God holds against the church is the spoken words of doubt and unbelief instigated by His people. Did you know that it was the words of doubt and unbelief that delayed Israel from reaching their promised land in the time that was originally designed? Don't miss your time!

Jesus refused to accept the fact that the season or the time of figs was not yet. He cursed the tree, not because it wasn't the right season, but because the tree refused to yield fruit. It wasn't even the lack of figs that caused Jesus to curse the tree; it was, however, the tree's refusal to yield to the authority of Jesus Christ.

When we listen, believe, and speak words that are contrary to the Word of God, we are keeping ourselves from our own inheritance. As long as a man or woman does not believe and continue to disobey the Word of God, they will not have authority and dominion over the principalities and powers of darkness. God's Word governs and extends beyond all principalities and powers. The Word of God reveals the name, person, and the character of God. When you speak the Word of God with faith you have all authority and dominion at your disposal. All you have to do is speak the Word.

The fig tree refused to yield to Jesus, the Word. The fig tree's refusal to yield fruit was in essence saying to Jesus that it would determine Jesus' fate of being hungry. Jesus then began to speak the words that determined the fate of the fig tree. The story of the fig tree also teaches us that no one or nothing has the last or final word except Christ.

Jesus, who is Alpha and Omega, the beginning and the end (Revelation 22:13), has the final word. No one determines our fate or what happens to us other than Christ. Moreover, God has already given us the power in our mouths to determine our own destiny (Proverb 18:21).

As fourth dimensional believers, we can speak to that stronghold of infirmities, lack, and poverty in our lives. Sickness, lack, and poverty do not determine our destiny of blessings, healing, and prosperity. What time is it? It is time for the anointed of Christ to start possessing the power and authority that is rightfully ours in the fourth dimension.

Holy Spirit

Holy Spirit, most precious are Thy ways,

Holy Spirit, angels sing Thy praise;

Holy Spirit, wrapped in a holy child,

Holy Spirit, living on Earth only a while;

Holy Spirit, You are the Christ in me,

Holy Spirit, only through this fourth dimension we can see;

Holy Spirit, the third person of the Godhead,

Holy Spirit, praise Him all nations, God is not dead

CHAPTER 22

The Church as a Living Organism

The church is a fourth dimensional organism in a third dimensional world. Scientifically speaking, an organism is a living and functioning body which is able to dramatically affect its environment and surroundings. The church is fourth dimensional in nature because its charter or constitution is from the dimension of the Kingdom of God. The governmental principles of the Christian church operate under the laws of God.

The church is a group of people called the body of Christ; believers of Christ are the church. The Apostle Paul said in 1 Corinthians 12:27-28, "Now ye are the body of Christ, and members in particular. And God hath set some in the church, first apostles, secondarily prophets, thirdly teachers, after that miracles, then gifts or healings, helps, governments, diversities of tongues."

Jesus is the head of the Church and we are His body. We are Jesus' hands, arms, legs, and feet which are created for mobility. As the body of Christ, we must be constantly in motion working to win the lost for Christ. A body not in motion will become atrophic and deteriorate.

The church is a living breathing organism. The church, as a body, feels, hurts, cries, laughs, and mourns.

It is more than an organization. An organization is man-made. Members of an organization are only links to other members of the organization through association as co-workers.; they have no personal or intricate connection with each other.

An organism is God-made. Man cannot create a living organism only God can. An organism is innately and intimately connected to everything else in the organism. If one part of the body experiences pain, the entire body is in discomfort. In an organization, it is highly possible that one department or sector of the organization may be totally unaware and oblivious to the problem affecting another department in the organization due to the discontinuity that exists in organizations.

The church is a unified body of believers whose mission and purpose on the earth supersedes the highest authority in the earth. The mission and purpose of the church is to bring the Kingdom of God to Earth. We, as the church, are to institute the laws of the Kingdom of God in the earth. Jesus said in Matthew 6:10, "Thy kingdom come. Thy will be done in earth, as it is in heaven."

No force in Earth or under the earth can overthrow or abolish the church's sovereignty. Jesus said in Matthew 16:18, "...Upon this rock I will build my church; and the gates of hell shall not prevail against it." In many respects, the church is a colony of the Kingdom of heaven. A colony represents a group of people with shared beliefs and aspirations governed by a higher power.

Just as the 13 original colonies in America were the providence of England, we who are the church are colonists from the Kingdom of God, the fourth dimensional world. As colonists of another world, we have been sent to impact and influence the political, educational, economical, governmental, and social organizations of this world through the power of the Holy Spirit.

The church represents the body of Christ. The Holy Spirit gives life to the church, just as God breathed life into our natural bodies. The Bible says in Genesis 2:7, "And the Lord God formed man of the dust of the ground, and breathed into his nostrils the breath of life; and man became a living soul."

The Bible says in 1 Corinthians 12:4-6, "Now there are diversities of gifts, but the same Spirit. And there are differences of administrations, but the same Lord. And there are diversities of operations, but it is the same God which worketh all in all."

The Holy Spirit breathes life into the church which allows the church to operate and function as a living body. Like the human body, the church has many members with different functions working together on a common goal mission.

The church has the workings that resemble the human anatomy. The veins and arteries of the church are filled with the blood of Jesus; it was purchased with the blood of Jesus Christ. The Bible exhorts saying, "Take heed therefore unto yourselves, and to all the flock, over the which the Holy Ghost hath made you overseers, to feed the church of God, which he hath purchased with his own blood" (Acts 20:28).

The blood of Jesus gives life. God said in Leviticus 17:11, "For the life of the flesh is in the blood; and I have given it to you upon the altar to make an atonement for your souls: for it is the blood that maketh an atonement for the soul."

The fourth dimensional church is covered by the blood of Jesus from the inside out. There is no way the enemy can penetrate the blood. God said in Exodus 12:13, "...And when I see the blood, I will pass over you, and the plague shall not be upon you to destroy you..."

The law of the Kingdom required the shedding of the blood of a living organism. Jesus became flesh to redeem the lost through His blood. Jesus was the perfect living organism. The Bible contends saying, "So the Word [Jesus] became human and made his home among us. He was full of unfailing love and faithfulness. And we have seen his glory, the glory of the Father's one and only Son" (John 1:14, NLT).

The only way sin could be forgiven was through the blood of Jesus. The Bible declares that, "...The law requires that nearly everything be cleansed with blood, and without the shedding of blood there is no forgiveness" (Hebrews 9:22, NIV).

The church is an eternal organism alive and well due to Christ, the head of the church. No organism can function effectively without a head. Jesus is the CEO of the church; it is not man-made. The church is the greatest living organism ever created by God through Jesus Christ. The only way to receive and experience life is through the church of Jesus Christ in the fourth dimension.

Holy Spirit

Holy Spirit, may the beauty of the Lord be upon us,

Holy Spirit, in Jehovah, our God, we trust;

Holy Spirit, hear what I have to say,

Holy Spirit, today will be a blessed day;

Holy Spirit, write Your love in my heart,

Holy Spirit, from now on the fourth dimension is Your part;

Holy Spirit, seer of the soul,

Holy Spirit, only Jesus can make me whole.

CHAPTER 23

Any Day Now

Have you ever sensed that there was something on the horizon that would change everything? Maybe you have felt that at any moment something would change your life forever. Perhaps you have sensed in your spirit that something is going to occur any day now. I have! I believe we are in the set time established by God.

The Bible says in Psalms 102:12-13, "But thou O Lord shalt endure for ever, and thy remembrance unto all generations; Thou shalt arise, and have mercy upon Zion: for the time to favor her, yea, the set time is come."

It is exciting and even stimulating to know that God has set an appointed time to favor and bless His people. God has not forgotten His people. Psalms 102:12 (above), says that God remembers all generations.

This means that God remembers His promises; He does not ever forget. The Apostle Paul says in Hebrews 6:10, "For God is not unrighteous to forget your work and labour of love, which ye have shewed toward his name, in that ye have ministered to the saints, and do minister."

This chapter has been written for fourth dimensional believers, especially to those who been faithful, unyielding, steadfast, and patiently enduring as believers of Jesus Christ. Are you one who has stood in faith on the Word of God, trusting, and believing for your breakthrough? If so, let's continue reading.

The Bible says in Joel 2:15, "Blow the trumpet in Zion (Jerusalem or the church), sanctify a fast, call a solemn assembly." The act of blowing a trumpet in Joel chapter 2 is to announce or herald the beginning, or season, of a special time. This special time in Joel chapter 2 was the beginning of the season of atonement.

The Day of Atonement signified that a time or season had come, whereby God would restore to His people all that had been lost or stolen regardless of the reason, that is, whether it was due to their own sins or through the work of the enemy. The public blowing of the trumpet in the ears of all the inhabitants of Jerusalem and in Judea marked the beginning of a type or season of Jubilee.

I am here to announce to you that the trumpet has sounded and this is your season of atonement. Your day of Jubilee and restoration has come!

Joel 2:15 goes on to say, "...Sanctify a fast." This means to prepare yourself spiritually for the supernatural. You cannot receive the revelation of God with a carnal mind, that is, with an unregenerate mind.

The Bible says in Romans 8:5, 7, "For they that are after the flesh; do mind the things of the flesh but they that are after the Spirit the things of the Spirit. Because the carnal mind is enmity against God; for it is not subject to the law of God, neither indeed can be."

Therefore, we must be sensitive to the Spirit of God by means of prayer and fasting. How can you recognize or discern the spiritual blessings of the Lord without being sensitive to the unction of the Holy Spirit? You must prepare yourself for what is coming!

In an event in 2 Kings chapter 3, we find three kings (King Jehoram, King of Edom, and King Jehoshaphat) who went up to fight the king and nation of Moab. And as they journeyed, they ran out of water on the seventh day's journey. As they wondered what they would do for water, King Jehoshaphat said in 2 Kings 3:11, "Is there not here a prophet of the Lord, that we may enquire of the Lord by him?"

King Jehoshaphat was really saying "Is there a prophet in the house?" They brought to King Jehoshaphat the prophet Elisha. The prophet Elisha said to bring him a minstrel–a praise musician. The Bible says and it came to pass when the minstrel played that the hand of the Lord (the anointing) came upon Elisha (2 Kings 3:15).

When the minstrel began to play the anointing of God came forth. You see, the anointing is not a shout or a dance. The anointing is the power and the glory of God. The anointing releases and breaks any stronghold or burden that restricts, confines, or holds us captive.

Sometimes when you don't know what to do, the best thing to do is to start singing praises unto God. God will, through praise, reveal the solution to your problem. Listen, it does not matter what you are going through or how unique or difficult your circumstances are. All you need is a Word from the Lord–just as God did it for King Jehoshaphat! God has the answer to every trial, dilemma, and situation we will face.

The Bible says in 2 Kings 3:15-16 when the minstrel played, Elisha prophesied to make the valley full of ditches. In other words, prepare ditches for the water that God is about to bring to you. Elisha goes on to say, "For thus saith the Lord, Ye shall not see wind, neither shall ye see rain; yet that valley shall be filled with water, that ye may drink" (2 Kings 3:17). The Bible says, and it came to pass in the morning that the valley was filled with water (2 Kings 3:20).

Prepare yourself for the blessing! You must prepare yourself for what is coming! The Word of God says in Isaiah 54:2-3, "Enlarge the place of thy tent, and let them stretch forth the curtains of thine habitations: spare not, lengthen thy cords and strengthened thy stakes; for thou shalt break forth on the right hand and on the left..." I like how the New Living Translation version says it, "Enlarge your house; build an addition. Spread out your home, and spare no expense! For you will soon be bursting at the seams. Your descendants occupy other nations and resettle the ruined cities" (Isaiah 54:2-3, NLT).

When the prophetic Word of God and the fullness of time aligned themselves together something supernatural happens. When the anointed Word of God and the fullness of time connect and become parallel, get ready to experience a revolution that will be world-changing. Get ready to experience a supernatural [gospel] explosion.

This chapter was written to make an important announcement: your wait is over! Something great is about to explode and blow up in your life! You are about to experience a supernatural explosion.

Amos 9:13 says, "Behold, the days come, saith the Lord, that the plowman shall overtake the reaper, and the treader of grapes him that soweth seed." What is a plowman? A plowman is an individual who plows or prepares the ground for crops or seeds.

The plowman is one who cultivates the soil, plants, and sows seed for a harvest. The Bible has a lot to say about sowing and reaping and the benefits of sowing and reaping. Even though chapter 9 of Amos is prophetic in nature concerning prophesies about the restoration and the blessing of Israel, a plowman characterizes one, who sows, in the Kingdom of God.

Believe it or not, it is a blessing to sow into the Kingdom of God. There are benefits to those who sow in obedience to the Word of God. The trumpet has sounded in the spirit. The time has come for those who have sown in the Kingdom of God. Because you have sown in times of abundance and in times of famine, your days of waiting for a harvest are over!

The days have come according to Amos 9:13 where the times of harvest and sowing will be simultaneous. The harvest and sowing season will be as one. What should be a season of sowing or waiting will be a season of gathering, reaping, and harvesting. This represents a perpetual season of abundance. Let me break it down further.

Your seed will increase, produce, and grow faster than it can be gathered and harvested. Imagine if you will, a reaper harvesting the crop as the plowman follows behind planting seed for the next year's harvest.

However, the Bible says that a time of supernatural blessings has come whereby the days will be so plentiful that the cycle for seed time and harvest will be as one (Amos 9:13). In other words, harvest season will not cease.

In essence, what should be a sowing season or a period of waiting and growing will be a season of gathering and harvesting. The days have come and now are that your next harvest will grow up before you finish gathering up your current harvest. Your season has changed!

Have you ever heard of a plowman or farmer who hates to sow seed into the ground in order to receive a harvest? No! Why then do some believers sow grudgingly? Because they do not believe that they will receive a harvest. We must learn to sow cheerfully in the Kingdom of God with the attitude of believing for an expected return. 2 Corinthians 9:7 says, "...God loveth a cheerful giver." Your attitude and willingness to sow will determine your level of receiving!

The Apostle Paul lets us know that there is something special to be gained with the right attitude of sowing and giving. In Philippians 4:18-19, Paul said, "But I have all, and abound; I am full, having received of Epaphroditus the things which were sent from you, an odour of a sweet smell, a sacrifice acceptable, well pleasing to God."

Paul said that the church of Philippi sowed unto him when no one else did. They gave continually and with liberality and cheerfulness of heart. Paul said because the Philippians did this for him, for the gospel sake, and for the advancement of the Kingdom of God, their tithes and offering have gone up to God as a sweet-smelling savor.

You see, the sowing of tithes and offerings is more than a monetary act; it is a holy sacrifice unto God. The act of sacrifice is not an outdated ritual characterized under the Old Testament. It is still applicable today.

Paul says that our sowing, whether it is tithes or offerings, go up to God as a holy sacrifice. Based on our generosity of heart and spirit, God shall show favor toward us and shall supply all of our needs according to His riches in glory by

Christ Jesus (Philippians 4:19). In other words, because you sowed, your needs shall be provided based on the availability of wealth and riches that flow in abundance in heaven.

In Malachi chapter 3, God himself teaches us of the doctrine of sowing and reaping. God said that if we would sow tithes and offerings, he would rebuke the devourer for our sake. In essence, if we are a sower (giver) when the enemy comes to destroy the fruits of our labor, God has promised to be our defense and protector (Malachi 3:10-11).

We are living in the season and in the fullness of the prophetic Word of the Living God. We all have heard of the cliché' or proverb, "He may not come when you want him, but He's always on time."

The good news for this season is that He is here! No waiting is required. The Bible says in Isaiah 65:24, "And it shall come to pass, that before they call; I will answer and while they are yet speaking, I will hear." The New Living Translation says, "I will answer them, before they even call to me; while they are still talking to me about their needs, I will go ahead and answer their prayers" (Isaiah 65:24, NLT)!

Before you get down on your knees or before you finish the first sentence of your prayer, the answer to your prayer has already been granted and manifested. The days have come where the prophetic Word of God and the fullness of time have synchronized together.

Imagine the Word of God and the prophetic Word of God as the hands on a clock. The time when the long hand and the short hand on a clock are directly synchronized together vertically is at 12 o'clock midnight. Midnight is the only time in the day when time stands between the past and the future. It is neither PM nor AM. However, in one minute's time, time will change from night to morning. Your time has changed from midnight to day!

Psalms 30:5 says, "For his anger endureth but a moment, in his favour is life: weeping may endure for a night, but joy cometh in the morning." It's morning time! Wipe your tears, brush your teeth, wash your face, and comb your hair! It's morning time!

Your night time is over! The Bible has a lot to say about time. In John 17:1, 4, Jesus prayed to the Father saying, "Father, the hour is come; glorify thy Son... I have glorified thee on the earth...And now O Father, glorify thou me with thine own self, with the glory which I had with thee before the world was."

Jesus was telling the Father that the time had come for him to receive glory and honor from him. Jesus was about to fulfill His purpose for redemption for all mankind. There comes a time when God will pour out His glory and blessing upon us when we have purposed in our heart to bring Him glory. Jesus was telling the Father, "It's my time." Listen, I am prophesying to you, "It's your time!"

I want you to know that the time has come for recompense in your life. What is recompense? Payback. What time or season is it? It's payback time! The Bible says in Proverb 11:31, "Behold, the righteous shall be recompensed in the earth."

Notice that the Bible did not say that the righteous will be recompensed or receive a payback in heaven. It said the righteous will be recompensed or paid back in the earth. God is about to make the devil pay back damages and wages that he has held up and delayed in your family for years. The Bible says in Isaiah 34:8, "For it is the day of the Lord's vengeance, and the year of recompenses [payback] for the controversy [trouble] of Zion."

In the book of 1 Samuel chapter 30, the Amalekites invaded the city of Ziklag where David and his men lived. The Amalekites had taken all their wives, children, animals, and possessions. In verse 8, the Bible says that David inquired of the Lord saying, 'Shall I pursue after them and overtake them?' God said, "Pursue: for thou shalt surely overtake them, and without fail, recover all" (1 Samuel 30:8).

Although you have experienced pain and troubles, you will recover. The good news is while you were waiting, trusting, believing, and holding on to God's word through faith, God was working on your behalf.

Oftentimes in times of trouble, we may feel that we are being torn apart on every side. Not knowing that God is performing [spiritual] open heart bypass surgery upon us. God knows that there are some defective arteries in our heart that are not functioning properly. The arteries are not bringing the proper spiritual blood-flow to the heart. Surgery is never comfortable and neither is spiritual surgery. God's surgery will make us better than we were before.

When Jesus performs open heart surgery through adversity, He implants and transplants His blood into us. This, in turn, creates in us a clean heart and a renewed a right spirit (Psalms 51:10).

There were times when you thought you were too weak and burdened to go on; however, God has implanted into your spiritual blood and DNA, supernatural power to overcome every spiritual adversity!

There's a song which says, "What can wash away my sin, nothing but the blood of Jesus."[1] It's okay to go under the scalpel when Jesus is your surgeon! Jesus can cut away a stony heart and give you a heart of flesh, like His own (Ezekiel 11:19). In your sickness, you shall recover. No wonder He is called the Great Physician.

Your best days are not behind you, but in front of you. You must believe 1 Corinthians 2:9 which says, "But as it is written, Eye hath not seen, nor ear heard, neither have entered into the heart of man, the things which God hath prepared for them that love him."

Paul is not simply talking about heaven. He is also talking about the manifold blessings restored upon the children of God on the earth.

I know that things may be difficult in your life; however, you have been anointed to make it through difficult times. The truth of the matter is you did not make it through the difficult times by yourself. God is the One who gave you the strength, power, and ability to go through.

Not only will you outlast every adversary, but you will overcome every obstacle. Anyone can quit. Anyone can give up when it gets hard. Anyone can get discouraged because it's taking a long time, but you must know you would not have the breath to breathe right now if God had not breathed a life of victory into your future!

There are more forces for you, in the fourth dimension than are against you in this world. Nothing that has happened to you can keep you from your God-given destiny. Every setback is a set up for a greater comeback.

I heard someone say, "Losers focus on what they are going through. Winners focus on what they are going to." What you are going through is the transportation or the vehicle to your destination.

God has turned your battlefield into a field of blessings. God will release a season of promotion, favor, and blessing upon you "any day now" in the fourth dimension.

Endnotes:

1. Lowry, Doane & Robert. "What Can Wash Away My Sin." New York: Biglow & Main, 1876.

Holy Spirit

Holy Spirit, Jesus the Redeemer of mankind,

Holy Spirit, praise God it's our time;

Holy Spirit, you will never grow old,

Holy Spirit, this is what the Scripture told;

Holy Spirit, past, present, and fourth dimension future,

Holy Spirit, we give all glory to Ya;

Holy Spirit, God's children's hearts belong to You,

Holy Spirit, for You only know the truth.

CHAPTER 24

Dreams

God uses a variety of modes or systems in which to communicate to us in the third dimension. He has never left us without having the means to communicate with us. One mode or way God speaks to us is through dreams. What are dreams? Dreams are mental images, ideas, sounds, and emotional sensations that occur involuntarily while in the stages of sleep.

God speak to us through dreams. Have you ever awakened from a dream? It may have been God speaking to you. Isaiah 50:4 (NIV) says, "...He [God] wakens me morning by morning, wakens my ear to listen like one being taught.

Dreams are dimensional portals God uses to communicate with us. Dreams are nothing new. Men have been having dreams since the beginning of time. The first recorded dream in Scripture was with a pagan king called Abimelech in chapter 20 of Genesis. The dream was based upon Abraham and his wife.

The Bible says in Genesis 20:2-3, "And Abraham said of Sarah his wife, She is my sister: and Abimelech king of Gerar sent, and took Sarah. But God came to Abimelech in a dream by night, and said to him, Behold, thou art but a dead man, for the woman which thou hast taken: for she is a man's wife."

In this dream, God made it crystal and poignantly clear to King Abimelech about Sarah, Abraham's wife. God said in essence, 'If you touch Sarah, you're dead!' In many dreams it can be difficult to decipher the meaning; however, in King

Abimelech's dream, God left no doubt in his mind to whom he was referring, as well as the consequence of what would happen if he did not obey Him. It is obvious that King Abimelech took the dream very seriously because he gave Sarah back to Abraham including cattle and great possessions.

The Bible says in Genesis 20:14, "And Abimelech took sheep, and oxen, and menservants, and womenservants, and gave them unto Abraham, and restored him Sarah his wife." God used a dream to teleport His message to a pagan king, who did not know Him, but yet the king obeyed God. The first dream recorded in the Bible represented an imminent warning.

John Paul Jackson, a renowned spiritual interpreter of dreams and visions, says that dreams convey meanings. They are parabolic in nature. In other words, they are like parables. Parables are succinct or summarized stories which illustrate or depict spiritual meanings. Dreams are like parables whose origin is from a spiritual dimension. They come as an experience or story. We are able to see various circumstances and situations in dreams which can move us about from one dimension to another.

Dreams are symbolic. They are usually not to be taken literally. Godly dreams are always in color which represents light. Light represents all colors. God is light (1 John 1:5-7). Therefore, God will always reveal Himself in color (light). Demonic and spiritual warfare dreams are usually in black and white.

Dreams reveal God's plans and purposes. God will often share with us the future of what is going to happen to us or to others.

Dreams can prompt us to accelerate in motion. Dreams can prompt us to act or move into motion. For an example Joseph, the earthly father of Jesus, was told in a dream by an angel to take the young child and His mother into Egypt because King Herod wanted to kill Him. When Joseph arose from his dream, he immediately took the young child and His mother by night and departed into Egypt. (Matthew 2:13-14).

Dreams can create order out of chaos. You can be instructed in a dream to do or not do something which can create order out of confusion and turmoil. For instance, unaware that they were being used by Herod to search for the Christ Child, the wise men from the East were warned, by God, in a dream. They were cautioned not to return to Jerusalem because King Herod desired to kill the young child (Matthew 2:12). Through a dream, God diverted the diabolical plan of King Herod.

God has dreams tell and warn the world about what's coming and how to get out of it. Joseph warned Pharaoh, who had a dream, of the impending famine which would come upon Egypt and the world. The prophet Daniel warned King Nebuchadnezzar, who had a dream, that he would lose his kingdom for a season. Nebuchadnezzar was taken from him for a season because he was lifted up in pride and did not give glory to God (Daniel 4:30-34).

Dreams allow us to be in more than one place at the same time. As with the fourth dimensional world, dreams are not linear nor do they follow a straight line. Dreams are fourth dimensional. They are not limited by space, matter, and time. You can be the current age of 50, but in your dream, you can be five years old again. You can travel thousands of miles without leaving your home in a dream.

Dreams can be a complex labyrinth; they can be intricately woven in the fabric of various dimensions. For instance, you can be in a dream and have a dream in the dream. Moreover, you can be in a dream having a vision or you can be in a vision having a dream. Daniel had a vision in a dream (Daniel 7:1).

Dreams are incredibly important. They launch people into ministry. They change the course of lives; they can alter and change destinies. They can position you in places you never thought possible. We spend one third of our lives asleep in dreams. Eight hours of 24 hours a day are spent in sleep. By the time you are 60 years old, you would have slept 20 years. There are 224 references to dreams and visions in the Bible. One-third of the Bible would not be there, if it were not for dreams and visions which interestingly correlate to one third of our lives of sleeping and dreaming.

Dreams can be induced and motivated by spiritual beings. Angels can visit us in dreams. The Holy Spirit also speaks to us in dreams.

There are levels and layers of meanings in dreams which can have multiple meanings. Dreams are given to allow God to change us. Dreams are spiritually driven and you must seek God for the interpretation.

Numbers 12:6-8 says, "...Hear now my words: If there be a prophet among you, I the Lord will make myself known unto him in a vision, and will I speak unto him in a dream." God speaks to us in dreams (parables) as Jesus taught the disciples.

According to Pastor Benny Hinn, when you have a dream that is not what you desire, you can rebuke the dream. In other words, you can rebuke it from coming to pass. If you are dreaming a dream and it is not in line with the Word of God for your life, you can rebuke the dream. Even while you are having the dream, you can rebuke the dream, if it is not of God. You can command your dreams to come into alignment with the Word and the Spirit of God.

God speaks to us in many forms and forums. Dreams represent one mode of communication God uses to speak to us. Are you a dreamer? Never discount your dreams. Dreams may very well be the way God chooses to communicate to you in the fourth dimension.

Holy Spirit

Holy Spirit, Jesus took on all my sins,

Holy Spirit, that I may have true love within;

Holy Spirit, my goal is to please Thee,

Holy Spirit, it is the Jesus in me;

Holy Spirit, my help is already here,

Holy Spirit, I know because in You in the fourth dimension

there is no fear;

Holy Spirit, the keeper of all time,

Holy Spirit, my life is and always will be Thine.

CHAPTER 25

It's In the Blood

There once was a popular commercial about Campbell's® soup advertising the vitamins and nutrition found in the soup. The theme slogan was, "It's in there!" What a bold statement about a $1.25 can of soup! The commercial portrayed soup as the best thing under the sun.

Although I personally love soup, I doubt if soup is the only thing you will need to live a healthy and productive life. However, there is one substance which has all the ingredients you need to live a full healthy and vibrant life forever, and that is the substance and power found in the blood of Jesus.

The Bible says in Exodus 12:13, "And the blood shall be to you for a token upon the houses where ye are: and when I see the blood, I will pass over you, and the plague shall not be upon you to destroy you, when I smite the land of Egypt."

Notice that the blood will be a token or sign. A sign represents something that conveys information or a command. In other words, the blood was a sign of salvation and redemption. God was letting His people know that salvation would come by a blood sacrifice.

Salvation, in lieu of destruction, came only to those who were under the blood. No power on Earth could protect from the principalities and powers of the enemy, other than the blood of Jesus. Many celebrate the Passover, Day of Atonement, or Communion by acknowledging the blood of Jesus Christ as the token or sign of salvation and redemption. The Bible has a lot to say about blood and sacrifice. From the beginning, we see animal sacrifices used as a means to cover the shameful and detestable conditions of sin. As a matter of fact, in the book of Genesis 3:21, we see God making coats of animal skins to clothe Adam and Eve.

With this act, God revealed to man that the cost of covering sin was the shed blood of an innocent victim. Throughout the Old Testament, which covers thousands of years, we see man using animals as a sacrifice to atone for the sins of mankind. Blood is absolutely necessary for our restoration. It was a constant reminder that the blood of an innocent victim was the price to take away sin.

The ritual of sacrifice was only a temporary method, at best, until a permanent solution could take place in the person of Jesus Christ who was, and is, the ultimate and permanent sacrifice for the sins of the world. In Revelation 5:6 the Apostle John writes, "And I beheld, and, lo, in the midst of the throne and of the four beasts, and in the midst of the elders, stood a Lamb [Jesus] as it had been slain..." The word slain is used here because wounds and blood covered His body.

1 Peter 1:18-19 says, "Forasmuch as ye know that ye were not redeemed with corruptible things, as silver and gold...But with the precious blood of Christ, as of a lamb without blemish and without spot." The Apostle Peter lets us know that the only means of being redeemed is through the precious blood of Jesus Christ.

The cost of redemption was bought by a great price – the blood of God. Jesus shed His blood as a sacrifice for us. Death was the only redeeming consequence of sin. The Bible says in Romans 6:23, "The wages of sin is death..." The reward or consequence of sin is death. Christ had to die because that was the only way that the law of sin could be fulfilled, that is, through death.

Exodus 12:13 lets us know that the blood over the Israelites' door posts covered them was symbolic of the blood of Christ. The blood acted as defense, protection, and power against harm. Christ is our protector and provider. When we are covered under His blood we take on the image of Christ. We become representatives and tokens of the blood of Jesus Christ.

As blood-washed believers, when we enter into a place, such as the workplace, every stronghold of the enemy ought to be subject to the blood that purchased our salvation. Every obstacle that we face should result in victory. The Apostle Paul writes in 1 Corinthians 15:57, "But thanks be to God, which giveth us the victory through our Lord Jesus Christ." We have the victory before the battle begins. There's a song which says, "Don't wait till the battles over, shout now, because in the end we're gonna win."[1]

The children of Israel were God's chosen people. We who have been blood-washed are also God's chosen. The Apostle Peter says in 1 Peter 2:9, "But ye are a chosen generation, a royal priesthood, an holy nation, a peculiar people; that ye should shew forth the praises of him who hath called you out of darkness into his marvelous light."

The only way to be born of the Spirit is to go by way of the cross. Jesus' blood covers our sins and brings us back in communion with God. Now, when God sees us, He no longer sees the iniquities, transgressions, and sins of man. What God sees is the blood of His dear Son, the blood that reaches out in love. When God sees the blood of His only begotten Son, He gravitates to the blood for the blood is a token of the love of His Son.

This is the same love that binds the Trinity (God, Father, and Son) together. The mystery of the Trinity can be found in the love of the Godhead. The mystery of the Trinity is love. When God sees the blood of love that flows through Emanuel's veins in and on you, the Spirit of God connects with your spirit.

Jesus said in John 15:7, "If you abide in me, and my words [spirit] abide in you, ye shall ask what ye will, and it shall be done unto you." This is because anything that the Son asks the Father, the Father gives to the Son.

Imagine having the blood of Jesus running through your veins. Now that we are born again, we have the blood of Jesus.

Several months ago, I read an article about a young man who was left, as an infant on the steps of a hospital. He grew up in an orphanage. He never knew his father, mother, or who his family was. In times past, he learned the value of hard work. Through hard work, he became successful and wealthy. To find out his roots and where he came from, he hired an investigator and learned that he was born on a Texas ranch.

Disguised as a common laborer, he got a job on the ranch where he was born. Because of his hard work, he moved up from laborer to assuming responsibilities on the ranch. He gained favor and was highly respected by the owner. As time went by, the man disclosed to the owner that he was wealthy and wanted to buy the farm. The owner of the ranch promptly refused. The owner stated that his ranch would not be sold, but will go to his blood relatives. It turned out that the owner was actually the wealthy man's father, who ended up giving him the ranch. The man gained possession of the ranch not by his works, but by his lineage.

Likewise, we are God's children not simply by works or good deeds, but by blood-relations. We can only obtain godly inheritance through the blood of Jesus. Christ must be blood-kin to us and we must be blood-kin to Him. When we bare the same blood of Christ we become heirs to the promised blessings God gave to Abraham. The Bible confirms the relationship we have in Christ and in the Abrahamic covenant by saying, "If ye be Christ's, then are ye Abraham's seed, and heirs according to the promise" (Galatians 3:29).

Being a blood carrier of Christ is more than a royal symbol or status. Christ's blood provides complete and immediate protection from harm. The blood of Jesus carries antibodies which battle and fight off infections and diseases of the enemy. Open up your eyes of faith and imagine God on the inside of you. If we could look through the eyes of faith, we would see that God inhabits these vessels [bodies] of clay. The Apostle Paul writes in 2 Corinthians 4:7, "But we have this treasure in earthen vessels, that the excellency of the power may be of God and not of us." We have these vessels of clay, but the all surpassing power that is in us comes from God and not from us. The power that resides in us is the Holy Ghost. Luke says in Acts 1:8, "But ye shall receive power, after that the Holy Ghost is come upon you..."

If you are going to be an effective and productive witness for Christ, you need the Holy Spirit. The Holy Spirit is our greatest advocate because He is our abiding and present helper. In fact, He is always on duty. The Bible says, "He will not suffer thy foot to be moved: he that keepeth thee will not slumber. Behold, he that keepeth Israel shall neither slumber nor sleep (Psalms 121:3-4)." The Holy Spirit never tires, gets weary, or sleeps.

While we are sleeping, He's standing guard over us against the adversary. He watches over our children in the midnight hour and while we are away on our jobs. He's the ultimate body guard and security system in and out of the home. He's present in the house and outside the house at the same time!

This is why we as believers should never worry–never have restless nights–because we have the spirit of God on the inside. He has all wisdom and knows how to work out our situations. We should sleep with the confidence that although weeping may endure for a night, joy comes in the morning (Psalms 30:5).

When we receive the Holy Spirit in our lives, we have the gift of Christ's blood. Christ's blood does more than cover, guard, and protects us as individuals. His blood covers our entire household. In fact, the blood of Jesus will even cover those who have not yet received salvation.

Before the children of Israel exited the land of Egypt, they were commanded to put the blood on the door post (Exodus 12:7, 13). Most of Israel did not have a personal relationship with God, but the blood protected them. The protection of the blood of Jesus is transferable. It will cover and protect our loved ones.

There is power in the blood of Jesus. There's a song written by André Crouch which says, "The blood that Jesus shed for me, way back on Calvary, oh the blood that gives me strength, from day to day, it will never lose its power. For it reaches to the highest mountain, and it flows to the lowest valley. The blood that gives me strength, from day to day, it will never lose its power..."[2]

The blood of Christ rebukes the hands of death and destruction in our lives. Paul said in 1 Corinthians 7:14, "For the unbelieving husband is sanctified by the wife, and the unbelieving wife is sanctified by the husband: else were your children unclean; but now are they holy."

The blood of Jesus purifies. Naturally speaking, blood on a garment can result in a virtually destroyed garment. Most of the time, the longer blood stays in a garment, the harder it is to rid the stain of blood. But the blood of Jesus does the opposite, the longer the blood of Jesus lingers on the garment called life, the cleaner that life becomes. When you wash something in detergent it takes the stain and dirt out. When you are washed in the blood of Jesus it takes the stain of sin out.

The prophet Isaiah said in Isaiah 1:18, "Come now, and let us reason together, saith the lord: though our sins be as scarlet, they shall be as white as snow, though they be red like crimson they shall be as wool." The blood of Jesus permeates and gains access to areas that are physically unreachable. It can wash and clean the filthiest mind. It can make new an adulterous, murderous, and lustful heart. King David can witness to a heart of this kind, but he also can witness that God will create in you a clean heart and renew a right spirit in you (Psalms 51:10).

When the Spirit of God sets residence in you, the spirit alters the DNA in the blood. DNA is responsible for how you look, your genetic make-up, heredity, and traits. Only the Holy Spirit can recreate, alter, and change that which has already been created. The Apostle Paul said in 2 Corinthians 5:17, "Therefore if any man be in Christ, he is a new creature: old things are passed away; behold, all things are become new."

There is a song by Tramaine Hawkins which says, "I am not the same; everything has changed, because of Christ."[3] Jesus' blood changes you inside and out. Paul said in Romans 8:29 that God has conformed us into the image of His Son.

Christ's blood has the power to transform. Now, we can have a new attitude and a new mind. The Apostle Paul says in Philippians 2:5, "Let this mind be in you, which was also in Christ Jesus." The things that you used to do, you don't do any more. The old church used to say, "I looked at my hands, my hands looked new, I looked at my feet and they did, too."

Physicians treat patients by taking a sampling of their blood. They can detect diseases and infirmities simply by extracting the blood of patients. In other words, medical problems and health issues can be found in the blood. This simple blood analysis also has spiritual implications. Just as diseases enter the body through defaulted ways and ultimately into the blood, sin also permeated the blood and bloodline of every individual.

Diseases are found in the blood. Sin is also found in the bloodline. Sin became such a permanent makeup of the bloodline that becomes synonymous with our DNA, genetics, and heredity. Christ shed His precious, virtuous blood to remedy our blood deficiency. In essence, God allowed a blood transfusion to take place between God and man through the blood of Jesus Christ, the God-Man.

From the days of Adam until today, man has suffered from [spiritual] anemia, the lack of blood to sustain life. Therefore, Jesus came to give us His blood so that we could live in communion and in relationship throughout eternity with Him.

The blood of Jesus is available to heal all those who will believe in Jesus. Isaiah 53:5 says, "But he was wounded for our transgressions, he was bruised for our iniquities: The chastisement of our peace was upon him; and with his stripes we are healed."

Stripes are lacerations, wounds, and cuts tearing the skin which reveal the blood. Imagine, if there is healing found in the hem of His garment, imagine what His blood will do (Luke 8:44)!

All that we will ever need is in the blood of Jesus. Jesus' blood cures us from the blood-anemia of sin. A person who suffers from anemia has a blood deficiency. As sinners, we suffered from the anemia of which required the blood of Jesus to make us whole again. If you suffer from any disease, spiritually or naturally, let the blood of Jesus heal you from all infirmities. His blood carries all the vitamins and nutrients you need to live forever with Him in the fourth dimension.

Endnotes:

1. Hawkins, Walter. "When the Battle is Over." Bud John Music Inc.,1985.

2. Crouch, André. "The Blood Will Never Lose Its Power." Manna Music, Inc., 1966.

3. Hawkins, Walter. "I'm Not the Same." Bud John Music, Inc., 1976.

Holy Spirit

Holy Spirit, forgive me if I've done wrong,

Holy Spirit, inside me there is a praise song;

Holy Spirit, Christ died to make men free,

Holy Spirit, salvation was meant to be;

Holy Spirit, before time had begun,

Holy Spirit, it was here in the Father and the Son;

Holy Spirit, my name is written on high,

Holy Spirit, together we will touch the sky.

CHAPTER 26

The Heart as a Dimension Portal

One of my favorite songs growing up as a child was: "Into my heart, into my heart, come into my heart, Lord Jesus, come in today, come in to stay, come into my heart Lord Jesus."[1] God uses the heart of man as a dimensional portal.

A dimensional portal can be described as a means in which God interacts, communes, and associates with man. Ephesians 3:17 (NLT) says, "... Christ will make his home in your hearts as you trust in him." David prayed that God would create in him a clean heart (Psalms 51:10). God desires to dwell in our hearts; however, our hearts must be clean.

The Bible defines the heart as the center of man's thoughts, intentions, and motives. The heart represents the true character of man.

Scientists are discovering new information and insights about the heart. There have been many incidents concerning the heart in the last few years. In one case, a woman received a heart from a donor. The heart transplant was very successful. However, after receiving the heart, the woman started to have nightmares, including the appearance of a car license plate throughout the nightmare. Every night she had the same nightmare and the flashing of a car license plate in her nightmare. The nightmare was so disturbing that she went to the police to find out about the license plate number.

The police found the car with the license plate number which matched the license plate number in her nightmare dreams. An investigation was conducted immediately because there was blood found on the back of the car and in the trunk of the car. The investigation revealed that before the donor died, she had been in a coma due to suffering from severe physical trauma.

After a blood analysis was conducted, it was revealed that the blood found on the car and in the trunk of the car matched the heart donor. The owner was arrested and sent to prison for murder. The owner of the car had beaten the woman severely, but she desperately fought back, and, in turn, some of his blood ended up on the car and on her when she was placed in the trunk. After the crime was solved, the woman with the donor's heart quit having nightmares. Incredibly, the donor's heart told the woman who was a recipient of the heart what happened and how she died.

Just as the heart was used to tell a woman about a horrific event, God uses the heart as well. The heart can speak and communicate. God uses the heart of man as a dimensional portal and entrance into the third dimensional world. In Revelation 2:23, Jesus said, "I am he which searcheth the reins and hearts..." God can enter the heart of every man.

God taught the prophet Samuel an important principle by which He evaluates the character of men. The Bible says in 1 Samuel 16:6-7:

> And it came to pass, when they were come, that he looked on Eliab, and said, Surely the Lord's anointed is before him. But the Lord said unto Samuel, Look not on his countenance, or on the height of his stature; because I have refused [rejected] him: for the Lord seeth not as man seeth; for man looketh on the outward appearance, but the Lord looketh on the heart.

What God sees and what man sees are usually two different things. Man can only look so far where God can look so much further. The prophet Samuel saw Eliab's height, physique, and appearance. God saw Eliab's heart of arrogance, disobedience, and love for himself and not for God. God does not associate Himself with ungodly men regardless of their outward appearances or abilities.

The heart is one of the main dimensional portals God sees through to judge and examine our will and intents. Jesus said in Matthew 5:8, "Blessed are the pure in heart for they shall see God." God said in Jeremiah 17:9-10 (NLT), "...I, the Lord, search all hearts and examine secret motives. I give all people their due rewards, according to what their actions deserve."

God searches the heart of man, not his family tree, credit score, or financial potential. God told the prophet Samuel that He had found a man after His own heart (1 Samuel 13:14). God chooses those who choose Him. God honors those who honor Him. God chooses those whose hearts are in close alignment with His.

Furthermore, God manipulates the heart of men to achieve His will and purpose. God can turn the heart of a king. The Bible says in Proverb 21:1, "The king's heart is in the hand of the Lord, as the rivers of water: He turneth it whithersoever he will." No heart is immune from the influence and the power of God.

No heart is ever so hardened that God can't manipulate it. No man is ever so powerful, great, high, exalted, or lifted up that God cannot humble him. God told King Nebuchadnezzar, because you were lifted up in pride based on the greatness of your power and dominion and did not honor the God of heaven, you will live and eat with the wild animals for seven years until you acknowledge God is sovereign over the kingdoms of men (Daniel 4:24-25).

Just as God can soften hearts, He can also harden hearts as a means to accomplish His will and glory. The Bible says, "And the Lord said unto Moses, When thou goest to return into Egypt, see that thou do all those wonders before Pharaoh, which I have put in thine hand: but I will harden his heart, that he shall not let the people go" (Exodus 4:21).

Exodus 9:12 says, "And the Lord hardened the heart of Pharaoh, and he hearkened not unto them; as the Lord had spoken unto Moses." Nine times the Bible records where God hardened the heart of Pharaoh.

The bottom line is that man is not in control of his own heart–God is. Even when man thinks he's acting completely on his own, there are forces at work to fulfill God's will and desires. God is the Great Puppet Master. He is the one, incognito, pulling the strings behind the curtain scenes of government, social, and political affairs.

The heart is a dimensional portal God uses as an instrument to exercise His authority and will on the earth. Therefore, freely give your heart to Him and for His glory in the fourth dimension.

Endnotes:

1. Clarke, Harry Dudley. "Come Into My Heart, O Lord Jesus." 1924

Holy Spirit

Holy Spirit, time and time again,

Holy Spirit, we may find ourselves victims of sin;

Holy Spirit, you are our Christ within,

Holy Spirit, the forgiver of all my sin;

Holy Spirit, I look only to you,

Holy Spirit, for your revelations are true;

Holy Spirit, He is the lover of my soul,

Holy Spirit, blessed heaven unfolds.

CHAPTER 27

How Long?

I have often heard people say, it is important to exercise patience and that patience is a virtue. But, is there a time when we should be patient no more? There is a famous quote from the late great Dr. Martin Luther King, the civil rights leader, which says, "There's a time when the cup of endurance runs over and men are no longer willing to be plunged into the abyss of despair."

King David experienced a time when his patience in waiting for God may seem to have run out. David said in Psalms 13:1-2 (NIV), "How long, O Lord? Will you forget me forever? How long will you hide your face from me? How long must I wrestle with my thoughts and every day have sorrow in my heart? How long will my enemy triumph over me?" These two verses strongly indicate that King David had been waiting for an extended length of time for God to act and move on his behalf.

In fact, we see in the above Scriptures an age-old question that seems to run throughout the entire chapter of Psalms 13: "How long?" Have you ever asked God the question, "How long concerning a particular issue?" If we would be honest with ourselves, we have probably asked this question countless times. King David, the writer of Psalms 13, is no exception. Undoubtedly, David asked on more than one occasion for God to deliver him from his afflictions and troubles, yet he had not seen the results of his petitions from God.

Have you ever prayed and prayed and didn't feel any closer to receiving your deliverance than from the first time you prayed? Has the same issue of life bombarded your thoughts, thinking, and meditation every waking moment? Have you been in a situation so long that you have all but surrendered to its debilitating effects? If these are your questions, feelings, and expressions, know that these are valid questions, and the question "How long?" needs to be addressed.

Before addressing this pertinent question of "How long?" let's look at several individuals who had been in a difficult state for a long time. In the book of John 5:2-9, it read:

> Now there is at Jerusalem by the sheep market pool, which is called in the Hebrew tongue Bethesda, having five porches. In these lay a great multitude of impotent folk, of blind, halt, withered, waiting for the moving of the water. For an angel went down at a certain season into the pool, and troubled the water: whosoever then first after the troubling of the water, stepped in, was made whole of whatsoever disease he had. And a certain man was there, which had an infirmity thirty and eight years. When Jesus saw him lie, and knew that he had been now a long time in that case, he saith unto him, wilt thou be made whole? The impotent man answered him, sir, I have no man, when the water is troubled, to put me into the pool: but while I am coming, another steppeth down before me. Jesus saith unto him, Rise, take up thy bed, and walk. And immediately the man was made whole, and took up his bed, and walked...

Notice in the above text that many people had been waiting at the Pool called *Bethesda*, meaning place or house of mercy. Just like the lame man, could it be that you have been at a place of mercy for a long time? Could it be that God's power to heal has always been available, but somehow you have been unable to reap the benefits?

Just like the lame man, have you ever thought that everybody seems to be getting blessed, but you? The lame man had an excuse for why he was not healed and delivered. His excuse was that someone else would go in before him, and he had no one to help him into the pool. What's your excuse? Do you have an excuse for why you are not healed, blessed, or prosperous? Is it someone else's fault? Let me say this as humbly as I know how: there are no excuses! Stop crying, it's time for you to get your deliverance! It does you no good to know that God can heal and not receive your healing from Him!

Bethesda means God's place of mercy and blessings, but the lame man and many others around the pool received none. He was near the pool of Bethesda, but yet not able to benefit from being there. There is a phrase that says, "So close, but yet so far!" This is a picture of many today who are experiencing pain, suffering, and heartache even though the power of God is here and available to heal and deliver. Did you know that as a child of the Most High God, you have been given power through the Holy Spirit to do as Jesus did during His 3½ year ministry? Jesus said in Luke 10:19, "Behold, I give unto you power to tread on serpents and scorpions, and over all the power of the enemy; and nothing shall by any means hurt you."

Notice in the Scriptures above, John 5:2-9, Jesus never addressed the excuses of the lame man. Jesus never entertains excuses, all He wants to know is, "Wilt thou be made whole?" There's a song that says, "In case you have fallen by the wayside of life; dreams and visions shattered, you're all broken inside. You don't have to stay in the shape that you're in; the potter wants to put you back together again, oh, the potter wants to put you back together again. In case your situation has turned upside down, and all that you've accomplished, is now on the ground. You don't have to stay in the shape that you're in; the potter wants to put you back together again, oh, the potter wants to put you back together again!"[1]

There's a woman in the book of Luke chapter 13 who was crippled and bent over for 18 years. Luke 13:11-17 says,

And behold, there was a woman which had a spirit of infirmity eighteen years, and was bowed together, and could in no wise lift up herself. And when Jesus saw her, he called her to him, and said unto her, Woman, thou art loosed from thy infirmity. And he laid his hands on her: and immediately she was made straight, and glorified God. And the ruler of the synagogue answered with indignation, because that Jesus had healed on the Sabbath day, and said unto the people, There are six days in which men ought to work: in them therefore come and be healed and not on the sabbath day. The Lord then answered him, and said, thou hypocrite, doth not each one of you on the sabbath loose his ox or his ass from the stall, and lead him away to watering? And ought not this woman, being a daughter of Abraham, whom satan hath bound, lo these eighteen years, be loosed from this bond on the sabbath day? And when he had said these things, all his adversaries were ashamed; and all the people rejoiced for all the glorious things that were done by him.

This crippled and bent over woman was in this debilitating state for eighteen years. This was not God teaching her a lesson on humility; this was a spirit of infirmity from satan!

I am reminded of another song which says "When Jesus comes, the tempter's power is broken; when Jesus comes, the tears are wiped away, he takes the gloom and fills the life with glory, for all is changed when Jesus comes to stay."[2]

Everywhere Jesus traveled during His earthly ministry, He changed the status quo, loosed and broke the powers of darkness, brought life where there was death, and brought liberty where there was bondage and captivity.

What we think, believe, and imagine as normal dysfunctions or the misfortunes of life, Jesus came to show us a life in Him that is full, whole, and complete. Jesus said in John 10:10, "...I am come that you might have life and that you might have it more abundantly."

The theme question in our text is: "How long?" In other words, how long should we live as defeated and defenseless victims in bondage and captivity? The answer should be long enough to realize, we do not have to live as puppets and pawns under the control and manipulation of the enemy.

In the book of John chapter 9, there was a man born blind from his mother's womb. The Bible reads:

> *And as Jesus passed by, he saw a man which was blind from his birth. And his disciples asked him, saying, Master, who did sin, this man, or his parents, that he was born blind? Jesus answered, Neither hath this man sinned, nor his parents: but that the works of God should be made manifest in him...when he had thus spoken, he spat on the ground, and made clay of the spittle, and he anointed the eyes of the blind man with the clay, And said unto him, Go, wash in the pool of Siloam, (which is by interpretation, Sent.) He went his way therefore, and washed, and came seeing" (John 9:1-3, 6-7).*

I am certain that this man believed that he would be blind his entire life, since he was born blind. He never imagined being able to see! This passage of Scripture teaches us that it does not matter how long or how bleak our circumstances are, Jesus can reverse every situation. Never place a period where God has placed a comma! God can do anything, but fail.

This passage from John chapter nine also lets us know, we may experience some adversities that are no fault of our own. Every problem and situation we experience in life is not always a result of sin! Sometimes it's so the work of God might be made manifest. Listen; if God can call Lazarus to life after being dead for four days He can call your situation to life regardless of how long you have been in it (John 11:43-44).

God asked Sarah, Abraham's wife in Genesis 18:14, a rhetorical question, "Is there any thing too hard for the Lord?" When you have the thought or question, "How long?" ask yourself the question, "Is there anything too hard for the Lord?" If you can answer the second question, "Is there anything too hard for the Lord?" correctly, perhaps the first question of "How long?" will soon be answered.

The question that David had in the scriptural text (above) was, "How long wilt God forget him?" (Psalms 13:1). God never forgets! The Bible says, "He [God] hath remembered his covenant forever, the word which he commanded to a thousand generations."

In other words, what God has promised, He will perform. He has promised to heal all your infirmity and deliver you from every captivity. The Bible says in Psalms 103:1-3, "Bless the Lord, O my soul: and all that is within me, bless his holy name. Bless the Lord, O my soul, and forget not all his benefits: Who forgiveth all thine iniquities; who healeth all thy diseases." If God healed a lame man who had been in the same condition, lame for 38 years, He'll heal you!

If you have been asking the old question, "How long?" maybe you are asking the wrong question. Instead of asking questions, why not start decreeing and declaring words of faith? Faith declarations such as, "Thus saith the Lord, tomorrow about this time or by this time tomorrow!" This is exactly what Elisha did when he faced overwhelming and impossible odds.

In 2 Kings 7:1, Elisha responded to the issue facing the destruction of Jerusalem by saying, "Hear ye the word of the Lord; thus saith the Lord, to morrow about this time shall a measure of fine flour be sold for a shekel, and two measures of barley for a shekel, in the gate of Samaria."

The prophet Elisha, the man of God, said that the entire city of Samaria would experience prosperity in 24 hours. When Elisha said this, there were thousands of Syrian military soldiers who had surrounded the city and besieged it for many months.

The prophet speaks a word of prosperity despite the existing major famine in the city, despite the practice of cannibalism, despite a donkey's head selling for 80 pieces of silver, despite a cup of dove's dung costing two ounces of silver, and despite a major take-over by the forces of the enemy (2 Kings 6:24-29). Within 24 hours, the words of Elisha came true!

If Elisha can decree a thing, so can we! The Bible says in Job 22:28, "Thou shalt also decree a thing, and it shall be established unto thee." If you are sick with a terminal disease, you can decree by faith according to the Word of God, saying, "I shall not die, but live, and declare the works of the Lord!" (Psalms 118:17).

In our scriptural text, David ends Psalms 13 by praising God. Perhaps the question is not "How long" will you have to wait for your deliverance, but how long has it been since you praised, blessed, and magnified the name of the Lord? David did not end Psalms 13 arguing and complaining, but he ended it on a high note of praise.

Praise is a reflection of one's faith. Can you praise God even in times of crisis? David said in Psalms 34:1, "I will bless the Lord at all times: his praise shall continually be in my mouth." The appropriate question may not be "How long?", but how grateful and thankful are we for God's mercy and grace toward us, even in the most hopeless, irreversible, and incurable conditions.

David trusted God and had faith to believe that the same God, who delivered him from King Saul and made him king, is the same God who will deliver him from all his present and future troubles.

Maybe you have been praying and believing for a long time for deliverance. God can still bring requests and petitions to pass. Don't write off your deliverance. Keep believing, Jesus has sent a message through this book to let you know that it will not be long. He has come! Will you dare to believe Jesus has come to heal, restore, and set you free today?

Why don't you lift your hands and say, "Yes, Lord, come into my heart, come into my heart, come into my heart, Lord Jesus, come in today, come in to stay, come into my heart, Lord, Jesus!" Listen, Jesus has come to deliver you just as He did for the man who had been lame for 38 years.

God wants to show us today in the fourth dimension that nothing is ever permanent. Jesus wants you to know that it's never too late for God to heal. We are living in the era and season of the fourth dimension. In the fourth dimension, there is no waiting period. The Holy Spirit is ready, able, and willing to heal, deliver, and set free in the fourth dimension.

Endnotes:

1. McKay, Varn Michael. "The Potter's House." His Eye Music,1990.
2. Rodeheaver, Homer. "When Jesus Comes." 1940.

Holy Spirit

Holy Spirit, You are the keeper of my soul,

Holy Spirit, You are the life that I hold;

Holy Spirit, my Jesus place within,

Holy Spirit, You washed away all my sins;

Holy Spirit, God the Father we love,

Holy Spirit, Jesus sent from above;

Holy Spirit, come and rest in me,

Holy Spirit, Your love is all they will see.

CHAPTER 28

The Specialist

There is a movie entitled, **The Specialist**, starring Sylvester Stallone, Sharon Stone, and James Woods written by Oliver Heidelbach. In the movie, Ray Quick (Sylvester Stallone) is personified as a master of explosives. He can eliminate anyone, anywhere, and at anytime. Ray Quick was the best of the best. He could create the most high-tech, advanced, unrecognizable explosive device and detonate it in a far remote place.

However, Ray Quick pales in comparison to the True Specialist–Jesus Christ. Ray Quick was a former CIA pyrotechnical expert. However, Jesus is the premier one and only CIA [Curer of Infirmities Anywhere] specialist. He can eliminate, destroy, and annihilate any known and foreign threats, dangers, or hazardous situations.

God can defend and protect like no one else. God is depicted as a Man of War. After God miraculously delivers the children of Israel by dividing the Rea Sea, Moses sang a song in commemoration of God's power and glory. Moses sang, "...For he hath triumphed gloriously: the horse [of Pharaoh] and his rider hath he [God] thrown into the sea" (Exodus 15:1). Never before had an entire cavalry force been engulfed and overthrown by the sea while going into battle. God used the sea to fight for Israel!

Exodus 14:25 reveals that the Lord caused problems for the Egyptians by disabling the wheels of the chariots. Any speedy escape to shore was made impossible. It was the perfect setup! No one can set the enemy up like God. God will have the enemy think he is winning when all the time he is losing. He is the perfect "set up" strategist! When the enemy finally realizes that it's a trap, it's too late! God is superior to any foreign and domestic force or adversary.

We serve a God who can do the impossible. He is omnipotent (all powerful), omniscient (all knowledgeable), and omnipresent (present everywhere). We should be confident that He will never fail us regardless of the circumstances and situation we face. Why? Because He loves us! Besides, to die for someone, as Jesus did, is the greatest demonstration of genuine unconditional love. Jesus said, "Greater love hath no man than this that a man lay down his life for his friends (John 15:13)."

No one specializes in knowledge, authority, and power like our God. From the beginning of time, we see God doing the impossible by creating worlds without end merely by the words of His mouth. The Bible says in Psalms 33:6-7, "By the word of the lord were the heavens made; and all the host of them by the breath of his mouth; he gathereth the waters of the sea together as an heap: he layeth up the depth in storehouses."

When your life is filled with impossibilities, when there are more questions than answers, when things are beyond your scope and range, it is without question time to go to the God who can do the impossible. If there are overwhelming odds in your life, there's a God that specializes in things impossible. Maybe the doctor has given you some bad news about your health or the health of a family member. Perhaps the medical diagnosis is deemed terminal and the prognosis is unfavorable. May be your friends have turned their backs on you, if you need a helping hand, God specializes in things impossible.

In the movie, "The Specialist," Sylvester Stallone may be a master at explosives, but God is a master and guru of all the arts. He can do anything, but fail! Why not call the One who specializes in things which are absolutely impossible in the fourth dimension?

Holy Spirit

Holy Spirit, we write to honor Thee,

Holy Spirit, You are Earth's Trinity;

Holy Spirit, before time had begun,

Holy Spirit, You knew the Father and the Son;

Holy Spirit, our lives will always be Christ,

Holy Spirit, because He paid the ultimate sacrifice;

Holy Spirit, be the witness on our behalf,

Holy Spirit, until we go and meet Him there at last.

CHAPTER 29

A Dream

I recently had a dream where thousands of people died all at once. This was due to a major war which had taken the life of many individuals. In the dream, I was able to see the dead. They appeared alive, but I knew they were dead. They knew they were dead, as well. There were hundreds and thousands who had recently died. They were boarding on what seemed to be transit buses or large capacity vehicles.

As one who is naturally curious, I went with them. In the dream, I knew that I had no business there, but I boarded the bus anyway. While on the bus, many of the individuals looked briefly at each other and turn away. They felt shame that they had died. The shuttle bus dropped them off at a large hanger or holding area with long tables inside. As they entered the lobby, there was a sign-in sheet, and many were signing in as they entered the building. Upon signing in, they went to the tables and sat down.

I found myself, unexpectedly, standing in front of the entire population of people. I felt a sense of urgency to tell them about Jesus and salvation. I told them that Jesus would soon come, and they needed to accept Christ before it was too late. As I was frantically telling them to repent, I could hear their thoughts. Even though they were not speaking, I could hear their thoughts as if they were speaking. Some were saying in their thoughts, "I don't want to hear this!" Others were saying, "If this is eternity or hell, I can live with this!"

I knew there was only a small window of opportunity for those who were lost to confess Christ. Those on the bus and in the cafeteria had not received Christ as their Savior. After what seemed to be about a minute and a half, many people dropped their heads on the table, one by one like dominoes. As their heads hit the table, a dark glow [halo] surrounded their heads. I knew they had crossed over into eternity without Christ. God allowed me to see briefly on the other side at the moment an individual dies.

Even though a person may not have accepted Christ during their lifetime, there is a brief moment before entering into eternity for a decision to be made about Jesus. The Holy Spirit revealed to me a mystery concerning those who do not know Christ at the time of death. That is, Jesus is so merciful that He will give you a brief moment in death to accept Him before the transition of eternity is complete!

I once read a passage which said, there will be three surprises in heaven: some of the people you thought didn't make it will be there, some of the people you knew made it won't be there, and thirdly, you'll be surprised if you make it!

The Bible declares in Job 33:14-17 (NLT), "But God speaks again and again, though people do not recognize it. He speaks in dreams, in visions of the night...He whispers in their ear...he keeps them from pride." In other words, God will give us a dream, but hide the instruction from us so that we do not become prideful. Yet, the Holy Spirit will lead us to do what we did not know was an instruction from God.

Other times, God will give us a dream and conceal the instruction in order for us to search for the interpretation or meaning. The Bible says in Proverb 25:2, "It is the glory of God to conceal a thing: But the honour of kings is to search out a matter."

It is "kingly" to have to search for the meaning or the interpretation of dreams. When you search or research a matter you will learn more about the matter, than just having someone give you the answer. In the interpretation of dreams, the journey of understanding can be more important than the destination.

When you have an experience with God or a revelation from God such as through dreams and visions, there is usually a cost-factor involved. Paul said in 2 Corinthians 12:1-5, 7 (NLT):

> *Let me tell about the visions and revelations I received from the Lord. I was caught up into the third heaven fourteen years ago. Whether my body was there or just my spirit, I don't know; only God knows. But I do know that I was caught up into paradise and heard things so astounding that they cannot be told. That experience is something worth boasting about, but I am not going to do it. But to keep me from getting puffed up, I was given a thorn in the flesh, a messenger from satan to torment me and keep me from getting proud.*

Because revelations of God were revealed to Paul, there was a cost or sacrifice attached to the magnificent and awesome experiences. Notice that the thorn in the flesh is related to the visions and revelations he experienced from God (2 Corinthians 12:7). God will never reveal His glory to you without placing you in a position of humility. Revelation will always come with humility. God desires no man to be lifted up in pride after receiving revelation and knowledge of Him. The Bible is clear concerning the ramifications of pride. Proverbs 16:18 says, "Pride goeth before destruction, And a haughty spirit before a fall."

When God gives you a greater revelation of Him He holds you accountable for that revelation. The Bible says in Luke 12:48, "...For unto whomsoever much is given, of him shall much be required..." God will provide little or very few options to you when He has abundantly revealed Himself to you. The Bible says in Hebrews 6:4-6 (NLT),

> *For it is impossible to restore to repentance those who were once enlightened—those who have experi-*

enced the good things of heaven and shared in the Holy Spirit, who have tasted the goodness of the Word of God and the power of the age to come—and who then turn away from God. It is impossible to bring such people to repentance again because they are nailing the Son of God to the cross again by rejecting him, holding him up to public shame.

Paul's heavenly vision of God left him with a thorn in the flesh. Jacob's encounter with God left him with a limp (Genesis 32:25). The revelation of God is not without sacrifice. However, the rewards are always greater than the sacrifice.

Dreams can reveal the answers and solutions to hidden secrets, mysteries, and the unknown. Dreams can reveal hidden mysteries which were known only to God in the fourth dimension.

Holy Spirit

Holy Spirit, here we are again,

Holy Spirit, trusting You to the end;

Holy Spirit, God's precious gift of the Trinity,

Holy Spirit, loving us from now to eternity;

Holy Spirit, take hold of my hand,

Holy Spirit, together we will stand;

Holy Spirit, it is the Jesus Christ in me,

Holy Spirit, for all men to see.

CHAPTER 30

Visions

The first recorded vision in the Holy Scriptures was given to Abraham, the father of faith, by God. In the book of Genesis, God showed Abraham the stars in the heavens, as a means to compare the number of descendants he would have, as well as the multitude of blessings God would give him. The Bible says:

> After this, the word of the Lord came to Abram [Abraham] in a vision: 'Do not be afraid, Abram. I am your shield, your very great reward'. But Abram said, 'O Sovereign Lord, what can you give me since I remain childless and the one who will inherit my estate is Eliezer of Damascus?' And Abram said, 'You have given me no children; so a servant in my household will be my heir.' Then the word of the Lord came to him: 'This man will not be your heir, but a son who is your own flesh and blood will be your heir.' He took him outside and said, 'Look up at the sky and count the stars—if indeed you can count them.' Then he said to him, 'So shall your offspring be' (Genesis 15:1-5, NIV).

The first vision recorded in Scripture represented a future promise by God to Abraham. Visions can be visual tools God uses for us to see and witness promised and future blessings.

Visions are another mode or method of communication of the fourth dimension. The Bible says in Joel 2:28, "And it shall come to pass afterward, That I will pour out my spirit upon all flesh; And your sons and your daughters shall prophesy, Your old men shall dream dreams, Your young men shall see visions."

This Scripture has nothing to do with old men and young men as it relates to chronological age, but to spiritual growth, development, and maturity. Joel 2:28 lets us know that dreams are more complex than visions. The understanding of dreams will be revealed to those who have knowledge and revelation of the Word of God.

What is a vision? A vision is an experience in which something or an event appears vividly or credibly to the mind usually due to divine influence.

According to John Paul Jackson, visions are often revealed to those who are less mature and inexperienced in the Word of God. Visions are more literal. It takes less interpretation or wisdom to understand a vision than it does a dream. In visions, what you see is what you get. In dreams, what you see is a symbol of what you get.

Notwithstanding, Pastor Benny Hinn reports that visions reveal God's nature. The nature of God refers to His characteristics, attributes, and qualities. The Bible says in Genesis 15:1, "After these things the Word of the Lord came unto Abram in a vision, saying, Fear not, Abram: I am thy shield, and thy exceeding great reward."

In Genesis 15:1, God let Abram [Abraham] know that He is both his protection and blessing. There is no need to look for security anywhere else other than in God. The Bible says in Psalms 18:1-3, "...The Lord is my rock, and my fortress, and my deliverer; My God, my strength, in whom I will trust; My buckler, and the horn of my salvation, and my high tower, I will call upon the Lord, who is worthy to be praised: So shall I be saved from mine enemies."

The president of the United States is protected by the U.S. Secret Service. Their job is to protect domestic, national, and world leaders against potential threats and terrorist activities. However, as a believer of Christ, you are more important to God than the president of the United States or any other domestic or foreign dignitary. When God is your body guard or protection, there is never any breach or compromise in security. The Apostle Paul said in 2 Thessalonians 3:3, "But the Lord is faithful, who shall stablish you, and keep you from evil."

God shares with Abram that He is his provision, supply, prosperity, and blessing. No one can bless us like God can. Many operate in the Kingdom of God by trying to bless themselves, only to come up short every time, but "can't nobody do you like Jesus!" God is speaking to us today, saying that He wants to be our "great reward," as He said to Abram.

Visions reveal God to us. In a vision, you can speak back to God. Notice what Abram replied to God in Genesis 15:2-3, "And Abram said, Lord, God, what wilt thou give me, seeing I go childless...behold, to me thou hast given no seed..." In a vision, there is communion and conversation with God.

God places great value on visions as He does dreams. God desires that His people have visions and revelations. The Bible says in Proverbs 29:18, "Where there is no vision, the people perish..." Visions belong to the righteous. Visions are a part of God's mode of communication in the fourth dimension.

Holy Spirit

Holy Spirit, God's love seen through You,

Holy Spirit, use this vessel to spread His truth;

Holy Spirit, His love never ending,

Holy Spirit, from past to the beginning;

Holy Spirit, His love has conquered all,

Holy Spirit, He saved me from the fall;

Holy Spirit, my ways are not His ways,

Holy Spirit, but with thee He will bless all my days.

CHAPTER 31

Limitless

There is a movie entitled **Limitless** by Neil Burger. In the movie Eddie Morra (Bradley Cooper) takes a pill which allows him to use 100% of his brain. In the movie, he wrote an entire novel in four days, learned foreign languages, the piano, and the stock market. He could remember everything he ever heard, read, or saw. As with any pill or drug, the drug NZT wore off which left Eddie Morra's brain operating back at its original limited capacity.

Science theorizes that the brain is the center of all conscious, mental, and subconscious activities. There is much debate about what percentage of the brain we use as humans. For all practical purposes let's assume based on popular beliefs that we only use 10-20% of our brain at any given time.

Notwithstanding, there is a brain-booster and cerebrum-enhancer which is a miracle breakthrough. There is no need to take a pill or tablet. Moreover, there are no chemical withdrawals, side effects, or harmful after-effects. This miracle brain-enhancer is called the Holy Spirit.

In fact, the Holy Spirit is called the Spirit of wisdom, knowledge, and understanding. The Bible says in Isaiah 11:2, "And the Spirit of the Lord shall rest upon him. The Spirit of wisdom and understanding, The spirit of counsel and might, The spirit of knowledge and of the fear of the Lord."A daily intake of the presence of the Spirit of God will produce far greater results than any brain pill or drug.

Jesus is our prime example of possessing the Spirit of wisdom even though He was the son of an unlearned carpenter. The Bible says in Mark 6:2-3:

And when the sabbath day was come, he began to teach in the synagogue: and many hearing him were astonished, saying, From whence hath this man these things? and what wisdom is this which is given unto him, that even such mighty works are wrought by his hands? Is not this the carpenter...here with us?

The Spirit of wisdom, given by the Holy Spirit, does not come from a man, book, library, or university, but from God. The Bible says in 1 Corinthians 1:25-27,

Because the foolishness of God is wiser than men: and the weakness of God is stronger than men. For ye see your calling, brethren, how that not many wise men after the flesh, not many mighty, not many noble, are called: but God hath chosen the foolish things of the world to confound the wise; and God hath chosen the weak things of the world to confound the things which are mighty.

The Holy Spirit will give us wisdom that no man can challenge or oppose. The Bible says in Luke 21:15, "For I will give you a mouth and wisdom, which all your adversaries shall not be able to gainsay [contradict] nor resist."

God, by the Holy Spirit, gave King Solomon His wisdom. The Bible says in 1 Kings 4:29-34 (NLT):

And God gave Solomon wisdom and understanding, and knowledge too vast to be measured. In fact, his wisdom exceeded that of all the wise men of the East and the wise men of Egypt. He was wiser than anyone else, including Ethan the Ezrahite and

*Heman, Calcol, and Darda–the sons of Mahol. His
fame spread throughout all the surrounding nations.
He composed some 3,000 proverbs and wrote 1,005
songs. He could speak with authority about all kinds
of plants, from the great cedar of Lebanon to the tiny
hyssop that grows from cracks in the wall. He could
also speak about animals, birds, reptiles, and fish.
And kings from every nation sent ambassadors to
listen to the wisdom of Solomon."*

Solomon will forever be known as the king who possessed the wisdom of God. There was no limit to Solomon's wisdom! The Holy Spirit is the only One who can make the brain function at 100%. The Holy Spirit is limitless, and He is the only one who can give you exceptional cognitive abilities.

Allowing the Holy Spirit to operate in our lives increases our capability, aptitude, and capacity. The Holy Spirit is the giver of our gifts and talents. The Bible says in 1 Corinthians 12:4-9,

*Now there are diversities of gifts, but the same Spirit.
And there are differences of administrations, but the
same Lord...For to one is given by the Spirit the Word
of Wisdom; to another the world of knowledge by the
same Spirit; To another faith by the same Spirit; to another the gifts of healing by the same Spirit.*

The Holy Spirit is the one who already knows our potential hidden talents and gifts. What better way to determine our talents and gifts than to invite the Holy Spirit in our lives?

Possession of the Holy Spirit in you creates unlimited potential. Jesus was filled with wisdom and the grace of God. Jesus possessed the Holy Spirit without measure. The Bible says in John 3:34 (NLT), "For he is sent by God. He speaks God's words, for God's Spirit is upon him without measure or limit."

Using gifts and talents you never thought you had is the expansion of utilizing more of the brain. It would appear that

Jesus had the capacity to utilize all of His brain. Scripture tells us that Jesus was answering and asking questions to the doctors and lawyers at the age of twelve before being baptized and anointed officially by the Holy Spirit.

With the aid of the Holy Spirit, we can discover talents we never knew we possessed. In fact, the Holy Spirit wants to equip us with new talents and abilities. The Bible says in Matthew 25:20-21, "And so he that had received five talents came and brought other five talents, saying, Lord, thou deliveredst unto me five talents: behold, I have gained beside them five talents more. His lord said unto him, Well done, thou good and faithful servant: thou hast been faithful over a few things, I will make thee ruler over many things..."

Before the fall, Adam, the ruler of Earth and made in the image of God could use 100% of his brain. The Bible says in Genesis 19, "...God formed every beast of the field, and every fowl of the air; and brought them unto Adam to see what he would call them: and whatsoever Adam called every living creature, that was the name thereof. And Adam gave names to all cattle, and to the fowl of the air, and to every beast of the field..." Adam had perfect memory and limitless brain ability. He had the ability to express himself orally as well as in written form. Adam's IQ was off the scale!

Adam had the ability to discern between the third and fourth dimensional world. Could it be that we lost the ability to discern the spirit world of the fourth dimension due to the sin of disobedience beginning with Adam?

God would not give us a brain with only the capacity to use only 20% with 80% of the brain useless. Somehow we have lost the ability in the brain to use it to the fullness of what God has created it for. Perhaps when God told Adam, "Ye shall surely die (Genesis 2:17)," his brain lost the capacity or power to regenerate and reproduce, leaving the brain vulnerable to the state of mortality and decay.

Could it be that we have no consciousness of the 80% of what's real? If we can only investigate what is tangible with the 20% of brain capabilities, perhaps the 80% of the brain used is meant to investigate, function, and interact in the intangible (fourth dimensional / spiritual) world.

May be the discrepancy of 20% versus 80% is indicative of the fact that we are 20% flesh and 80% spiritual. In other words, we are more of a spiritual being than a physical being. If 20% of man's brain can create the advance technological age in which we live, imagine what the ability to harness the power of 100% of the brain would do!

The Holy Spirit is limitless. He is able to do exceeding and abundantly above anything we can imagine. The Bible says, "Now to the one who can do infinitely more than all we can ask or imagine according to the power that is working among us" (Ephesians 3:20, ISV).

Have you ever asked the Holy Spirit to increase your brain and mental capacity? If not, why not? Do it today! He is waiting to answer your call in the fourth dimension.

Holy Spirit

Holy Spirit, our purpose is to please Him,

Holy Spirit, you know the heart of them;

Holy Spirit, love conquers all,

Holy Spirit, for He died that we may recover from the fall;

Holy Spirit, You know what to do,

Holy Spirit, speak silence to my heart and teach me Your truth;

Holy Spirit, Counselor, Helper, Comforter to man,

Holy Spirit, You already knew His plan.

CHAPTER 32

A Midnight Cry

Midnight has always been a time of mystery and intrigue. Many mystery novels have depicted a conundrum of activities happening at midnight. Authors often begin their suspense novels and episodes with phrases like, "When the clock struck midnight or at the stroke of midnight." Midnight is the moment in time that is neither night nor day. The Bible depicts the time of Christ's return as unpredictable and mysteriously occurring at midnight. The Bible says in Matthew 25:5-6, & 10-13,

> *While the bridegroom tarried, they [the virgins] all slumbered and slept. And at midnight there was a cry made, behold, the bridegroom cometh: go ye out to meet him...And while they [the five virgins who needed oil] went to buy, the bridegroom came, and they that were ready went in with him to the marriage; and the door was shut. Afterward came also the other virgins, saying, Lord, Lord open to us. But he answered and said, verily I say unto you, I know you not. Watch therefore, for ye know neither the day nor the hours wherein the Son of man cometh.*

Notice in the above scriptural text, the bridegroom tarried [waited]. No one knew exactly how long it would take for the bridegroom's arrival. For the five [foolish] virgins, the bridegroom did not come at the time that they had expected. Based upon the limited oil in their lamps, they assumed he would arrive much earlier than he did. Although unsure when the bridegroom would arrive, the five wise virgins were prepared in case of delay. This parable is a lesson about preparation to meet the bridegroom, Jesus Christ.

This parable lets us know of the importance of being prepared. Five virgins were prepared while five virgins were not. We must be prepared and ready for when Christ returns. All issues of preparation must be settled prior to His coming. There will be no time to complete any last minute details after He arrives. Five were called "foolish" because they were not adequately prepared to meet the one they that had looked forward to spending time with at the wedding.

Don't be one of the foolish ones! Our preparation to meet Christ must start today, not tomorrow. Tomorrow might be too late. Come to Jesus while you still have time. The Holy Spirit is speaking to you right now. The Bible says in Hebrews 3:7-8, "Wherefore (as the Holy Ghost saith, to day if ye will hear his voice, harden not your hearts..."

The Scripture above indicates that the cry or call to meet the bridegroom was at midnight. Midnight is an odd time to have a wedding ceremony. This suggests that Christ will return when we all [wise or foolish] will least expect Him. Jesus said in Matthew 24:36-42 (NLT):

> However, no man knows the day or the hours when these things will happen, not even the angels in heaven or the Son himself. Only the Father knows. When the Son of Man returns, it will be like it was in Noah's day. In those days before the flood, the people were enjoying banquets and parties and weddings right up to the time Noah entered his boat. People didn't realize what was going to happen until the flood came and swept them all away. That is the way it will be when the Son of Man comes. Two men will be working together in the field; one will be taken,

the other left. Two women will be grinding flour at the mill, one will be taken, the other left. So be prepared, because you don't know what day your Lord is coming.

Notice in Matthew 25:10 (above), the limited time between the bridegroom's arrival and the door closing. The time when the bridegroom arrived and the door closing were nearly the same. There was no way those who were not ready had the faintest chance. When the door [of opportunity] closes, it will not be reopened. Either you are ready to go with Christ to the wedding supper or you are left behind. A midnight cry is about to be made. Will you be ready?

Jesus said no man knows the day or the hour when Christ returns. Notwithstanding, He does say that we would know the times and seasons. Jesus said in Luke 21:10, 28 (NIV) "...Nation will rise against nation and kingdom against kingdom. There will be great earthquakes, famines and pestilences in various places, and fearful events and great signs from heaven...when these things begin to take place, stand up and lift up your heads, because your redemption is drawing near." Just simply observe the conditions around us. We are living in the times and seasons surrounding Christ's coming. The conditions are ripe for His return.

Paul said in 1 Thessalonians 5:1-2, "But of the times and the seasons, brethren, ye have no need that I write unto you, for yourselves know perfectly that the day of the Lord so cometh as a thief in the night." Can you see clearly now? Paul lets us know that we should be able to discern the times and seasons in which we live. Those who are believers in Christ should not be taken off guard or surprised when Christ returns.

We know that the time is near for Christ's return but is there any additional evidence that narrows down Christ's return, other than wars and earthquakes mentioned in the Bible? Of course! It is important to know that the Old Testament is filled with foreshadows of events in history that also picture something coming in the future. An example of foreshadowing is when Abraham sacrificed his son Isaac on Mount Moriah. God said in Genesis 22:2, "Take now thy son, thine only son Isaac, whom thou lovest, and get thee into the land of Moriah; and offer him there for a burnt offering upon one of the mountains which I will tell thee of." We know that this event actually happened, but this was also a picture of what God would do with His Son on the cross to offer Him for the sins of the world.

The Bible says in 2 Peter 3:8, referring to the second coming of Christ, "But beloved, be not ignorant of this one thing, that one day is with the Lord as a thousand years and a thousand years as one day." Many Biblical scholars believe that the creation in Genesis chapter one is also a foreshadowing of what was to come. In other words, God was showing us how long we would have on the earth before the last Adam [Christ] would reign in dominion on the earth.

The Bible says in chapter 1 and 2 of Genesis that God created the heavens and the earth in six days and on the seventh day He rested from creation of the earth. Why would God take six days to create the earth and rest on the seventh? He could have easily said on the first day let there be light, let the waters under the heavens be gathered together, let the dry land appear, let the earth bring forth the living creatures, and let us make man all on the same day. But He didn't! He purposely made use of seven days. Perhaps this too is another pattern or a foreshadow of what was to come.

Biblical scholars theorized that from the creation of Adam to the birth of Jesus Christ is 4000 years. We all know that from Christ's birth which was approximately 3 A.D. to the current date is over 2000 years. If the biblical scholars' theory is correct, from the creation of Adam to our present time is approximately 6,000 years.

The Bible says in Psalms 90:4, "For a thousand years in thy [God's] sight are but as yesterday when it is past, and as a watch in the night." Therefore, could it be that six days of creation was to indicate to us the time man would have on this earth would be about 6,000 years? With the seventh day of rest picturing the 1000 year millennial reign when Christ would set up His earthly Kingdom. Notice the Bible says that God rested on the seventh day. The Bible says in the book of Revelation, Christ would "rest" on the throne of David for a thousand years (Revelation 20:4). Listen to what Genesis 2:2-3 says,

> *And on the seventh day God ended his work which he had made; and he rested on the seventh day from all his work which he had made. And God blessed the seventh day, and sanctified it because that in it he had rested from all his work which God created and made.*

Do you think God became tired of creating during the six days of creation? No! Rest here is symbolic or foreshadowing of something happening in the future. When Christ comes during the 1000 year reign, it will be a time of righteousness, peace, and rest from all the turmoil which previously existed on the earth.

It is important to note that days and years are seen differently from God's perspective than man's perspective. Notice again 2 Peter 3:8 says, "...One day is with the Lord as a thousand years and a thousand years as one day."

Even during the Garden of Eden, God's Word stands true. God commanded Adam in Genesis chapter two that the day he ate of the tree of good and evil, he would surely die. Therefore, as far as God is concerned, Adam died the same day he ate of the tree of good and evil. God said in Genesis 2:16-17, "...The tree of the garden thou mayest freely eat, but of the tree of the knowledge of good and evil, thou shalt not eat of it: for the day that thou eatest thereof thou shalt surely die."

In God's eyes, Adam died the day God told him not to eat of the Tree of Good and Evil. How? No one has lived a day (or a thousand years) in God's eyes. God commanded the day Adam ate of the tree that he would surely die. The oldest man recorded in history is Methuselah who lived to be 965 years old (Genesis 5:27). No one has lived a day or a thousand years in

God's sight. This decree from God will stand until Christ reigns on the earth in Jerusalem during the millennium.

In the millennium, "No longer will babies die when only a few days old. No longer will adults die before they have lived a full life. No longer will people be considered old at one hundred! Only the cursed [sinners] will die that young!" (Isaiah 65:20, NLT). The Bible also says,

> *The wolf also shall dwell with the lamb and the leopard shall lie down with the kid; and the calf and the young lion and the fatling together; and a little child shall lead them. And the cow and the bear shall feed; their young ones shall lie down together, and the lion shall eat straw like the ox. And the suckling child shall play on the hole of the asp, and the weaned child shall put his hand on the cockatrice' den (Isaiah 11:6-8).*

God deals with time in the Bible differently than we do. When God measures events in time, He measures time by sevens. God created the world in six days with the 7th day being a day of rest. Sevens are significant on God's calendar and timetable.

According to the Old Testament law, the Jews were commanded to rest every seven days. The 7th week after the Passover, they celebrated the big Feast of the Rest. The 7th month, they celebrated the biggest Feasts of the Rest. Every 7th year, the Jews celebrated the Rest of the Land. Every 49th year (which is 7x7) is the year of Jubilee, where the land rests as well as liberty for the people is declared.

Therefore, it makes perfect sense that God would set up a time or a 7,000 year period for man to occupy this earth with the last 1000 years being a time of rest. When Jesus comes back to set up His earthly Kingdom, it will be for a thousand years. His earthly Kingdom was spoken of in Revelation 20:4-6 (NLT) which says,

...And I saw the souls of those who had... not worshipped the beast or his statute, nor accepted his mark on their forehead or their hands. They all came to life again and they reigned with Christ for thousand years. This is the first resurrection. (The rest of the dead did not come back to life until the thousand years had ended.) Blessed and holy are those who share in the first resurrection. For them the second death holds no power, but they will be priests of God and of Christ and will reign with him a thousand years.

The second coming of Christ is the most important day on God's calendar. God wants us to know about it, including the timing. The Book of Hosea, written by an Old Testament prophet, spoke of Christ's return in Hosea chapter six. Hosea talked about Israel, God's chosen nation, who has always rejected him.

Hosea 6:1-2 says, "Come and let us return unto the Lord, for he hath torn, and he will heal us; he hath smitten, and he will bind us up. After two days will he revive us, in the third day he will raise us up, and we shall live in his sight." In other words, when Jesus came Israel rejected Him as their Messiah, so God scattered the nation all over the world.

For approximately 2000 years, there was no nation of Israel, but God said after two days or 2000 years He would revive the people of Israel and they would live in His sight. We see that the scattered nation of Israel is being gathered together right before our eyes. In 1948, Israel became a nation again! This is very important because God is reviving the nation of Israel because Jesus is coming back to set up His earthly Kingdom.

We know from the books of the Old Testament that there were many different nations of the world such as the Canaanites, Jebusites, Amorites, Hittites, Amalekites, and many others; all of which have long dissipated and have been forgotten. Only the Israelite nation has survived. Why? Because

God said they would and because they are God's chosen people! No other nations have been preserved, only the Jews.

God must fulfill the Kingdom prophecies He made with Israel. Many of the Jews still reject Christ. How long would they reject Christ? For 2,000 years! At the end of the two days or 2000 years, the Bible says that Israel will receive Christ as their long-awaited Messiah. The 2,000 years mark is about to end. The second coming events of Christ are about to begin!

The second coming event is also foreshadowed in Exodus chapter 19 when God told Israel to get clean and wait for two days because on the third day He would come down in the sight of all the nation. Listen to Exodus 19:10 (NASB), "The Lord also said to Moses, Go to the people and consecrate them today and tomorrow, and let them wash their garments; and let them be ready for the third day, for on the third day the Lord will come down on Mount Sinai in the sight of all the people." This Scripture suggests that God would revisit Israel after two days (or 2,000 years).

Another foreshadowing of Christ's return is found in John chapter 11. Jesus waits two days before going to raise Lazarus from the dead. Let's read John 11:3-6,

> Therefore his sisters [Mary and Martha] sent unto him [Jesus], saying, Lord, behold he whom thou lovest is sick. When Jesus heard that, he said, this sickness is not unto death, but for the glory of God, that the Son of God might be glorified thereby. Now Jesus loved Martha and her sister, and Lazarus. When he had heard therefore that he was sick; he abode two days still in the same place where he was.

Why would Jesus stay and minister in the place where He was for two days instead of coming to the rescue of the one whom He loved? Because this was a picture of how God would turn His back on the nation of Israel for 2000 years [or two days] and start reaching out and ministering to the rest of the world, through the New Testament Church. These events in the

Bible are not mere coincidences, or thrown in the Bible for our amusement, or to take up space. These events are indicators or timings of Christ's return.

Furthermore, in Matthew 17:1-2, Jesus took Peter, James, and John up apart from the rest of the group to the top of a mountain. Let's read the verses together, "And after six days Jesus taketh Peter, James, and John his brother, and bringeth them up into a high mountain apart, and was transfigured before them: and his face did shine as the sun, and his raiment was white as the light."

Three disciples, Jesus' inner circle, are given a preview of His second coming. Notice what the Bible says, after six days Jesus took Peter, James, and John apart from the rest of the group. In other words, after six days or 6,000 years, Jesus will reign on Earth as He was seen transfigured on the mount in the sight of Peter, James, and John. Is God trying to tell us something we need to know?

Certainly! Remember from Adam to Christ is 4,000 years and the time of the church period is 2,000 years. Six thousand years has been completed; we are entering into the millennium time period in which Christ will return to reign on Earth.

This chapter is sending out a "Midnight Cry." A cry of repentance has been sounded. Judgment is coming soon! Judgment is not a new concept in the Bible. In Genesis chapter six, it says that there was a great population explosion and the earth was corrupted and filled with violence. Sounds like the world we live in today, doesn't it? Notice what the Bible says in Genesis 6: 1, 12, 13,

> *And it came to pass, when men began to multiply on the face of the earth...And God looked upon the earth and behold it was corrupted, for all flesh had corrupted his way upon the earth... And God said unto Noah, the end of all flesh is come before me, for the earth is filled with violence through them, and behold, I will destroy them with the earth.*

God wiped out the whole earth's population with a flood and only eight people survived.

God judged the cities of Sodom and Gomorrah because of their rampant sexual sins, homosexuality, and perversion in Genesis chapter 19. Sounds like our world today, doesn't it? Genesis 19:24-25 says, "...The Lord rained upon Sodom and upon Gomorrah brimstone and fire from the Lord out of heaven, and he overthrew those cities, and all the plain, and all the inhabitants of the cities, and that which grew upon the ground." Only three persons survived the judgment of the cities of Sodom and Gomorrah: Lot and his two daughters.

In both cases of the days of Noah and Sodom and Gomorrah, the unbelievers were taken by complete surprise, but the believers were not! Why? Because they knew that judgment was coming. Very soon there will be a judgment on the earth, like never before, just prior to the return of Christ which the Bible calls the Great Tribulation (Revelation 7:14).

God is telling us that our time is about up. This current existence will not go on forever. Sometime very soon Israel will turn to Jesus as their Messiah and Christ will come back to earth and begin His reign.

God has not left us without a message or evidence of His return. His message or letter which signifies His return is the Holy Bible. The Bible is the greatest book ever written. Paul, an apostle of Jesus Christ, declared in 2 Timothy 3:16-17, "All scripture is given by inspiration of God, and is profitable for doctrine for reproof, for correction, for instruction in righteousness; that the man of God may be perfect, thoroughly furnished unto all good works."

The Bible's message is so simple that it can be summed up in a few verses. Yet at the same time, the Bible has so much depth that one can study verse by verse and chapter by chapter for a lifetime and never come close to fathoming all of its truths and revelations.

A midnight cry has been heralded throughout the third and fourth dimension. God has announced to His people that He is ready to return. Angels are being summoned to perform judgment as recorded in the book of Revelation. Fourth dimensional believers are preparing to meet the bridegroom. A cry has been made. Are you ready to meet the bridegroom, Jesus Christ, when He comes?

Holy Spirit

Holy Spirit, You're that warm-blooded Spirit in me,

Holy Spirit, when in the night You help me to see what the future

will be;

Holy Spirit, through dreams and visions God speaks to me,

Holy Spirit, forever angels are watching You see;

Holy Spirit, having dominion in life was meant for me,

Holy Spirit, by Your power has all this come to be;

Holy Spirit, the fourth dimension by night I can see,

Holy Spirit, by dreams and by visions nothing will grieve me.

CHAPTER 33

The Holy Spirit

Although the modes of communication such as angels, dreams, visions, and prayers are significant, the chief mode of communication to God, other than the Word of God, is the Holy Spirit. He is the representative of the Godhead on planet Earth. The Holy Spirit is the chief communicator of the fourth dimension to the third dimension, and vice versa. Jesus said, "Nevertheless, I tell you the truth: it is to your advantage that I go away, for if I do not go away, the Helper will not come to you. But if I go, I will send him to you" (John 16:7, ESV).

Just as Jesus was God on Earth, wrapped in flesh, the Holy Spirit is the Spirit of God on Earth. The Scripture says in 1 Corinthians 2:11, "For what man knoweth the things of a man, save the spirit of man which is in him? Even so the things of God knoweth no man, but the Spirit of God."

The reason that the Holy Spirit is the greatest communicator between God and man is that the Holy Spirit knows the mind of God. He can share with us what is in the heart of God. That is, how God feels about us and what is God's desire for us. The Holy Spirit is the next best thing to being seated at the right hand of the Father.

The Holy Spirit is the mind of God. When we allow the Holy Spirit to reign supreme in our lives, He transforms our minds into the image of Christ (Romans 12:2). The more we think like Christ, the more we become like God.

The Holy Spirit is our present and personal helper. The Bible says in Romans 8:26,

> *Likewise the Spirit also helpeth our infirmities [weaknesses]: for we know not what we should pray for as we ought: but the Spirit itself maketh intercession for us with groaning which cannot be uttered. And he that searcheth the hearts knoweth what is the mind of the Spirit, because he maketh intercession for the saints according to the will of God.*

In other words, the Holy Spirit is the key communicator between God and man. He is the great intercessor. When we do not know what to pray for, He knows and prays for us. The Holy Spirit knows what God thinks, and He shares with us what is on God's heart. He also shares with God what is on our hearts. The closer and more intimate we become with the Holy Spirit, the more we will be able to know what God thinks the moment He thinks it!

The Holy Spirit is the Commander General of all the modes of communication to the Father. He is the author and creator of spiritual dreams and visions. The Holy Spirit directs the flow of information, intelligence, and communication that constantly streams from the fourth dimension to the third dimension, and vice versa.

The Holy Spirit is the "Commander in Chief" of the cherubim, seraphim, and the angels of the Lord. He is the "Five Star" General of the military and armed forces of God while on the earth. The Holy Spirit is here to make Earth a sovereign state for God, the Father. A sovereign state is a state with a defined territory on which it exercises internal and external sovereignty.

In other words, the Holy Spirit has set residence on the earth to ensure that "the kingdoms of this world are become the kingdoms of our Lord, and of his Christ..." (Revelation 11:15). The Holy Spirit is here on Earth to root out violence, anarchy, and terrorism of the devil.

Satan is the terrorist behind the malicious and vicious attacks on the nations of the earth. He has an "occupied force" in every community, city, state, and nation (Daniel 10:13). Satan and his forces occupy the earth illegally (Psalms 115:16).

Osama bin Laden, who was the most-wanted terrorist on the earth, is not the one behind inordinate evil, wickedness, and calamity; it is satan. However, the Holy Spirit has been deployed on the earth until the population and government of Earth, including the forces of darkness, become subject to the sovereign will of God.

If you want to know the True and Living God, you must first be introduced to the Holy Spirit. He knows the mind of God. The Holy Spirit is God. If there is something you want to share with God, tell it to the Holy Spirit. He is also the "Commander in Chief of Communication" in the fourth dimension.

Holy Spirit

Holy Spirit, five seven three three seven,

Holy Spirit, Thou has revealed this to us from heaven;

Holy Spirit, You were sent from Jehovah's throne,

Holy Spirit, now God's children will never be alone;

Holy Spirit, our eyes are focused on Thee,

Holy Spirit, You hold the Master's key;

Holy Spirit, the number of the day,

Holy Spirit, You direct our perfect way.

CHAPTER 34

A Love Letter

Have you ever thought to yourself, "Does anyone really love me?" We all know that individuals may say they love you, but their actions and behavior may paint a different picture. Perhaps you have considered these questions: "Does anybody really care about me? Am I just another face among billions of people in the world? Am I really special or just a result or product of two individuals coming together? Does anyone love me unconditionally?"

David, the King of Israel, let us know that there is only one who truly loves us. The Bible says in Psalms 139:17-18, "How precious also are thy thoughts unto me, O God: How great is the sum of them! If I should count them, they are more in number than the sand: When I awake, I am still with thee."

King David, who is the author of the Scripture above, says that there's not a moment that goes by that God doesn't think about you. From the time you wake up in the morning until the time you go to bed at night, and all in between, you are always on God's mind. What is God thinking? The thoughts that God has are thoughts toward you. The thoughts toward you are thoughts of blessing and prosperity. God said in Jeremiah 29:11, "For I know the thoughts that I think toward you, saith the Lord, thoughts of peace, and not of evil, to give you an expected [prosperous] end."

Along with the Bible, the Holy Spirit has penned a love letter just for you. This brief love letter was written and submitted through this book by the Holy Spirit. He wants you to know the Father and the Son in a more intimate way. When was the last time you went on a date with Jesus? He longs and yearns to know you in a very special way.

Moreover, God does not want you to just be His private secret-lover. He is not exclusive or selfish. God wants you to share Him with the world. Neither does He want to be your "part-time lover," that is, when you don't have anything else to do.

God wants to have an up-and-close intimate relationship with you. He said in Revelation 3:16, "So then because thou art lukewarm, and neither cold nor hot, I will spue thee out of my mouth." God doesn't like part-time, lukewarm, relationships. He wants you to know that you have always been His first love. Even when you weren't thinking of Him, He was constantly thinking of you. God is mad, head-over-heels about you!

Listen to the short love letter message God writes to you through the Holy Spirit:

'To my beloved bride: I know it's been a long time since we've talked, but I've missed you! And since you haven't talked with me lately, I have sent this love letter to let you know you have always been on my mind. We can make it work this time. I've never stopped loving you. I've always been with you gazing at a distance. I've been eagerly waiting to hold you. You belong to me. I talk to my beloved Son, Jesus, about you every day in heaven. We had a discussion about you just before you read this letter. You are always at the top of my "most beloved" list. I want you to know how much I love you. When the law required death because of your sins, I asked my only begotten Son to take your place (John 3:16).'

'And because He loves you too, Jesus gladly agreed to die in your stead. That's how much He and I love you! When I gave you my only Son, I gave you My everything! There's no one that can take your place (Romans 8:32)!'

'You see the spectacular display of stars in the heavens? I did that for you! Do you see the beautiful autumn trees and leaves? I did that for you! Do you feel the warmth of the sun on your face? I did that for you! Do you see the wonderful display of colored flowers in the spring? Do you smell the perfumed fragrance of flowers and roses in the summer rain? I did all that for you! Just for you!'

'I often dream about us together during the marriage supper. For the Bible says, "...Blessed are they which are called into the marriage supper of the Lamb" (Revelation 19:9). I have planned an awesome feast, second to none! You are My special preferred bride. I am sending you a personal invitation now to meet with Me at the marriage supper. Will you agree to attend? It will be most memorable! It will be a dining experience that will take your breath away!'

'You will be treated like the queen (bride) that you are. But before coming to heaven, I want to give you a little taste of heaven on Earth. Just an appetizer of what is in store for you. You know that house, furniture, car, estate, land, business, and jewelry you've been longing for? I am going to give it to you as an engagement present. You are going to be swept off your feet when you witness all of the gifts I have in store leading up to the wedding ceremony! Why? Because there is no bridegroom like Me! No bridegroom, dead or alive, can woo his bride like I can! What is your taste and preference? I can "wine and dine" you like no other (Psalms 34:8)!'

'This marriage has been pre-arranged since the beginning of time. I knew your name before your mother and father named you. Jeremiah 1:5 says, "Before I formed thee in the belly I knew thee, and before thou camest forth of the womb I sanctified thee..." It was I who placed your name in your parent's hearts as what to name and call you.'

'I have commanded a guardian angel to watch over you, everyday, never to leave your side. I refuse to leave you unprotected. The Bible says in Psalms 34:7, "The angel of the Lord encampeth round about them that fear him and delivereth them."'

'I created you. Psalms 8:5 says, "For thou hast made him [man] a little lower than the angels [God] and hast crowned him with glory and honor, thou madest him to have dominion over the works of thy hands; thou hast put all things under his feet."'

'I sent my Holy Spirit to live in you, so that you and I can live [now] together forever, not when you arrive in heaven, but right now!'

'As king and queen, you are seated next to me in heaven. Ephesians 2:6 says, "And God raised us up with Christ and seated us with him in the heavenly realms in Christ Jesus."'

'As your dear King and Husband, I will always be eternally true to you. Just as I have a great capacity to forgive, I have a great capacity to hurt, too! My heart is sensitive and easy to break. Have you ever had a broken heart because your dearest love had forsaken you? Hosea 5:3 (NLT) says, "I know what you are like, O Israel! You have left me as a prostitute leaves her husband; you are utterly defiled."'

'My heart breaks when my bride leaves me for another lover. Have you ever been rejected and forsaken? How can you say you love Me when you never talk with Me? How can you say you are in love with Me when you don't even know Me? My heart is crushed when My bride neglects and disobeys My words and commandments.'

'A good bridegroom always wants to please His bride. A good bride should always want to please her bridegroom. Need love? I can show you what true love is all about. Remember, I don't just have love; I am love (1 John 4:8)!'

'I want you to know I love you very much and want to speak with you today! As evidence of my love, I left 66 books, 1189 chapters, 31,102 verses, and 774,746 words expressed in a formal love letter, called the Bible, just for you. It is the longest and greatest love letter ever written.'

'I knew this day would come. I've been anxious to contact you. Again, I love you! Will you accept this invitation to make me your lover, Lord, and Savior? Will you invite Me into your heart today? Listen, just between you and Me – Heaven is not heaven without you as My bride!'

'Will you share this letter with others, who may not have read this special love letter invitation? I know I can count on you! Can we meet today? We can meet now in the fourth dimension. I am now waiting at the door for you in the fourth dimension!'"

Holy Spirit

Holy Spirit, time speaks of change,

Holy Spirit, but love is never out of range;

Holy Spirit, some may come and others may go,

Holy Spirit, but only in the Godhead is it so;

Holy Spirit, satan thought it was over,

Holy Spirit, but our Heavenly Father sent Another;

Holy Spirit, the second person of the Trinity,

Holy Spirit, Redeemer, Savior, is His identity.

CHAPTER 35

God-Talk

Have you ever eaves-dropped on someone's conversation? Perhaps you overheard your parents talking to each other which were different than the way they talked to you. Better yet, have you ever heard God-talk? God-talk is diametrically different from man-talk. Let's eaves-drop and listen in on God's conversation and talking points He had with the children of Israel. God said in Isaiah 40:25-26, 28-29 (NIV),

> To whom will you compare me? Or who is my equal?" says the Holy One. Lift your eyes and look to the heavens: Who created all these? He who brings out the starry host one by one, and calls them each by name. Because of his great power and mighty strength, not one of them is missing. Do you not know? Have you not heard? The LORD is the everlasting God, the Creator of the ends of the earth. He will not grow tired or weary, and his understanding no one can fathom. He gives strength to the weary and increases the power of the weak.

Does that sound in any way like God is unsure of Himself? This is not God bragging. A person who brags is someone who exaggerates in an attempt to make himself look better than he really is. God doesn't brag, neither does He exaggerate. He simply states the facts and truths about Himself and what He is able to do. God is in a category all by Himself!

God-talk is distinctive. God-talk, as we will discover, is different from man-talk. Just listen to the news and the mass hysteria in the media as an illustration of man-talk. Man-talk is filled with doubt, uncertainty, and anxiety. Man-talk is usually composed of vain words, lies, and empty rhetoric.

God, who is the Sovereign King, talks sovereign. His words and commandments are matchless, unparalleled, unprecedented, and unrivaled. When God opens His mouth, His words are filled with truth, glory, and dominion.

God never says, "I don't know how I am going to do that." Nor does He say, "Wow, this is going to be difficult." Or, "How can I make this work?" Neither does He say, "What am I going to do now? Or what am I going to do?" These words of uncertainty are not a part of God's vocabulary and repertoire.

You can't make God, the Sovereign King, sweat. God is not in heaven wringing and rubbing His hands together in uneasiness and worry. Naturally, when things seem to be out of control, it simply means that things are beyond our power, capacity, and ability to handle it. God doesn't have that problem. There's nothing impossible with God (Luke 1:37). He has the power to do the impossible. Every problem and situation you face is completely solvable with God.

If you have a problem, God has a solution. God never perspires. His pulse and blood pressure never rises. "God is not a man..." (Numbers 23:19). However if God was human, His blood pressure would always be a perfect 120/80 regardless of the surrounding circumstances and situations. God is always "cool, calm, and collected." He never looks or sounds stressed out or nervous. You can't create or design a problem that He can't solve.

God talks without boundaries, limits, or constraints. God talks on a supernatural level not a natural level. His words are filled with confidence, faith, and assurance. There is not a thread, hint, or glimmer of doubt in God's words or when He speaks.

When God asks a question it's not for him to solve or figure out, but for us. God asked Sarah a question at the age of 90 (Genesis 17:17), long after the age of child bearing, saying, "Is any thing too hard for the Lord..." (Genesis 18:14)?

God wants us to believe that He can do what has never been done before (Ephesians 3:20). What's possible for you is not based on what other people have done, accomplished, or achieved. God wants you to believe for something that has never been documented throughout the pages of history. In fact, God wants to work through you something that He has never done before.

You must believe that no mountain is too high, no valley too low, no river too wide, and no ocean too deep for our God. Psalms 113:5-8 (NLT) says:

> *Who can be compared with the Lord our God, who is enthroned on high? Far below him are the heavens and the earth. He stoops to look, and He lifts the poor from the dust and the needy from the garbage dump. He sets them among princes, even the princes of his own people!*

To believe for the supernatural, we must talk supernatural. Jesus said, "For by thy words thou shalt be justified, and by thy words thou shalt be condemned" (Matthew 12:37). We can never rise higher than the level or position of our words.

You can't say you think on a supernatural level but talk on a natural level. What you think is what you will say. Jesus said, "The good man brings good things out of the good stored up in him, and the evil man brings evil things out of the evil stored up in him" (Matthew 12:35, NIV) .

The Apostle Paul said, "Only let your conversation [words and actions] be as it becometh the gospel of Christ..." (Philippians 1:27). We must learn and adopt the native language of Christ. The problem is we usually don't talk God-talk. God-talk is the language of faith.

Moreover, God-talk is filled with authority and power. The Bible says Jesus' words were with power. Luke 4:32 says, "And they were astonished at his [Jesus'] doctrine: for his word was with power." The writer of Hebrews says, "The Son is the radiance of God's glory and the exact representation of his being, sustaining all things by his powerful word... (Hebrews 1:3, NIV)"

The Apostle Paul demonstrated God-talk throughout his teachings, sermons, and preaching. Paul said, "...My speech and my preaching was not with enticing words of man's wisdom, but in demonstration of the Spirit and of power." You can tell when God speaks because He will back up His words with signs and wonders.

God said in Isaiah 55:11 (NASB), "So will My word be which goes forth from My mouth; It will not return to Me empty, Without accomplishing what I desire, And without succeeding in the matter for which I sent it."

God often talks in two forms: singular and plural. He is able to speak and perform independently on His own. However, when He wants to do or create something special, He uses the word, "us," such as "Let us make man..." (Genesis 1:26).

God includes the God-head [Son and the Holy Spirit] in His decision-making activities. He teaches that your talk should not always be singular that is about you, but should include others. No one is an island [not even God]; no one stands alone.

There are two models of talk: **self talk** and **audible talk**. Let's begin with the latter of the two. **Audible talk** is what people hear us say.

Self talk is the talk we have within our inner self. Our self talk reflects our inner self. It may be surprising to find that most self talk, what we say to ourselves, is usually negative. Sometimes, we can be our own worst critic.

Although we may never fully discuss openly what we say [inwardly] to ourselves, self talk [the conversation we have with ourselves], defines who we really are. The Bible says "For as he thinketh in his heart, so is he..." (Proverb 23:7).

Our inner self reflects who we really are, not the image

we portray on the outside. Jesus was able to see into the inner-self of the scribes and Pharisees. Jesus said, "Woe to you, teachers of the law and Pharisees, you hypocrites! You are like whitewashed tombs, which look beautiful on the outside but on the inside are full of dead men's bones and everything unclean" (Matthew 23:27, NIV).

Oftentimes, it is not what happens to us on the outside, that devastates us, but on the inside. The most destructive war is the war which rages on the inside. It is the "war of the interior." Due to inner struggles, personal hurts, and intrinsic pains, many people implode from the inside out.

Do you battle conflicting and opposing views which continually bombard your mind? Are you deeply depressed and tormented on the inside, but pretend that you are filled with joy and happiness on the outside? You are not alone. Millions are experiencing outcries from their inner voice.

Although we may be able to muffle, suppress, and silence our inner voice from others. It cannot be hidden from God. He hears self talk–the language of the heart. The heart does not lie. God said, "...These people [the children of Israel] come near to me with their mouth and honor me with their lips, but their hearts are far from me..." (Isaiah 29:13).

The heart is the barometer by which God measures the worthiness and value of a man. God said to Samuel, "...For the LORD seeth not as man seeth; for man looketh on the outward appearance, but the LORD looketh on the heart" (1 Samuel 16:7).

God listens more to our self talk than He does our audible talk–what we say out loud. You may think you are having an inner conversation with yourself, but you have an audience. The Bible says, "The LORD knows the thoughts of man ... (Psalms 94:11, NIV).

Our thoughts have a voice and God is listening! Luke 11:17 (NIV) says, "Jesus knew their thoughts ..." In fact, God knows our thoughts afar off. Psalms 139:2-3 says, "Thou knowest my downsitting and mine uprising, thou understandest my thought afar off. Thou compassest my path and my lying down, And art acquainted with all my ways." God is actively listening to our thoughts, not just what's coming out of our mouths.

Positive self talk helps build our self image and our self perception. Self talk is directly related to our outward performance and success. Self talk must not be based solely on positive thinking, but on the Word of God.

Negative self talk represents doubt and unbelief. If we allow negative self talk to take root, grow, and mature, we will become the image of the negative. Negative self talk can be highly destructive. Negative talk is saying to ourselves what is contrary to the Word of God. Negative self talk is the opposite of faith. Romans 14:23 (ESV) says, "...For whatever does not proceed from faith is sin. Sin always brings destruction.

When we talk on a natural level, it's a talk about how we can do it. But when we talk on a supernatural level, it's a talk about how God can do it. We must uniformly speak on a spiritual dimension. The Apostle Paul said in 1 Corinthians 2:13 (NIV), "This is what we speak, not in words taught us by human wisdom but in words taught by the Spirit, expressing spiritual truths in spiritual words."

Talking on a spiritual and supernatural dimension is supported by the Words of Jesus. Jesus said, "It is the Spirit who gives life; the flesh is no help at all. The words that I have spoken to you are spirit and life" (John 6:63, ESV). Only the Word of God unleashes the supernatural power of God.

We are the sum of our thoughts and words, just as God is the epitome of His Word (John 1:1). We become more like God when His words become our words. The Word of God will change and alter any negative self talk and create godly thoughts.

Hebrews 4:12 (NIV) says, "For the word of God is living and active. Sharper than any double-edged sword, it penetrates even to dividing soul and spirit, joints and marrow; it judges the thoughts and attitudes of the heart." The Word of God has the power to cut and divide asunder any negative, self defeating thoughts at the root.

To exercise God-talk is to read and speak God's Word. When the prophets of old would say, "Hear ye or thus saith the Lord," they were demonstrating God-talk. In other words, they were only repeating what God had said. Therefore, when we read and speak the Word of God concerning our healing, deliverance, and prosperity, we are only repeating what God has already said.

We have God-talk, but we also have man-talk. Problems often arise when we allow man to talk to us more than God. Man-talk comes in a myriad of forms. One form is through popular television "talk" shows.

Instead of talking to God, we turn on Tyra Banks, Jerry Springer, Ricki Lake, Oprah Winfrey, Dr. Phil, Ellen DeGeneres, Dr. Oz, Judge Judy, and Howard Stern. These talk shows are simply a new form of soap opera entertainment for TV. We listen to everyone's opinion, but God's.

These talk shows may be able to give good advice, but no advice is superior to God's. Which advice will you choose? We can choose man's advice or God's.

There's a song written by Harrison Johnson which says. "Some folks would rather have houses and land, Some folks choose silver and gold, These things they treasure, And forget about their souls, I've decided to make Jesus my choice..."[1] Which talk is more important to you: God-talk or man-talk?

When you start talking like God, supernatural miracles and wonders will begin to take place. For example: Abraham not only believed God, he began to talk like God.

Romans 4:17 says, "(As it is written, I have made thee a father of many nations,) before him whom he believed, even God, who quickeneth the dead, and calleth those things which be not as though they were."

Abraham, like God, began to call those things that were not as if they existed. This is what brought Isaac into the world – God talk. Abraham allowed "God-talk" to become his "self-talk." Abraham's self talk [what he believed and said in his heart] was directly in alignment with God-talk.

God-talk has the power to bring what is divided, dead, or in chaos into divine alignment. Abraham allowed the seed of the Word of God [which was the promise of a son] to take root in his heart which produced the desired fruit [his son].

The seed of the Word of God is designed for hostile and adversarial environments. We are currently experiencing hostility throughout our nation and the world. There is no better time than now to speak the Word of God in all manner of conversation. The seed of the Word of God will change any environment.

The Word of God is a seed. Jesus said in Luke 8:11 (NIV), "This is the meaning of the parable: The seed is the Word of God. Like a mustard seed, "which indeed is the least of all seeds: but when it is grown it is the greatest among herbs, and becometh a tree, so that the birds of the air come and lodge in the branches thereof (Matthew 13:32)." The Word of God has the power to influence environments, atmospheres, habitats, and territories.

The Word of God, like a mustard seed, may not physically or naturally appear significant. However, if you allow it to take root, it will change the entire landscape of your life.

Faith-talk is God-talk. Because Jesus is God, Jesus introduced the concept and the power of faith. No one taught more about faith before Christ. In fact, Jesus taught on faith throughout His ministry.

Jesus said, "...If ye have faith as small as a grain of mustard seed, ye shall say unto this mountain, Remove hence to yonder place, and it shall remove; and nothing shall be impossible unto you" (Mathew 17:20). God talk is a talk of faith.

Jesus said in Mark 11:22, "...Have faith in God." We are to believe as God believes. Faith is a spirit which is intrinsic to God. What makes us God's people is the spirit of faith. Ephesians 2:8 says, "For by grace are we saved through faith; and that not of yourselves: it is the gift of God."

Our kinship with God, through Christ, is faith. Second Corinthians 4:13 says, "We having the same spirit of faith, according as it is written, I believed, and therefore have I spoken; we also believe, and therefore speak."

When we speak in faith we are acting and behaving like our Father, God. Romans 4:17 says, "...Even God, who quickeneth the dead, and calleth those things which be not as though they were."

Faith-talk is the language of God. It is the common component of every believer's spoken word regardless of their native language. When we speak in faith, we speak as God speaks. Furthermore, when we possess the same spirit of faith as God, we take on His divine nature. When we take on God's divine nature, we possess His divine power. According to 2 Peter 1:3 (ESV), "[God's] divine power has granted to us all things that pertain to life and godliness, through the knowledge of him who called us to his own glory and excellence."

God is talking now. Can you hear? God dictated this chapter, through the medium of the Holy Spirit for you as evidence. Are you on the right frequency to hear His voice? If not, set your frequency on faith through repentance and prayer. He is ready to talk and take your call in the fourth dimension.

Endnotes:
1. Johnson, Harrison. "I Have Decided to Make Jesus My Choice."

Holy Spirit

Holy Spirit....His presence of sweet joy is now complete,

It is the fruit that blesses and defeats;

This Truth for always my soul has known,

That the feeling of joy is what Christ had preserved and sown;

Holy Spirit....Listen to the sound of my heartbeat,

Beautiful rhythm in the fullness of joy it speaks;

It's the place where happiness forever lives,

It's the place where the smiling spirit appears;

Holy Spirit....Come dance, sing this precious melody with me,

So joyous, peaceful and worry free;

No more bound by the cares of this life,

Now I have the joy of the Lord, a part of the Lamb's sacrifice;

Holy Spirit....In profit this wonderful day in joy has been,

When He came and dwelt eternally within;

Holy Spirit....For now I feel this power of heaven's community You send,

The joy of the soul is the strength God recommends.

CHAPTER 36

Is There Anything Too Hard for the Lord?

We live in a limited, inhibited, and restrictive world. Although there have been many scientific discoveries, advancements in medicine, innovative breakthroughs in engineering, and cutting-edge technology, there are still fundamental occurrences man has no power or ability to manipulate or control. These phenomena include terminal diseases, natural disasters, epidemics, and death.

There are certain things and events in this world which cannot be accomplished or performed candidly. There are many limitations in this finite and obscure world. Some things are beyond the scope of human ingenuity and natural intelligence. In other words, there are things which are virtually impossible–but not to God.

There is a biblical account in which angels bring an incredible message from God that Abraham and his wife, Sarah will have a son. Genesis 18:9-10, 12-14 says:

> And they [heavenly beings] said unto him, Where is Sarah thy wife? And he [Abraham] said, Behold, in the tent. And he said, I will certainly return unto thee according to the time of life; and lo, Sarah thy wife shall have a son. And Sarah heard it in the tent door, which was behind him. Therefore Sarah laughed within herself, saying, After I am waxed old shall I

*have pleasure, my lord being old also? And the Lord
said unto Abraham, Wherefore did Sarah laugh, saying
Shall I of a surety bear a child, which am old? Is any
thing too hard of the Lord?*

At the time of the three heavenly beings' visitation,
Abraham is now a hundred years of age and his wife Sarah is
ninety years old (Genesis 17:17). Undoubtedly, the Scriptures
[above] entail many years of past emotional hurts, desires,
hopes, and dreams that have long died.

Isn't it strange that God will bring up the things that
have hurt you the most in the past–things that you once longed
for with all your heart only to be denied time and time again?
However, it is important to know, if God brings it up or dis-
cusses it with you, He has a breakthrough planned for you! God
never brings up an impossible issue without having a supernatural solution to the problem.

The stigma that defined Sarah was "the barren one."
Everyone knew and identified Sarah as the one who could not
bear any children. Sarah and Abraham were blessed with gold,
silver, cattle, and land, but the thing that Sarah desired most
was a child. Isn't ironic that you can be blessed on one hand
and seemed to be cursed on the other? Have you ever said to
yourself, "Yes, God has blessed me, but I still need a blessing in
certain areas of my life?"

Sarah accepted the fact that she will never bear children. As far as Sarah was concerned, her prayers to God for a
child fell on deaf ears. God refused her requests and now any
possibility of bearing a child has long past.

Imagine what was going on in Sarah's mind when she
heard the impossible news that she will have a son. Listen to
what Sarah possibly said to herself as the angels gave the news
of her bearing a son.

I can imagine Sarah saying to herself, "Ain't this something! Another preacher now come along and says I will have a
son. Where were these three preachers 60 years ago? Why
couldn't this announcement occur when I was at the age to conceive? Now you bring up something that didn't happen 60 years

ago, and now you say that I will bear a son when I am over the age to even bear children? You fellas must be at the wrong residence!"

Sarah realized that there were two impossibilities here: one, she had been barren throughout her life and secondly, she is now too old to have children, even if she wasn't barren! For Sarah, this was too incredible to believe. Imagine getting such as absurd announcement. Sarah's only response was to laugh. However, God wasn't joking! Listen, God can give you a blessing that will blow your mind and have you cracking up!

The Word of God declares to us today that the things we have long desired shall conceive and give birth (Habakkuk 2:3). Just like the three company of angels which spoke to Abraham and Sarah–Christ, the Father, and the Holy Spirit bear witness to our long awaited promises. In fact, the things that you have stopped praying for, the things that time itself says is too late, the things that circumstances and situations say will never happen, and the things that nature says are impossible, shall come to pass.

The Holy Spirit has come to let you know that the things that have been birthed in your spirit shall come forth alive! Let's listen to the conversation between Jesus and Martha after Lazarus has been dead for four days in John chapter 11.

Martha tells Jesus that time has brought about a change and certain things have come into place and fruition that even He cannot alter or change. Notice what Martha says to Jesus in John 11:21, "...Lord if thou hadst been here my brother had not died."

However, we must know that anytime Jesus shows up, a change will come. He specializes in things impossible. He can bring dead things to life!

Are there things in your life that have died? Are there things that you have prayed for and because so much time has elapsed it is now impossible to be revived or resurrected?

Have you ever asked yourself, "God where are you?" Where is the God of Abraham, Isaac, and Jacob? Where is the God of Elijah? Note that if God delays His coming, He's got something far greater than your prayer requests! Isn't it wonderful to know that Jesus will come?

"Jesus saith unto her [Martha], Thy brother shall rise again. Martha saith unto him, I know that he shall rise again in the resurrection at the last day. Jesus said unto her, I am the resurrection, and the life: he that believeth in me, though he were dead, yet shall he live" (John 11:23-25)

In verse 23 of John 11, Jesus tells Martha that her brother shall rise again. In verse 24, Martha declares, "I know he shall rise again in the resurrection at the last day." Jesus then begins to share with Martha that He is able to do what she had believed in the past, right now.

Jesus tells Martha in verse 25, that He is the resurrection and life. In essence, Jesus says to Martha that the One whom she is standing face to face with controls life and death. Jesus holds the past, present, and future in His hands. Jesus is saying to us as He did 2000 years ago that He is the resurrection and the life. Why not ask Him, right now, what you believed for in the past, but didn't receive? He is able to do right now what did not happen in the past!

In verse 39, we see Martha not fully comprehending what Jesus is saying because she objects to Jesus commanding to take away the stone from the tomb of Lazarus. In essence, Martha was saying: 'it's too late to pray, it's too late to heal him now, for Lazarus has been dead for four days.'

What we need to understand today, as Martha learned, that regardless of what did not happen yesterday or in the past, Jesus is still the "I am that I am" (Exodus 3:14). God is still everything that you need and desire. He is still the Resurrection and the Life (John 11:25). He is still the Good Shepherd (John 10:11). He is still the Bread of Life (John 6:35). He is still healing and health for the body (Isaiah 58:8).

You don't have to wait until the resurrection at the last day before Jesus shows up, for He is here right now! Don't stand in His awesome presence and not ask Him for what you need and desire, to do so is to not know who He is. He can do right now that which seems to be impossible. He is here today! When Jesus shows up, every petition is granted and every desire is fulfilled.

Today is the day of His visitation!" Jesus has come. There's a song that says, "When Jesus comes, all satan's power is broken." In fact, Jesus has heard your prayers for employment and your prayers for a better salary. He has heard your prayers for healing. He has heard your prayers for ministry. He has heard your prayers for more faithful members in the church. He has heard your prayers for signs and wonders. Moreover, He has heard your prayers for a new vehicle. He has heard your prayers for a new home. He has heard your prayers for your child to attend the school of their choice. He has heard your prayers for financial prosperity.

God told Sarah and Abraham that He was about to give them what they always wanted–a son! God has given us everything we need–His Son!

Christ has come to give you the things you've always wanted. There is not anything too hard for the Lord of the fourth dimension.

Heavenly Father

Heavenly Father, we will never let You go,

You are the only God we know;

All that we have we freely give,

For in our faith we must live;

Blessed Creator from above,

Sealed in Jesus Christ, our First Love;

Father, we come as we are,

Needing more of You, in our hearts;

If only faith, works for You,

Then believing will carry us through;

Committed to Your blessed Love,

Living in the Kingdom from above;

Blessed and highly favored are we,

Joined to the royal priesthood destiny.

CHAPTER 37

Your Greatest Defeat Will Be Your Greatest Victory

Defeat is the essence of loss. Nothing hurts worst than the loss of a job, the loss of an income, the loss of a loved one, the loss of one's faculties [mental abilities], or the loss of one's health. The Bible tells us that we will all experience loss. Solomon declared, "To everything there is a season, and a time to every purpose under the heaven. A time to get, and a time to lose..." (Ecclesiastes 3:1, 6).

Loss is often seen and viewed in a negative connotation; however, loss is not always a bad thing. In fact, loss can be a wonderful blessing. God created the body to have four major systems: nervous system, respiratory system, circulatory system, and the digestion system. One of the most important of these systems is the digestive system. Without it, we would not have any way to lose the excess waste from the body. Our body would be filled with toxins and poisons which would cause severe harm and death. Therefore, losing waste and harmful refuse in the body is one of the many remarkable system designs of God.

According to Solomon (Ecclesiastes 3:1, 6 above), loss and gain are two variables on the same spectrum. The same can be said of defeat and victory. Defeat and victory are two sides of the same coin. Depending on which side the coin is on, you can have victory or defeat. In the same way, God can turn [or flip] any defeat into victory.

God often uses what we think is a complete failure, and use it, to give us total victory. Your greatest disappointments may turn out to be the "perfect set up" in which God uses to bring glory and honor to His name. Nobody can "set you up" for success like God can!

God is the Great Manipulator behind the "turn of events." When things happen unexpectedly in your favor or when you receive a financial blessing out of nowhere, this can be a sure sign that God has written Himself into the equation of your circumstances. Yes, God will rewrite the script of your life.

Your life is not beyond repair. God will take what should have cursed you and bless you with it. What should have brought you infirmity, God will take it and bring healing. What should have destroyed you, God will take it and restore you. Your life is not over until God says it over.

There are many individuals in the Bible who thought that their lives were over due to the countless mistakes made in their past. Samson, one of the judges of Israel, whom God gave great strength and power to defeat Israel's oppressors, is a perfect example.

After disregarding, ignoring, and dishonoring his Nazarite vow, Samson was defeated primarily by a woman called Delilah. His hair was shaved and his eyes were gouged out; Samson suffered his one and only defeat. Although this was his only defeat, it was the worst defeat anyone could experience. The great and powerful Samson experienced tremendous shame, ridicule, scorn, and humiliation. One would think that Samson's life was over. It looked like the champion of the Israelites was reduced to a piece of meat–blind, helpless, hopeless, and disgraced.

Once proud, audacious, and fearless, Samson was only a shell of his former self. The wonderful thing about the story of Samson is that although Samson messed up, having no one to blame but himself, God used his greatest defeat to create his greatest victory. The Bible says,

> But the Philistines took him, and put out his eyes,
> and brought him down to Gaza, and bound him with

fetters of brass; and he did grind in the prison house. Howbeit the hair of his head began to grow again after he was shaven. And it came to pass, when their hearts were merry, that they said, Call for Samson, that he may make us sport. And they called for Samson out of the prison house; and he made them sport [ridiculed and made fun of him]: and they set him between the pillars. And Samson said unto the lad that held him by the hand, Suffer me that I may feel the pillars whereupon the house standeth, that I may lean upon them. And Samson called unto the Lord, and said, O Lord God, remember me, I pray thee, only this once, O God, that I may be at once avenged of the Philistines for my two eyes. And Samson took hold of the two middle pillars upon which the house stood, and on which it was borne up, of the one with his right hand, and of the other with his left. And Samson said, Let me die with the Philistines. And he bowed himself with all his might; and the house fell upon the lords, and upon all the people that were therein. So the dead which he slew at his death were more than they which he slew in his life (Judges 16:21-22, 25-26, 28-30).

Although Samson experienced a horrific defeat by the hands of his enemies, Samson had one good fight left in him; he wasn't through yet!

Don't ever give up. Regardless of how dark your present condition looks, you have one good fight left in you! This fight is going to take you to ultimate victory.

What satan does not know or understand is that the saints of God are at their best when facing impossible odds. When the enemy backs us in a corner, we come out fighting! Satan has not figured out that when he comes against a child of God, it only brings defeat and loss to his kingdom. Satan is a defeated cherub, and bully, who has not learned a single lesson concerning the righteous. The worst thing he can do is bother a child of the King.

When satan picks on you, get excited! Satan will not choose just anyone to try to defeat. If he has selected you for warfare, it is because you are special to God!

Satan executes opposing strategies against what God's desires are for us. If you are sick, it's because God desires for you to be well. If you are experiencing financial difficulties, it's because God desires that you experience financial prosperity. If you are unemployed and jobless, it's because God desires that you have a top-level, high income, position. If you have been bombarded consistently with trouble, it's because God has designed an unusual long-term peaceful and prosperous future for you.

On the other hand, if the devil has not messed with you in years, it's because you are not a threat! Satan is not at odds with those who possess a laissez-faire and callous attitude toward God and His Kingdom.

Satan threatens those who threaten his kingdom. He attacks those who attack his kingdom. This is what happened to Job. It wasn't just Job's good fortune that caused satan to want to harm Job; it was Job's influence in the earth for God. Satan never revealed to God the real reason why he wanted to attack Job, but God knew. In fact, God knows that Job is on satan's mind when satan presents himself before God.

The Bible says, "Now there was a day when the sons of God came to present themselves before the Lord, and satan came also among them. And the Lord said unto satan, Hast thou considered my servant Job, that there is none like him in the earth, a perfect and an upright man, one that feareth God, and escheweth evil?" (Job 1:6, 8).

God told satan why Job was on His mind [in verse 8 above]: it was because of his influence in the earth. Job possessed godly virtues. He had impeccable character; he was known as one having a godly reputation throughout the earth. Job was credible, trustworthy, and righteous. His godly influence affected the hearts and minds of countless people. Satan knew that Job posed a serious threat to his kingdom. Job's life and devoted worship to God caused many to seek after the God whom he served.

Satan, unsurprisingly, painted a negative picture of Job and why Job served God. The Bible records,

> *Then Satan answered the Lord and said, "Does Job fear God for no reason? Have you not put a hedge around him and his house and all that he has, on every side? You have blessed the work of his hands, and his possessions have increased in the land. But stretch out your hand and touch all that he has, and he will curse you to your face" (Job 1:9-11, ESV).*

Satan has nothing good to say about us, the children of the Most High God. All the good that we do, he tries systematically to pervert and distort it.

God knows that what satan says is a lie. John 8:44 (NIV) says, "...When he [satan] lies, he speaks his native language, for he is a liar and the father of lies." The native language of satan is lies.

Nevertheless, God allowed satan to test Job's faith and devotion to Him. God, in His infinite wisdom and knowledge, knew that Job would serve Him even if Job didn't have a dime. It was never about the money and possession with Job; it was all about his dedication to God.

Satan desperately wanted to destroy Job's influence for God in the earth. One of satan's main strategies was to use Job's, so-called, friends to attack his image, credibility, reputation, and character (Job 4:5-8) which is what makes up one's influence. To destroy someone's influence is to destroy what one holds dear, believes, loves, and admires.

Satan destroyed Job's children, livestock, estate, and wealth (Job 1:13-19). Everything satan saw, in Job's life as a blessing and a threat against his kingdom, he destroyed. When allowed, satan uses the same strategy against us. Satan did not destroy Job's wife because he would soon use her as a pawn in his continuous strategy to defeat Job (Job 2: 9-10).

Temporary evidence may indicate that satan is winning in our life, but the conclusion or the end result will be totally different. God's promises cannot be evaluated or concluded in a limited span of time. However, as time goes by, you will see that God is faithful to His promises. The Bible says God is faithful to what He has promised (Hebrews 10:23); God always comes through.

The longer the enemy's attacks last, the longer your time of victory and deliverance. God uses time as well as physical substance to compensate us when we hold fast to Him in faith. In other words, if the devil has stolen years from you, he will have to give back those years. God said in Joel 2:25, "...And I will restore to you the years that the locust hath eaten, the cankerworm, and the caterpillar, and the palmerworm, my great army which I sent among you."

Moreover, often times, God gives back or restores in double portions. God said in Isaiah 61:7 (NASB), "Instead of your shame you will have a double portion, And instead of humiliation they will shout for joy over their portion. Therefore they will possess a double portion in their land, Everlasting joy will be theirs."

God always rewards those who stand on His Word in the midst of adversity and spiritual turbulence. The Bible says that "He [God] is a rewarder of them that diligently seek him" (Hebrews 11:6). If you have been under satanic attack, you have a reward coming!

Satan is rather slow in his thinking and judgment. He has not yet figured out that when he places resistance and burdens on the shoulders of a believer, it only makes him stronger. In fact, his worst mistake ever was placing the weight of a cross on the shoulder of Jesus. Killing Jesus and nailing him to a cross was a fatal mistake on satan's part. First Corinthians 2:8 (NASB) says, "The wisdom which none of the rulers of this age has understood; for if they had understood it they would not have crucified the Lord of glory."

This unforeseeable error, on the part of satan, to allow Jesus to be crucified cost satan and his kingdom hordes the keys to hell, death, and the grave. Jesus declared in Revelation 1:18, "I am he that liveth, and was dead; and, behold, I am alive for evermore, Amen; and have the keys of hell and of death."

Jesus took the keys to hell, death, and the grave. The only way to get the key of hell was to go to hell. Jesus took the key of death. The only way to get the key of death was to die. Jesus took the key of the grave. The only way to get the key of the grave was to be buried. Jesus satisfied all the requirements to obtain complete authority in heaven and in Earth.

Victory over hell, death, and the grave can only be obtained through experiencing hell, death, and the grave. You can only get victory through battle, warfare, conflict, and struggle. You can only experience triumph through adversity.

Satan thought that his greatest victory was when he crucified Jesus and nailed him to an old rugged cross. The Bible says Jesus died a criminal's death (Matthew 27:44). However, satan's greatest victory was his greatest defeat because three days later, early Sunday morning, Jesus rose from the dead (Mark 16:9).

Jesus went down to hell and back. You may be going through hell right now, but you are coming back. I love the 1984 science fiction action film, **The Terminator**, starring Arnold Schwarzenegger.

In the movie, Arnold Schwarzenegger, portrayed as a cyborg assassin that would often say the immortal words, "I'll be back!" When he came back, he would always come back with a vengeance, killing everything in sight with automatic assault weapons and heavy artillery producing mass destruction.

Jesus also declared that He would be back. The Bible says, "From that time forth began Jesus to shew unto his disciples, how that he must go unto Jerusalem, and suffer many things of the elders and chief priests and scribes, and be killed, and be raised again the third day" (Matthew 16:21).

There's a song written by Dallas Holm which depicts Jesus saying, "...I'll rise again, there's no power on Earth, can tie me down, I'll rise again, death can't keep me in the ground. Go ahead and bury me, but very soon I will be free. 'Cause I'll rise again..."[1] Jesus got up from the grave with all power in His hand.

Jesus' worst day turned out to be His best day. Hebrews 5:8, 9 (NLT) says, "Even though Jesus was God's Son, he learned obedience from the things he suffered. In this way, God qualified him as a perfect High Priest, and he became the source of eternal salvation for all those who obey him."

No one can strategize what looks like complete disaster and doom, and turn it into triumph, but God. He can take the worst defeat and turn it into the greatest victory. When satan seems to have the victory in your life, look out, God is about to raise you up in victory over every circumstance and demise.

In 2004, an American reality television show debuted on NBC called, **The Biggest Loser**. The reality show centers on overweight contestants. The overweight contestant who lost the highest percentage of weight received a grand prize of thousands of dollars in cash.

God sometimes features us in a contest with satan, as He did Job, so that we too can "lose weight." Resistance often causes weight loss. The trials of satan make us stronger and leaner.

The Apostle Paul admonishes us to "lose weight" so that we can run our race effectively. Hebrews 12:1 (NLT) says, "...Let us 'strip off every weight' that slows us down, especially the sin that so easily trips us up. And let us run with endurance the race God has set before us." There are things that we must lose or must die in us, in order for us to live the way God intends for us to live.

Just as in the reality show, The Biggest Loser, when we "lose the weight" and the sin during trials and adversities–we gain. The battle, which God allows us to fight with the devil, helps us to work out the "excess weight" we don't need. We, therefore, become "lean mean fighting machines."

As believers, we are always better after an ornery [difficult] experience. The people of God are better having gone through a fiery trial than before. Romans 8:28 (NASB) says, "And we know that God causes all things to work together for good to those who love God, to those who are called according to His purpose." After the affliction, we are healthier, stronger, faster, and more energetic than ever. We win and satan loses, for he is the biggest loser of all!

Nothing brings out sheer excitement, thrilled emotions, and the spirit of victory than when an opponent or team comes from "sudden death" to win the national championship match and game. This is usually how God works, as well. In the first three quarters, God will allow the devil to think he's in control of the game; however, late in the fourth quarter, God will pull the greatest upset in history. God loves a great comeback.

Oftentimes, our greatest loss can be our greatest discovery. The Bible shares with us that Isaiah lost someone dear to him, King Uzziah. Isaiah writes, "In the year that king Uzziah died I saw also the Lord sitting upon a throne, high and lifted up, and his train filled the temple" (Isaiah 6:1).

Theologians and biblical scholars believe that Isaiah was of the royal blood line of King Uzziah's court. Isaiah lost someone whom he highly respected and was dear to him. Isaiah was discouraged and disillusioned after the loss of his honorable king. According to 2 Chronicles chapter 26, King Uzziah was one of the greatest kings to sit on the throne of Judah. He reigned for fifty-two years and did what was right in the sight of the Lord (2 Chronicles 26:3-4).

However, one day King Uzziah's heart was lifted up within him. King Uzziah became proud and arrogant. He was not satisfied in being the king of Judah; he wanted to be a priest, as well. He burned incense in the temple which was consecrated and only to be performed by the priests. King Uzziah, due his insolence and transgression, was struck with leprosy and later died (2 Chronicles 26:16-23).

After Uzziah's death, the young Isaiah was bewildered and distraught. What had always brought him security and confidence was dead. Isaiah never imagined that what he thought was the worst moments in his life would turn out to be his greatest moments.

In Isaiah 6:1 [above], Isaiah correlated King Uzziah's death with seeing God. What he assumed was his greatest loss ended up being his greatest discovery. He thought he had seen and experienced the greatest person there was, King Uzziah, until he saw the Lord! King Uzziah did not come close in comparison to the King of kings and the Lord of lords.

Defeat and loss can be the catalyst for change. This change can usher in success and victory in your life. Oftentimes it's the bitterness of defeat that creates a relentless drive for victory and success. If you have never tasted defeat, you may become complacent and satisfied with where you are. Subsequently, you may never possess an appetite for victory.

We are overcomers. The Word of God declares, "For everyone who has been born of God overcomes the world. And this is the victory that has overcome the world—our faith (1 John 5:4, ESV). It is our faith that will give us the victory. Our faith in God shall overcome every situation and circumstance we encounter in this world.

The Apostle Paul describes us as more than conquerors. Romans 8:37 says, "Nay, in all these things we are more than conquerors through him that loved us." You cannot be an overcomer void of obstacles and difficult circumstances.

Oftentimes, obstacles and difficulties try to bind us and place us in captivity. However, we are victors, not victims. A victor cannot be bound. He will always triumph in all circumstances. 2 Corinthians 2:14 says, "Now thanks be unto God, which always causeth us to triumph in Christ."

A victor is not one who is free of problems, but one who gains the victory in every conflict. The victory that we possess in Christ creates everlasting freedom and liberty.

Are you eternally free today? There's a song which says, "I am free! Praise the Lord, I'm free. No longer bound, no more chains holding me. My soul is resting, it's just another blessing."[2]

In John chapter 11, after Jesus miraculously raised Lazarus from death's stronghold and the grave's grasp, there was still the natural linen cloths and wrappings which held

Lazarus' mouth, hands, and feet. Therefore Jesus said, "...Loose him, and let him go" (John 11:44).

God does not want anything hindering us or keeping us in bondage. Ultimate victory is achieved only when we are set free from all forms of bondage whether it is financially, emotionally, mentally, or physically. It's time for an "extreme maker." God wants to turn every negative situation in your life around.

Only God can turn what was meant for your evil and turn it into your good. Joseph said to his brothers, "As for you, you meant evil against me, but God meant it for good in order to bring about this present result, to preserve many people alive" (Genesis 50:20, NASB).

Although man is unaware, God is often the manipulator behind man's thoughts, decisions, and actions. The Bible says, "The king's heart is in the hand of the Lord, as the rivers of water: he turneth it whithersoever he will" (Proverbs 21:1). God was the One who influenced Pharaoh to make Joseph prime minister. Pharaoh would have never made Joseph prime minister, on his own, without divine intervention (Genesis 41:38-44).

God is the "Master and Turner of Events." He alone can manipulate the events of the past, present, and future. God is the controller and operator of time, places, and events. Regardless of how chaotic your life may seem, God is still in control.

He can turn day into night and night into day. God said in Amos 8:9, ESV, "I will make the sun go down at noon and darken the earth in broad daylight." God can turn your midnight into day. He wants to turn the light on in your midnight. Having a bad day? A bad week? A bad month? A bad year? God can turn it all around.

God is the Great Transformer. He took a convicted murderer and wanted fugitive named Moses and made him the prince and leader of His people Israel (Exodus 2:12-14:31). Moses performed many of the greatest miracles found in the Bible.

If God did it for Moses, He can do it for you. God can transform you from a pauper to a prince. First Samuel 2:8 (NIV) says, "He raises the poor from the dust and lifts the needy from the ash heap; he seats them with princes and has them inherit a throne of honor. For the foundations of the earth are the Lord's; upon them he has set the world."

Are you ready to be transformed? Transformation is available to all believers of the fourth dimension. He can transform your life at any moment. Your greatest days are ahead of you, not behind you. Experiencing defeat is not the end. God can convert any defeat into victory. Today, believe by faith that your greatest defeat will be your greatest victory.

Endnotes:
1. Holm, Dallas. "Rise Again." Going Holm Music, 1977.
2. Brunson, Rev. Milton. "Praise the Lord, Hallelujah, I'm Free."

Heavenly Father

Heavenly Father, if compassion is what You seek,

It is here in the meek;

Your children know Your heart,

When we awake, it is our part;

Love is shown wherever we go,

Blessing everyone even those we don't know;

If compassion, Father, is what You seek,

Here we are, ready to greet;

The kindness that we share,

It's a part of the Christian affair;

With lovingkindness did You draw,

Bringing generations in from afar;

Heavenly Father, if the fruit of the Spirit is the make of the day,

Then look no further, this is our way.

CHAPTER 38

Your Everything

In 1977, Andy Gibb created a popular hit song called, *"I Just Want to Be Your Everything."*[1] A portion of the lyrics are as follows,

> *For so long, You and me been finding each other for so long, And the feeling that I feel for you is more than strong...Take it from me, If you give a little more then you're asking for, Your love will turn the key, Darling mine, I would wait forever for those lips of wine, Build my world around you, darling, This love will shine...Watch it and see, If you give a little more then you're asking for, Your love will turn the key, I, I just want to be your everything, Open up the heaven in your heart and let me be, The things you are to me and not some puppet on a string, Oh, if I stay here without you, darling, I will die, I want you laying in the love I have to bring, I'd do anything to be your everything.*

Although the song and lyrics above is a secular song, it can represent and reflect God's thoughts and words toward us, His children. As the song above states, "For so long," God has been waiting for a love relationship with us. It has always been God's eternal plan to have a unique "love" relationship with man. From eternity past, it has always been about us and God.

Since the world began, it was God's desire that we have an inherent relationship with Him.

Jesus said in Matthew 25:34 (NLT), "...The King will say ...Come, you who are blessed by my Father, inherit the Kingdom prepared for you from the creation of the world." Those who will inherit the Kingdom of God are those who love God.

Notwithstanding, the entire struggle between good and evil comes down to a love story between God and man. The strength and power of love is only revealed during times of struggle, pain, and conflict. As in many love and romance novels, an antagonist or rival usually come along who disrupts, tears down, and reaps havoc on a perfectly harmonious and beautiful relationship.

This is what happened in the case of God and man. In the book of Genesis an antagonist, called satan, showed up in the Garden of Eden and placed Adam and Eve at odds with God. Satan posed a question to Eve saying:

> ...Hath God said, Ye shall not eat of every tree of the garden? And the woman said unto the serpent. We may eat of the fruit of the trees of the garden: But of the fruit of the tree which is in the midst of the garden, God hath said, Ye shall not eat of it, neither shall ye touch it, lest ye die. And the serpent said unto the woman. Ye shall not surely die; For God doeth know that in the day ye eat thereof, then your eyes shall be opened, and ye shall be as gods, knowing good and evil (Genesis 3:1-5).

When satan poses a question to us, about what God has said in His Word [as he did Eve], he is not seeking clarity but confusion. Satan is the author and creator of confusion (1 Corinthians 14:33). Satan is a deceiver. Revelation 12:9 (ESV) says, "...That ancient serpent, who is called the devil and satan, the deceiver of the whole world..."

Satan's subtle and crafty words painted God as the antagonist instead of himself. As a result of Adam and Eve's disobedience, they were banned from the Garden of Eden and eternally separated from God (Genesis 3:24).

Although God's Word declared death for all mankind (Romans 6:23), God's love refused to quit. The love romance didn't end there. The elements of a love story between God and man continue throughout the pages of the Old and New Testament.

Love can be seen through the annals of history from Genesis to Malachi. Love would find a way to uphold the law, but also bring man back in relationship with God. Galatians 4:4-5 says, "But when the fulness of the time was come, God sent forth his Son, made of a woman, made under the law, To redeem them that were under the law, that we might receive the adoption of sons."

Jesus represents the law and the love of God. God's ultimate pursuit of romance with man comes in the person of Jesus Christ. The Bible says, "For God so loved the world, that he gave his only begotten Son, that whosoever believeth in him should not perish, but have everlasting life" (John 3:16). Jesus' death and sacrifice acts as a court injunction, which gives us [an eternal] reprieve from death, hell, and damnation.

Upon further discovery, the entire Bible can be seen as a romantic novel written before creation and into the future. This romantic love novel, called the Bible, is about God and man. They represent the two main characters in the novel. This romantic novel was inspired and written by God Himself (2 Timothy 3:16). God, who has spoken from eternal past to the present, says, "...I have loved you with an everlasting love; I have drawn you with unfailing kindness" (Jeremiah 31:3, NIV).

The romantic love depicted in the Word of God is seen as a special love that exists between a bridegroom and His bride. Throughout Scripture, Christ is described as the bridegroom and we as His bride. Revelation 19:7 (ESV) says, "Let us rejoice and exult and give him the glory, for the marriage of the Lamb [Christ] has come, and his Bride [the church] has made herself ready."

A romantic love story consists of at least five elements: plot, romance, drama/conflict, hero, and villain. We will also experience these elements throughout our lives. The plot represents God's plan for our life. The question is will we follow God's perfect plan for our lives, or will we pursue an alternative?

Our life represents a love story. Like a romantic love story, we will find that our life story is filled with drama, conflict, and adversity.

Second Corinthians 4:8-9 (NLT) says, "We are pressed on every side by troubles, but we are not crushed. We are perplexed, but not driven to despair. We are hunted down, but never abandoned by God. We get knocked down, but we are not destroyed."

Because our life is a love story, it will always be filled with drama. There's no way around it! The Bible says, "Man [mankind] that is born of a woman is of few days, and full of trouble (Job 14:1).

Moreover, a romantic love story has a hero and a villain. The Bible reveals to us that Jesus is our Hero and satan is the villain. A hero in a story is the champion, defender, and conqueror. Christ is our hero. The Bible says, "He defends the cause of the fatherless and the widow, and loves the alien, giving him food and clothing" (Deuteronomy 10:18, NIV).

A villain is one who is the major adversary in a story. Satan [the devil] is called our adversary. The Apostle Peter said, "Be sober, be vigilant; because your adversary the devil, as a roaring lion, walketh about, seeking whom he may devour (1 Peter 5:8).

Jesus, our Hero, Savior and Deliverer, said, "The thief [devil] cometh not, but for to steal, and to kill, and to destroy: I am come that they might have life, and that they might have it more abundantly" (John 10:10).

Jesus, who is "Earth's mightiest hero," came down from heaven to rescue us from the hands of the evil villain, satan. We did not find God; He found us, through Christ, and rescued us.

Galatians 3:13 (NLT) says, "But Christ has rescued us from the curse pronounced by the law. When he was hung on the cross, he took upon himself the curse for our wrongdoing.

For it is written in the Scriptures, Cursed is everyone who is hung on a tree."

Christ who is the Prince of Peace came and rescued us–the "damsels in distress"–from the dungeon of our arch nemesis. All mankind was held in a dungeon, unable to free themselves, from satan's stronghold and death's eternal grip.

> *That is why the Scriptures say, When he ascended to the heights, he led a crowd of captives and gave gifts to His people. Notice that it says he ascended. This clearly means that Christ also descended to our lowly world. And the same one who descended is the one who ascended higher than all the heavens, so that he might fill the entire universe with himself (Ephesians 4:8-10, NLT).*

Christ went down into the kingdom of darkness and released all who were in Christ. He came to free those who were dead and those who were alive from the captivity of satan.

The events of our love story are being written each day of our lives. Each day represents a new chapter in our lives. In addition, each day represents the opportunity to choose between the hero and villain. Our choice, of who we will love, is contingent upon who we choose to obey.

Jesus said, "Whoever has my commands and obeys them, he is the one who loves me. He who loves me will be loved by my Father, and I too will love him and show myself to him" (John 14:21, NKJV).

Obedience is the demonstration of love. The Apostle Paul said, "Don't you realize that you become the slave of whatever you choose to obey? You can be a slave to sin, which leads to death, or you can choose to obey God, which leads to righteous living" (Romans 6:16, NIV).

We are all romantically in love with something; rather it is with God and not the things of this world. The Apostle John said, "Love not the world, neither the things that are in the world. If any man love the world, the love of the Father is not in him" (1 John 2:15).

Life is designed to be a love story between you and God. However, satan wants deliberately to break up that relationship. His sole purpose and desire is to keep man in sin. Satan knows that sin will keep us away from God and God away from us. The Bible declares, "But your iniquities have separated between you and your God, and your sins have hid his face from you, that he will not hear" (Isaiah 59:2).

Satan does not want you to be with God and he does not want God to be with you. Satan wanted God to give us a "certificate of divorce" and to declare eternal separation. Instead, Jesus graciously volunteered to be our "marriage counselor," intermediary, and liaison between God and man. First Timothy 2:5 says, "For there is one God, and one mediator between God and men, the man Christ Jesus." Jesus bridged the gap and separation that held both God and man at bay.

As the man in the love ballad, quoted earlier, cries out to his lover, Jesus also cries to us, saying, "I just want to be your everything, open up the heaven in your heart and let me be, the things you are to me and not some puppet on a string..."

The song continues, "...Open up the heaven in your heart..." Until we can physically be with God, He sees our heart as "heaven," the place where He can dwell with us. The Word of God declares that God desires to dwell in our hearts. Ephesians 3:16-17 (NLT) says, "I pray that from his glorious, unlimited resources he will empower you with inner strength through his Spirit. Then Christ will make His home in your hearts as you trust in him. Your roots will grow down into God's love and keep you strong."

God lives in the realm of eternity. However, in order to live in our hearts, He has placed eternity in our hearts. The Bible says "...He [God] has put eternity into man's heart..." (Ecclesiastes 3:11, NKJV).

God wants us to love Him as He loves us. However, we must choose to love Him. God has given us free choice. We were created with free will. We are not "some puppet on a string."

Inversely, God is not "some puppet on a string" that we can demand or control His behaviors and actions at whim.

Based upon many of the contemporary and popular sermons on television and in the media, one would think God is simply an inanimate "treasure chest" filled with money, gold, and silver. If that is the case, then we can be viewed simply as "gold-diggers" seeking God only for money or what we can get out of Him. Notwithstanding, God must be viewed holistically.

If there are any "puppets on a string," it is us. Quoting prosperity Scriptures from the Bible is not going to get us wealth and prosperity, if there is no obedience and love in the relationship between you and God.

In the time of the prophet Samuel and Israel's rebellion against God, the children of Israel thought that they could win the battle against the army of the Philistine by fetching the Ark of the Covenant from Shiloh. They were certain that having the Ark would guarantee them victory.

The Israelites thought that they would use the Ark of the Covenant as a "rabbit's foot" or "good luck charm." They were highly mistaken. Thirty thousand Israelites were killed and the Ark of the Covenant fell into the hands of the Philistines, Israel's enemies (1 Samuel 4:4-10).

During the time of the prophet Isaiah, the children of Israel tried a similar tactic through words, but heartless worship. God rebuked them and said, "...These people come near to me with their mouth and honor me with their lips, but their hearts are far from me. Their worship of me is made up only of rules taught by men" (Isaiah 29:13, NIV).

The children of Israel learned that God is not some "magic charm" that they could use when needed, and place back on a shelf after use. It is a lesson we need to learn today. We must not insult God's intelligence through tactics of manipulation, trickery, craftiness, cunning, and short-cut maneuvers.

The truth of the matter is God wants to be "our everything," not "our something." Often times, we unknowingly place God in a separate category in our lives. When we need Him, we'll call Him. Other than that, He is separate from our lives. Our behavior often reflects that we want God to perform only certain isolated tasks. Other than that, He is not invited or welcomed in other area of our lives.

The reason the Bible says that David was loved my God is because God was truly "his everything." David serenaded God as if God was his lover. First Samuel 13:14 (NASB) says, "...The Lord has sought out for Himself a man after His own heart, and the Lord has appointed him as ruler over His people..." David was a man who sought after the heart of God; he pursued and tugged on the heart-strings of God.

David wrote in Psalms 27:4, "One thing have I desired of the Lord, that will I seek after; that I may dwell in the house [presence] of the Lord all the days of my life, to behold the beauty of the Lord, and to inquire in his temple."

If there's anything two lovers want is to be in each other's presence. Being together takes precedent over money, houses, and land. It's not about the money and wealth with God; it's about love and relationship.

With David, it was all about intimacy. God's presence was intoxicating to David; He was David's addiction. David was addicted to Love. David expressed his love for God through praise and worship. Our praise and worship to God represents intimacy. Our intimacy with God is not one-sided; He shares in our intimacy with Him. Psalms 22:3 says, "But thou art holy, O thou that inhabitest the praises of [His people] Israel. When we get intimate with God, He gets intimate with us.

We often try many tactics in an attempt to get to God's heart. But the only way to get to God, who is love, is through love. Love is the key. First Corinthians 13:13 (NLT) says, "Three things will last forever–faith, hope, and love–and the greatest of these is love." If you want to seek God, seek His love. Love responds to Love.

The love song above says, "If we give a little more...your love will turn the key." Jesus echoes the same sentiments saying, "Can you love me just a little more?" It is our love for God that turns the key and unlocks the vault to the promises of God. Have you ever pray this simple prayer? "Lord, teach me how to draw closer to you. I want to love you more each day. Show me the path of your love."

The Word of God teaches us the secret to a successful, blessed, and Spirit-filled life. That is to love God. Jesus said, "...Thou shalt love the Lord thy God with all thy heart, and with all thy soul, and with all thy mind. This is the first and great commandment" (Matthew 22:37-38).

We are commanded to love God. Obedience to the commandment of love creates the key to prosperity. Psalms 84:11 says, "For the Lord God is a sun and shield: the Lord will give grace and glory: no good thing will he withhold from them that walk uprightly."

The key to prosperity is in who you love. There a popular cliché which says, "It's not what you know, but who you know." Christ loved us so much that he gave His life for us. Listen, you can give without loving, but you can't love without giving. God is love (1 John 4:8). Christ freely gave us His life. When we freely give our life to Him, we are expressing our love toward Him.

We were created to have fellowship with God. We are joined together with Christ. Jesus said, "I am the vine, ye are the branches: He that abideth in me, and I in him, the same bringeth forth much fruit: for without me ye can do nothing" (John 15:5). We cannot live without God. Acts 17:28 (NLT) says, "For in him we live and move and exist."

God has invested everything in the life of man. God sees us as His most prized possessions and treasures. God said in Malachi 3:17, "And they shall be mine, saith the Lord of hosts, in that day when I make up my jewels..."

The song by Andy Gibbs quoted earlier continues saying, "Darling mine, I would wait forever for those lips of wine." God also sees us as His "darlings." Not only did David know of the love of God, he taught his son Solomon to love God.

The Song of Solomon are dedications to the intimacy of God's love. Song of Solomon 1:2 (NLT) says, "Kiss me and kiss me again, for your love is sweeter than wine."

Love doesn't see the bad only the good. Song of Solomon 4:7 (NIV) says, "All beautiful you are, my darling; there is no flaw in you." Although we have sinned, because of Christ, God sees no fault in us. Second Corinthians 5:21 says, "For he hath made him to be sin for us, who knew no sin; that we might be made the righteousness of God in him."

Christ built His world around us. Jesus said, "...Upon this rock [the confession that Jesus is the Messiah] I will build my church (the people of God); and the gates of hell shall not prevail against it."

Man is the focal point of God's divine designs, plans, and thoughts. God said, "I will make my home among them. I will be their God, and they will be my people" (Ezekiel 37:27, NLT).

Christ built His entire life and Kingdom around man. Job said in Job 7:17-18 (ESV), "What is man, that you make so much of him, and that you set your heart on him visit him every morning and test him every moment?"

The feelings that God has for us is strong. Romans 8:32 says, "He that spared not his own Son, but delivered him up for us all, how shall he not with him also freely give us all things?" God sacrificed His only begotten son for us. What unimaginable love!

In fact, the cross is not just a symbol of death, but love. The cross is a sign and symbol of love. The cross has horizontal and vertical lines that stretch in all four directions: North, south, east, and west. This means that the cross has the power to touch and embrace, the souls of man, from eternity past to eternity future. The cross represents God's love which has been extended to man throughout eternity.

God, our bridegroom, is in heaven. We, His bride, are on the earth. Although we are currently experiencing a love romance with God from a distance, soon God will come for His bride. Jesus said, "...I go and prepare a place for you, I will come again, and receive you unto myself; that where I am, there ye may be also" (John14:3). Can you stay faithful, true, and chaste to God until He returns?

God is worthy and deserves to be "our everything." He has done "everything to be our everything." There's a song that says, "What more can he do, what more can Jesus do, well he done laid the foundation, open up the way, what more can he do!"[2] Does your life reveal that Jesus is your everything?

Your life represents a love story. A love story can have a tragic ending or a happy ending. How it ends depends on who you choose as your lover, bridegroom, and eternal soul mate. Will you choose the one who broke up the relationship you had with God in the beginning? Or will you choose the One who chose you before the world began?

The Bible says God chose us before the world began. Ephesians 1:4 says, "According as he has chosen us in him before the foundation of the world, that we should be holy and without blame before him in love."

Salvation is the greatest love story created and written in the universe. Could it be that God decided to create the greatest love story of all times? Tina Turner sings a song which says, "What's love got to do with it?"[3] Love has everything to do with it! It was love that brought us back in right standing and fellowship with God.

We are born of God through love. First John 4:7 says, "Beloved, let us love one another: for love is of God; and every one that loveth is born of God, and knoweth God." Love enables us to live a new life in Christ.

A new life is a Spirit-filled life in the fourth dimension. The fourth dimension is the spiritual dimension where perfect love, peace, and hope reside. It is a realm where the love of God is shared abroad in our hearts (Romans 5:5). Come and experience a new way of living where Christ is "your everything," found only in the fourth dimension.

Endnotes:

1. Gibb, Barry. "I Just Want to Be Your Everything." RSO Records, 1977.

2. Author unknown. "What More Can He Do?"

3. Britten, Terry & Graham Lyle. "What's Love Got to Do With It?" Capitol Records, 1984.

Heavenly Father

Heavenly Father, greatness is found in You,

Everyday our benefits are renewed;

Great is Thy faithfulness,

Mercy is Thy gracefulness;

Love is Thy middle name,

Salvation lives in every vein;

Father, mere words cannot express,

The perfection of Your Holiness;

Thankful and grateful are our ways,

Honor and respect end our days;

Seek and You shall find,

All of You is in our minds.

CHAPTER 39

The Fourth Man

Growing up as a child boy in elementary school, I always liked to be the first in line. It was cool that everyone else followed behind and after me. The world places a great deal of emphasis on being first. We learn at an early age that being first place in finishing a race or completing a competition always brings fame and glory to the victor. However, God did not always see "being first" as the best or the greatest. In fact, Jesus said the first shall be last and the last shall be first (Matthew 20:16). God often places the greatest emphasis on the last, instead of the first. In God's eyes, it's the last man that is to be honored.

King Nebuchadnezzar would learn something about the last man, which he called the fourth man, in his attempt to execute the three Hebrew boys for failing to bow down to his golden image.

In Daniel chapter 3, the three Hebrew boys were tied up and thrown in the fiery furnace after refusing to bow down to the golden image upon the request of King Nebuchadnezzar. The Hebrews boy refused to compromise in their worship to God.

When you will not allow anything to minimize your commitment, devotion, and allegiance to God, He will stand with you in midst of whatever you are going through. Never think you are standing alone when you stand up for Christ. There are more with us than against us. The Bible says, "…If God be for us, who can be against us?" (Romans 8:31).

When Stephen stood up in the face of persecution and death, Jesus stood up with him from His eternal and glorious throne in glory. Christ allowed Stephen to see Him stand as Stephen stood up in the face of death for the gospel of Jesus Christ.

The Bible says in Acts 7:54-60,

> When they heard these things, they were cut to the heart, and they gnashed on him [Stephen] with their teeth. But he, being full of the Holy Ghost, looked up stedfastly into heaven, and saw the glory of God, and Jesus standing on the right hand of God. And said, Behold, I see the heavens opened, and the Son of man standing on the right hand of God. Then they cried out with a loud voice, and stopped their ears, and ran upon him with one accord. And cast him out of the city, and stoned him and the witnesses laid down their clothes at a young man's feet, whose name was Saul. And they stoned Stephen, calling upon God, and saying Lord Jesus, receive my spirit. And he kneeled down, and cried with a loud voice, Lord, lay not this sin to their charge. And when he had said this, fell asleep.

When we stand and not bow, Christ stands with us. The three Hebrew boys did not bow so then they could not burn. The Bible does not say that the fire had no power; it said that the fire had no power over the three Hebrew boys (Daniel 3:27). The fire still had power to burn, destroy, and annihilate. The Hebrew boys were immune to the fire and its crippling effects. They became fireproof.

Hebrew boys were thrown into a living hell. The Bible says the furnace was heated up seven times higher (Daniel 3:19) than normal. Sometimes the devil will turn up the heat in our lives. Excessive heat will determine what we are truly made up. There's an old saying which says, "If you can't stand the heat, get out of the kitchen."

Trials are never meant to destroy us, but to strength us. Whatever we go through, we become immune to it. In other words, what should have killed you, will made you stronger. Like the mighty men who threw the Hebrew boys in the fire, what killed other people will strengthen you (Daniel 3:20).

As the king looked on, the Bible says:

> Then Nebuchadnezzar the king was astonied, and rose up in haste, and spake, and said unto his counselors, Did not we cast three men bound into the midst of the fire? They answered and said unto the king, True, O king. He answered and said, Lo, I see four men loose, walking in the midst of the fire, and they have no hurt; and the form of the fourth is like the Son of God" (Daniel 3:24-25).

King Nebuchadnezzar was amazed at the three Hebrew boys who continued to live and thrive while in the midst of a fiery furnace. However, what truly amazed the king the most wasn't the three Hebrew boys, but the fourth man. King Nebuchadnezzar came face to face with the true king, King Jesus. Jesus is the only King who is omnipotent [all-powerful], omniscience [all-knowing], and omnipresent [present everywhere at the same time].

King Nebuchadnezzar found out that there is a King who is not only invincible and indestructible, but has the power to protect those who serve and worship him from all harm, including the fiery furnace.

As long as the fourth man was in the fire, nothing could harm the three Hebrew boys. God said in Isaiah 43:2, "When thou passest through the waters, I will be with thee; and through the rivers, they shall not overflow thee: when thou walkest through the fire, thou shalt not be burned; neither shall the flame kindle upon thee."

As long as we have the presence of the fourth man in our lives nothing can harm us. The disciples witness firsthand the power of Christ, the fourth man, in the Gospel of Mark. Mark 4:37-41 (NLT) says,

Jesus was sleeping at the back of the boat with his head on a cushion. But soon a fierce storm came up. High waves were breaking into the boat, and it began to fill with water. The disciples woke him up, shouting, Teacher, don't you care that we're going to drown? When Jesus woke up, he rebuked the wind and said to the waves, Silence! Be still! Suddenly the wind stopped, and there was a great calm. Then he asked them, Why are you afraid? Do you still have no faith? The disciples were absolutely terrified. Who is this man? they asked each other. Even the wind and waves obey him!

Jesus was not only teaching them about power of faith, He was also teaching the disciples to know, without a shadow of a doubt, that if He was present with them nothing could harm them.

It's the presence of God which makes the difference. Moses knew the significance and the power of God's presence. Moses prayed to God saying, "...If your presence is not going [with us], don't make us leave this place (Exodus 33:15, GW).

Just as Jesus spoke to the wind and the sea, I believe Jesus spoke to the fire before the Hebrew children entered into the fire and said, "Fire, do no harm to my servants." Please understand that God did not cool the fiery flames or the fire as some has said, suggested, or reasoned. In fact, the Bible tells us the fire was extremely hot. Daniel 3:20, 22 says,

And he [Nebuchadnezzar] commanded the most mighty men that were in his army to bind Shadrach, Meshach, and Abednego, and to cast them into the burning fiery furnace. Therefore because the king's commandment was urgent, and the furnace exceeding hot, the flame of the fire slew those men that took up Shadrach, Meshach, and Abednego.

These two Scriptures let us know that God did not cool the flames, for if He had, the mighty men of King

Nebuchadnezzar would not have died. Something else is at play here. It is apparent that the fire is selective in what and who it would hurt or burn up. Yes, God can speak to nature and the natural elements [fire, water, earth, and wind] and they will obey Him.

Because of God's presence in the life of the three Hebrews boys, no weapon formed against them would prosper (Isaiah 54:17). Listen, you don't need a million dollars or to know people of influence to be blessed and prosper, all you need is God's presence with you.

The Bible says that when Joseph was sold into slavery that God was with him. Genesis 39:1-2 says, "And Joseph was brought down to Egypt; and Potiphar, and officer of Pharaoh, a captain of the guard, an Egyptian, bought him of the hands of the Ishmeelites , which had brought him down thither. And the Lord was with Joseph, and he was a prosperous man..."

Now, Joseph wasn't prosperous because he had money, influence, status, or fame in Egypt. Joseph was a slave having no rights or privileges. He was prosperous because God was with him. In other words, godly prosperity is not defined by monetary value, economic worth, or earthly possession, but by the presence of God.

Regardless of what happened in Joseph's past, because God was with him, his life would never be the same again. When God is with you, look out, your life will never be ordinary or the status quo. Do not look or expect to have a meager human existence when God is with you. Your life will forever change. When God is with you, life will be never ordinary, but extraordinary. Is God with you?

Moreover, God's presence will always bring you into the presence of great men. Because God was with Joseph, Joseph had a date with Pharaoh, the most powerful man on the face of the earth. Genesis 41:14-15 says,

> *Then Pharaoh sent and called Joseph, and they brought him hastily out of the dungeon: and he shaved himself, and changed his raiment, and came in unto Pharaoh. And Pharaoh said unto Joseph, I have*

dreamed a dream, and there is none that can interpret it: and I have heard say of thee, that thou canst understand a dream to interpret it.

When God's presence is with you, you don't have to contact or try to "rub shoulders" with great men. Great men will contact you! Because God's presence was with Joseph, Pharaoh made contact with Joseph, instead of Joseph contacting Pharaoh. God's presence enabled Joseph to interpret Pharaoh's dreams to the minutest and microscopic detail, perfectly without the slightest margin of error (Genesis 41:25-32).

The interpretation of dreams was God's gift to Joseph. The Bible says, "A gift opens doors for the one who gives it and brings him into the presence of great people" (Proverb 18:16, GW). If God is with you, you have a destiny with greatness!

The presence of God is the key which opens the door to success and victory. God's presence is more valuable than silver and gold. King David continually sought after the presence of God. David said, "...I had rather be a doorkeeper in the house of my God, than to dwell in the tents of wickedness" (Psalms 84:10).

The three Hebrew boys met the manifest presence of God, the Son, in the fire. King Nebuchadnezzar noticed that the presence of the fourth man was not the presence of a mortal [natural] man (Daniel 3:25). The glory of this fourth man superseded the effects that resonated from natural fire. The presence of the fourth man illuminated through the fiery furnace.

The fourth man stood out above the rest of the men in the fire. His presence was no doubt more bright and brilliant than the fiery fire itself. In fact, there was a staunch difference between the fourth man and the other three men. King Nebuchadnezzar described the fourth man as looking, not like an angel, but the Son of God (Daniel 3:25).

In fact, Jesus is at home in the fire. The Bible says that God is a consuming fire (Hebrews 12:29). The hotter the fire, the more comfortable God is. The greater the heat of adversity and situation in your life is when God is at His best.

Oftentimes, the place we will encounter the supernatural presence and the glory of God is in the "fire" of life. We will often experience the miraculous and supernatural move of God during our greatest adversity.

The Bible says that the four men were walking in the fire (Daniel 3:35). "Walking" in the fire represents victory over the circumstances. We must continue to walk in faith above our situations, for we walk by faith and not by sight (2 Corinthians 5:7).

Our faith gives us the victory. First John 5:4 says, "For whatsoever is born of God overcometh the world: and this is the victory that overcometh the world, even our faith."

Don't allow your circumstances to walk over you. Our faith can walk on any situation. You can walk on any circumstance. If Peter can walk on the tumultuous waters, induced by contrary and adversarial winds on the Sea of Galilee, based on the Word of God, we, too, can walk on the trials of life which try to engulf us!

King Nebuchadnezzar found that there was a power greater and above anything known on planet Earth. God was letting the king know that he could not fight against or destroy what He has blessed and anointed. God's anointed was with the three Hebrew boys. Instead of persecuting the Hebrew boys any further, king Nebuchadnezzar blessed and honored them (Daniel 3:28-30). Wise decision!

The more God's people are persecuted by the enemy, the more God will show up. The more the enemy turns the heat up, the more God will manifest His power, presence, and glory. The number "4" denotes the revelation of God namely His creative works and manifestation. It was the fourth man that set the three Hebrew boys' bands loose; it wasn't the fire that burned up the bands from their hands and feet. It was Jesus the Son of God who set them free. The Bible says, in John 8:36, "If the Son therefore shall make you free, you shall be free indeed."

A man counted as "fourth" does not mean much in today's society. We only acknowledge those who come in first or among the top three. In Olympic completion, we often acknowledge and honor those who win first place, second place, and third place. First place recipients receive a gold medal. Second place receives the silver. Third place receives the bronze. The fourth place man receives nothing.

The newspapers and media headlines do not honor or acknowledge those who came in fourth place. The record books do not list the names of those who placed fourth in their competitions.

Likewise Jesus, who is the God of all creation, came to Earth with no reputation. The Bible says He gave Himself no reputation and took on the form of a servant. Instead of praise and exaltation, He was scorned and ridiculed (Philippians 2:7).

When Jesus was born into the world, there was no ticker-tape parade in the streets of Jerusalem honoring His birth and arrival on planet Earth. In fact, no one even noticed His arrival, prophesied in the book of Isaiah, until foreigners from the east came in search of Him.

Don't worry if you ever become a millionaire or that your name never appears on the Fortune 500 most successful list of the world's influential, wealthy, and prestigious individuals. You don't have to be ranked number one by man to be first in the Kingdom of God (Matthew 18:4).

It doesn't matter where you start in life or where people say you rank or belong. Maybe you were born in poverty, squalor, and obscurity. Maybe people have counted you out as being last or irrelevant. The good news is God doesn't count like man.

Two of America's most popular and beloved [pastime] sports are basketball and football. In basketball and football, the fourth quarter is the signature, critical, and most significant quarter. It doesn't matter how poor an opponent scored in the first three quarters. The fourth quarter determines who will experience victory or defeat.

You may have opened out of the starting gate of life at a slow crawl. You may have been told that your fate is sealed and you will never amount to anything. However, God determines our fate and future not man. Your life is not over until God says it's over.

God often waits until the fourth quarter to do His work. How do you know you are in the fourth quarter? When all seems lost and you are in a state or place of no return–welcome to the fourth quarter!

God loves a good comeback! The fourth quarter represents the final round. Because you waited on God, God will give you strength and power to run the fourth quarter with supernatural might and fortitude. Isaiah said, "But they that wait upon the Lord shall renew their strength they shall mount up with wings as eagles; they shall run and not be weary; and they shall walk and not faint" (Isaiah 40:31).

We are in the fourth quarter, the last and final quarter of the end times. However, we can take comfort to know that the "fourth man" is here with us. There may be fiery trials ahead; however, like the Hebrew boys, Christ will meet us at our greatest need. Only by standing in faith and commitment with the "fourth man", Jesus Christ, can we declare victory and triumph in the fourth dimension.

Heavenly Father

Heavenly Father, the Holy Spirit has Your eyes and the spiritual

eyes of man,

He sees the supernatural and He knows what's in Your hands;

He is our Helper, our Companion and our Friend,

We know Him because we feel Him within;

Father, Jesus Christ is the Lover of our souls,

His life is the life all men must hold;

Thank You for sharing all of You,

Father, Son, and Holy Spirit of Truth.

CHAPTER 40

Tomorrow

In 1982, Aileen Quinn played as a little orphan named, Annie (also the name of the movie). **Annie** has become a classic film and Broadway hit musical. The movie depicts a little orphan singing the legendary song, "Tomorrow."[1] In the play, Annie sings the chorus saying: *"...The sun will come out tomorrow, so ya gotta hang on 'til tomorrow, come what may. Tomorrow! Tomorrow! I love ya tomorrow! You're always a day away! Tomorrow! Tomorrow! I love ya tomorrow! You're always a day away!"*

The song encourages one not to give up. Even when things get tough, we must press on. There's an old idiom which says, "Troubles don't last always." Although tomorrow is not guaranteed to anyone, God has promised better days for those who love Him.

No one wants to experience struggles or troubles. However, struggles and troubles are an integral part of life. Job 5:7 says, "...Man is born unto trouble, as the sparks fly upward." This verse from the book of Job lets us know that we don't have to look for trouble to experience it, trouble will inevitably find us.

Although life's struggle may not be unavoidable, God often uses our struggles to strengthen, bless, and enrich our lives. The Apostle James admonishes us not to run from adverse circumstances, but to embrace them as a disciple of Jesus Christ. James 1:2-4 (NLT) says,

Dear brothers and sisters, when troubles come your way, consider it an opportunity for great joy. For you know that when your faith is tested, your endurance has a chance to grow. So let it grow, for when your endurance is fully developed, you will be perfect and complete, needing nothing.

When we face difficulties in life we must not focus all our attention on the experience, but on what the outcome from the experience will bring. However, often times our attitude during times of affliction and distress are just the opposite of what the Apostle James exhorts. James encourages us to "count it all joy." Our attitude is often that of sadness and sorrow when experiencing divers temptations. The Apostle James realized and knew that we cannot be strengthened without the struggle.

To try to have strength without resistance and struggle, is like asking God for rain without the thunder and lightning. Every promotion and elevation in God requires a test of adversity. When you ask God to empower you with His anointing, He will take you through resistance training. Asking God for His anointing in the absence of experiencing the forces of resistance is like praying for a harvest without plowing up the soil and planting the seed.

Your yesterday and today may have been filled with unavoidable struggles, but tomorrow you will be stronger after going through it. You will be stronger after the sickness. You will be stronger after the bankruptcy. You will be stronger after the divorce.

There's a strength that can only come through struggle. God has not forsaken you. He is not trying to kill or destroy you. He knows what we do not often realize which is: trials come to make us strong. The Apostle Peter teaches us "That the trial of your faith, being much more precious than of gold that perisheth, though it be tried with fire, might be found unto praise and honour and glory at the appearing of Jesus Christ" (1 Peter 1:7). Our trials and struggles strengthen us; they do not weaken us. You cannot have strength without the weight of resistance.

When adversarial winds blow in your life, God will use those adverse winds to provide you with lift and thrust. In order for a plane to take off, it must have enough force acting upon it to compensate for its own weight. Sometimes the enemy will create forces on every side. God will, in turn, use these adversarial forces the same way that an air plane obtains flight. The four aerodynamic forces that act upon an airplane are lift, weight/gravity, thrust, and drag. Lift is an upward acting force. Weight/gravity is a downward acting force. Thrust is a forward acting force. Drag is a backward acting force. These four forces are simultaneously acting against the airplane which gives it flight.

Like an airplane, you may feel like you are experiencing oppositional forces on every side. However, God is actually elevating you during this process. When contrary winds are hitting you on every side, God is lifting and thrusting you to a higher dimension. You will ascend to heights unknown and beyond your expectations.

Unknown to Joseph, but being placed in a pit, sold into slavery, accused of attempted rape, and jailed for a crime he didn't commit was the process God used to elevate Joseph. God used the contrarian winds in Joseph's life to sky rocket and airlift him from a foreign slave prisoner to prime minister of Egypt.

Another simple illustration of elevation can be seen in the case of a kite. A kite cannot take flight into the air and soar until contrary and adverse winds blow against it. Winds must blow in opposing directions before a kite receives lift and thrust.

As believers of Christ, the struggles of life create the aerodynamic ability of flight. God said in Isaiah 40:31 (NLT), "But those who trust in the Lord will find new strength. They will soar high on wings like eagles. They will run and not grow weary. They will walk and not faint."

You will be lifted up by the very winds which tried to keep you down. God uses adversity in order for us to fly on wings as an eagle. Soaring high is not just for the birds and eagles. It's time for us to fly like the eagles.

If you never experience adverse winds, you can never soar with the eagles. Furthermore if you have never encountered the imposing forces of evil, it may be because you and the adversary are moving in the same direction.

Amos 3:3 (NLT) says, "Can two people walk together without agreeing on the direction?" You can't feel much wind resistance when you are going in the same direction as the wind.

When you are moving in the opposite direction of wind, you can feel resistance. Adversarial kingdoms move in opposing directions. When you are in God's Kingdom, you will come in conflict with satan's kingdom. Jesus said, "...The Kingdom of Heaven has been forcefully advancing, and violent people are attacking it" (Matthew 11:12, NLT). Every believer of Christ will experience demonic opposition.

The good news is God has promised to turn our dark moments into brighter days. The Bible says, "For his anger lasts only a moment, but his favor lasts a lifetime! Weeping may last through the night, but joy comes with the morning" (Psalms 30:5, NLT).

You may be down and out today, but tomorrow's coming! Just because someone is down today, tomorrow can be an entirely different story.

Your life consists of three major parts: past, present, and future. Don't believe that there are only two parts–your past and present. You still have another major part of your life that you have yet to experience and enjoy–your future.

Your past has already been written; you can't change it or delete it. Your present is being written today. But your future tomorrow has yet to be written. What will your future tomorrow look like? It does not have to end in defeat.

In fact, your future has three versions: a version written by satan, a version written by you, and a version written by God. Yes, satan has a plan for your future, as well. Satan's plan leads to your death and destruction. Psalms 9:17 says, "The wicked [those who do not follow God's plan] shall be turned into hell, and all the nations that forget God."

Man has a plan for his life as well but it, too, leads to death. Proverbs 14:12 says, "There is a way which seemeth right unto a man, but the end thereof are the ways of death." Only

God's plan gives life. God's plan is reliable, trustworthy, verifiable, and perfect for your life.

God's plan leads to prosperity and a bright future. God declared in Jeremiah 29:11 (NIV), "For I know the plans I have for you, declares the Lord, plans to prosper you and not to harm you, plans to give you hope and a future." Which future plan of tomorrow will you choose? Only you can decide what it will be. The choice is yours!

You may presently be in a horrific situation in your life with no hope for tomorrow. However, "tomorrow" is speaking to you. Yes, tomorrow has a voice. It is the voice of the Holy Spirit. He says," Don't give up. I am only a day away." Tomorrow says, "Your story does not have to end in tragedy." You can change the outcome of your life by looking on toward tomorrow.

Hebrews 12:2 says, "Looking unto Jesus the author and finisher of our faith..." Jesus stands at the door of our tomorrow. When we come to the door of our tomorrow, we will see that tomorrow is not just a time or a chronological event, but a person. In John chapter 11, Jesus reveals to Martha that what she was hoping in a distant tomorrow was standing right there in front of her.

Martha said to Jesus, "...I know that he [Lazarus] shall rise again in the resurrection at the last day. Jesus said to her, I am the resurrection, and the life..." (John 11:24-25). Jesus makes it clear to Martha [and to us] that He is the "time of the resurrection." Jesus represents tomorrows and all future events. Martha's hope for tomorrow was in the person of Jesus Christ. Her tomorrow was right there in her today. Our tomorrows are in Jesus.

Don't underestimate the power and glory of tomorrow. In a time when the nation of Israel had converted to cannibalism to survive the besiegement of the Syrians, Elisha responded saying, "...Listen to the word of the Lord! This is what the Lord says: About this time tomorrow 24 cups of the best flour will sell for half an ounce of silver in the gateway to Samaria. And 48 cups of barley will sell for half an ounce of silver" (2 Kings 7:1, GW).

The prophet Elisha declared a time of great prosperity in a time of great poverty and misery. The prophet Elisha teaches us that it does not matter how devastating our present or past has been, tomorrow can change everything. The solution to your problem is in your tomorrow.

The Bible says, "It happened exactly as the man of God told the king, 48 cups of barley will sell for half an ounce of silver. And 24 cups of the best flour will sell for half an ounce of silver. This will happen about this time tomorrow in the gateway to Samaria" (2 King 7:18, GW).

Your future tomorrow may be unknown to you, but it is well-known to God. God has a plan and purpose for your tomorrow. Isaiah 14:27 says, "For the Lord of hosts hath purposed, and who shall disannul it?"

No one can stop God's future plans for your life. Nothing you have done or haven't done can cancel what God has planned for you. God has already taken into account all the enemy's attacks that are set up against you. Every negative circumstance and setback in your life has already been figured into the equation of victory. What God has purposed in your future tomorrow will come to pass!

God is bigger than any adversity. He is bigger than any trial. He is bigger than any foe. God is bigger than any bankruptcy. He is bigger than any sickness. God is bigger than any injustice done unto you. He is bigger than any lie. He is bigger than any affliction. God is bigger than any misfortune you can experience. Isaiah 59:19 says, "...When the enemy shall come in like a flood, the Spirit of the Lord shall lift up a standard against him."

God has promised to never fail us. Hebrews 13:5 (NASB) says, "...He [God] Himself has said, "I will never desert you, nor will I ever forsake you" God will always be with us regardless of the prevailing circumstances we experience.

There are new levels and dimensions to our destiny. You have not touched the surface of what God has planned for your tomorrow. First Corinthians 2:9 says, "But, as it is written, "What no eye has seen, nor ear heard, nor the heart of man imagined, what God has prepared for those who love him." Your tomorrow is always brighter than your past and present.

The fight you are experiencing today is over your to-morrow, not your today. Satan is a long-term thinker; he thinks futuristically not just for the "here and now." We are experiencing difficulties from the enemy because of our future. Satan fears your future tomorrow, not your today. You are experiencing anxiety because of your present condition. Satan is experiencing anxiety over you future!

Many people fail to realize that they cannot die before they fulfill their divine purpose in the earth. Your divine purpose is as permanent and fixed as the law of gravity. The law of gravity states that what goes up must come down. It has not changed since the beginning of time. Gravity will be the same tomorrow as it is today. As you are alive today, you will be alive tomorrow until your purpose is completed.

However, satan will make you feel that today is the beginning of the end for you. Satan is a liar! The Bible declares in Psalms 118:17, "I shall not die, but live, and declare the works of the LORD."

You will be able to tell others about what God has done for you. This, in turn, will bring in more lost sheep into the Kingdom of God. The test you experienced and endured will result in a testimony thereby creating gain for the Kingdom of Light and loss for the kingdom of darkness.

Your blessed tomorrow creates a major opposition against satan's kingdom. Therefore, he already has or he will release the hounds of hell to oppose, hinder, and discourage you from reaching your divine purpose and destiny in the earth. Many of God's people, in recent years, have experienced an all-out-attack from the devil. He has thrown everything he could against you and your family, including the kitchen sink! Nevertheless, you have withstood every attack.

The Word of God teaches us to stand in the midst of opposition and adversity. Ephesians 6:13 says, "Wherefore take unto you the whole armour of God, that ye may be able to withstand in the evil day, and having done all, to stand. Stand therefore..."

Every person's divine purpose of God in the earth creates havoc and destruction upon the kingdom of darkness. If you are not building up the Kingdom of God, you are in opposition to the Kingdom of God. Jesus said in Matthew 12:30 (NLT), "Anyone who isn't with me opposes me, and anyone who isn't working with me is actually working against me." Are you going to fulfill your divine purpose in the earth against the devil or fulfilling your own purpose?

Satan has existed for eons. He knows what we often don't know. His experience concerning the future is far more knowledgeable and mature than ours. We exist for a few years; satan has existed from eternity past.

Satan's eyes are on your future tomorrow, where are your eyes? In the past? In the present? We must look beyond on our past and present and see our glorious future. The Apostle Paul encourages us to look past our present condition and see a future tomorrow which only God could create.

Paul said in Romans 8:18, "For I reckon that the sufferings of this present time are not worthy to be compared with the glory which shall be revealed in us." Paul admonishes us that nothing in our past will compare to the glory of our tomorrow.

The enemy's plan is all about the future, not just today. The enemy knows it's not about today, but tomorrow. The enemy will have us so fixated, depressed, and overwhelmed on what happened yesterday or today that we cannot use our eyes of faith on the promises of God for tomorrow.

You cannot steer and advance forward looking backwards. Moreover, you cannot move and travel toward your next divine destination with your eyes fixed looking through the rear view mirror, in the vehicle of life. The past is called the past for a reason. The past is not your present or your future. There's absolutely nothing we can do about the past. Past failures are like spilled milk. God has wiped up the spilled milk [past failures] off the floor. In other words, He has forgiven you. Now move on!

Notwithstanding, we cannot even rely on our past good deeds as a substitute or excuse for not living righteous and holy today. The Apostle Paul said in Galatians 5:7 (NLT), "You were running the race so well. Who has held you back from following the truth?"

Today is the day of salvation not yesterday or the past. Second Corinthians 6:2 (NLT) says, "...Indeed, the 'right time' is now. Today is the day of salvation."

Don't rely on your past successes to advance you toward your divine destiny. Your past is the past. It is not your present or future. When Jesus raptures the church, He will be looking for those who are ready to enter into the marriage–not those who were ready yesterday. That was the difference between the five wise and the five foolish virgins. Five were ready when the bridegroom came and five were not (Matthew 25:1-13). The foolish were ready the day before, but were not ready when the bridegroom came. Don't be foolish by living in the past and being unprepared for the present and future.

Moreover, the five foolish virgins tried to borrow oil from the five wise virgins. Matthew 25: 8-9 says, "...The foolish said unto the wise, Give us of your oil; for our lamps are gone out. But the wise answered, saying, Not so; lest there be not enough for us and you: but go ye gather to them that sell, and buy for yourselves."

The prepared virgins were wise enough to know that one cannot depend on another to inherit the Kingdom of God. Every person must give an account for himself. We must work out our own salvation. Philippians 2:12 says, "...Work out your own salvation with fear and trembling." If Christ comes today, will you be ready?

Don't live in the past. Many people are currently living their present and future in the yester years. Their present has become tainted, contaminated, and cursed because they steadily focus on the disappointments and failures of the past.

We cannot mix the past with our future. You must draw a line between your past and your future tomorrow. You cannot put old wine in new bottles. Jesus said, "...No man putteth new wine into old bottles; else the new wine will burst the bottles, and be spilled, and the bottles shall perish. But new wine must be put into new bottles..." (Luke 5:37-38). Your past will contaminate your future, if you do not let go of the past.

It is the devil's desire to poison your future if you allow him to play the excerpts of your past on the movie screen of your mind. We must adapt a new way of thinking. We must have a newness of mind. Romans 12:2 (NLT) says, "...Let God transform you into a new person by changing the way you think. Then you will learn to know God's will for you, which is good and pleasing and perfect."

The first transformation of the mind is to know, without a shadow of a doubt, that you have been forgiven. The Word of God exhorts saying, "There is therefore now no condemnation to them which are in Christ Jesus..." (Romans 8:1). No one who is forgiven can be condemned.

We must forget our past, as it relates to our sins, which has been forgiven. God said in Hebrews 8:12 (NLT), "...I will forgive their wickedness, and I will never again remember their sins." If God can forget our sins, why can't we? God has thrown our sins in the sea of forgetfulness. Don't go fishing in the sea to pull up what God has thrown out!

You can't grow in Christ with a condemned mentality. The Apostle said in Philippians 3:13 (NLT), "...I focus on this one thing: Forgetting the past and looking forward to what lies ahead." People who live in the past never accomplish their goals, objectives, and assignments God has given them. This is one of satan's subtle techniques. Satan will try to use our past against us. If not vigilant and mindful, your past can rob you of the glorious future–tomorrow God has in store for you.

Your tomorrow is your future. You are only one day from your future. God is not through blessing you. Listen, you are a day away from your deliverance, healing, breakthrough, and prosperity. Your maximum of yesterdays will be your minimum of tomorrows. Your yesterday will pale in comparisons to your tomorrow.

A better tomorrow is not guaranteed to everyone. A brighter tomorrow and future is designed for those who humble themselves in obedience and submission to God. The Bible says, "Humble yourselves, therefore, under the mighty hand of God so that at the proper time he may exalt you, casting all your anxieties on him, because he cares for you" (1 Peter 5:6-7, ESV).

Your blessings are on tomorrow. We should be waiting with high expectations and sheer excitement about tomorrow. It is not the time to throw in the towel and quit because of the tribulations of the past. God is coming to deliver you tomorrow. Galatians 6:9 (NLT) says, "So let's not get tired of doing what is good. At just the right time we will reap a harvest of blessing if we don't give up."

It's high time to live for Christ for our redemption draweth nigh. Romans 13:11 says. "And that, knowing the time, that now it is high time to awake out of sleep: for now is our salvation nearer than when we believed."

Don't hold your head down in defeat. Look up! Jesus said, "...Look up, and lift up your heads; for your redemption draweth nigh" (Luke 21:28). Don't worry or fret your tomorrow will bring with it divine favor, healing, prosperity, deliverance, power, promotion, and breakthrough.

Listen, someday soon in our future tomorrow, there will be no more heart-aches, no tears, no pain, no sorrows, no grief, and no suffering. Christ has promised to wipe away every tear from our eyes on tomorrow. The Bible says, "He [Jesus] will wipe away every tear from their eyes, and death shall be no more, neither shall there be mourning, nor crying, nor pain anymore, for the former things have passed away" (Revelation 21:4, ESV).

As a fourth dimensional believer, use your faith. Get you some sunglasses and shades. You will need them because your tomorrow will be so bright. As the song from Annie goes, the sun will shine on tomorrow, so hang in there until tomorrow. There is always a brighter tomorrow for those who are heirs of God in the fourth dimension.

Endnotes:

1. Strouse, Charles & Martin Charnin. "Tomorrow." Edward H. Morris & Co. Inc.; Strouse Charles Publishers, 1976.

Heavenly Father

Heavenly Father, we want to be followers of Christ,

For in Him is the only way, the only truth and the only light;

Our souls long for that day,

When He returns and all sin is passed away;

His way is the way that we seek,

For He knows the voice of His sheep;

Father, the Holy Spirit has brought us thus far,

Blessing Your children from near and far;

Enjoying the journey as we go,

Guided by the power of the Holy Ghost;

In following the way of the cross,

Redeeming Your children, all that are lost.

CHAPTER 41

Guardian Angels

The fourth dimension was created by God before the creation of the universe. The fourth dimension is the realm of the eternal Kingdom of God and angelic beings. Before time, matter, and space ever existed, the heavenly realm stood alone in eternity, accompanied by angelic beings and supernatural creatures (Job 38:6-7).

Angels are mentioned and revealed throughout the entire Bible. In fact, angels are mentioned about 108 in the Old Testament and 165 times in the New Testament. They are agents of God. Just as the United States has federal agents, such as the FBI, heaven has heavenly agents called angels. These angelic beings, from eternity past, are the servants of the Lord. Angels are servants of God and of salvation.

The Bible says in Hebrews 1:14 (NLT), "But angels are only servants. They are spirits sent from God to care for those who will receive salvation." Angels guard and protect all who honor and reverence God. While others may become victims of the enemy, God's angels protect the children of God.

The Bible says, "Because thou hast made the Lord, which is my refuge, even the most High, thy habitation; There shall no evil befall thee, neither shall any plague come nigh thy dwelling. For he shall give his angels charge over thee, to keep thee in all your ways (Psalms 91:9-11)." There is a place in God where the devil, the forces of darkness, including plagues cannot terrorize you.

I have experienced the presence of angels. During the summer of 2010, my son, L.G., and I were preparing to cook hamburgers and hotdogs on the grill on the back patio. L.G was 6 years old. As I lit the grill, flames of fire blew out like a flame-thrower hitting L.G directly in the face. L.G started screaming. I knew he was hurt because I saw the fire hit him directly in the face including his eyes, nose, and mouth. I immediately ran into the kitchen and placed cold water on his face. I feared the worst. I knew his face would receive some form of degree burns. I was convinced he would be permanently scarred. He would have facial burn scars for the rest of his life, due to his father's negligence in safety. My wife and I rushed him to the emergency room. The doctor examined L.G. and found no signs of scar tissues or any indication of burns. I believe, without a doubt, that a guardian angel protected L.G. from harm! God has placed fourth dimensional beings, called heavenly angels, to guard, protect, and shield us from harm in the third dimension.

An even greater illustration of guardian angels as protectors of men can be found in 2 Kings Chapter 6. During the times of the kings of Israel, the man of God Elisha was the target of a diabolical Syrian attack. The king of Syria had previously discovered that the prophet Elisha was the one who was revealing his plans of attack against the king of Israel (2 Kings 6:8-10). The enemy, inspired by the devil, was sent to seize Elisha from Dothan. The king of Syrian sent thousands of horses, chariots, and armed soldiers to retrieve one man. The Bible says that the Syrian army compassed the entire city. Second Kings 6:14-17 says,

> *Therefore sent he [the king of Syria] thither horses, and chariots, and a great host: and they came by night, and compassed the city about. And when the servant of the man of God was risen early, and gone forth, behold an host compassed the city both with horses and chariots. And his servants said unto him, Alas, my master! How shall we do? And he answered, Fear not: they that be with us are more than*

they that be with them. And Elisha prayed, and said,
Lord, I pray thee, open his eyes, that he may see.
And the Lord opened the eyes of the young man; and
he saw: and, behold, the mountain was full of horses,
and chariots of fire around about Elisha.

The army of Syria invaded Israel to abduct the prophet Elisha by military force. However, things did not go as the Syrian army had planned. Unbeknownst to the army of Syria, there was the unseen [physical] presence of a military battalion of angels, not only in the city of Dothan, but the angels of God covered the entire region, even the mountains of Israel.

God sent an entire battalion of angels to protect His servant Elisha. God will do the same for us. Angels of the Lord were waiting for the Assyrian army to make one charge against the house of Elisha. However, instead of the Syrian army being annihilated by the angelic forces, the prophet Elisha prayed that the men be struck with blindness. Elisha's petition was granted (2 Kings 6:18). Therefore, the army of Syria was spared due to the intercession of Elisha.

Angels have been placed on assignment from God in the earth. They have a distinct mission. The mission of angels is to protect the intergalactic security of heaven and the church on the earth. They assist in providing intelligence, law enforcement, and judicial support. Their mission is to protect and defend the Word of God, the gospel, and salvation against terrorists, attacks, and threats of the enemy. Most importantly, angels are sworn to protect those who are heirs of salvation in the fourth dimension.

Holy Spirit

Holy Spirit, what love I have found in You,

Holy Spirit, sent from heaven's blessed truth;

Holy Spirit, we know who You are,

Holy Spirit, the presence of God near and far;

Holy Spirit, dwell in my soul,

Holy Spirit, You're all-knowing from the days of old;

Holy Spirit, my eyes are on You,

Holy Spirit, Jesus' gift sent so true.

CHAPTER 42

Conclusion

God has never left us or forsaken us, not even for a moment. Although sin has separated us from God, His angels are a constant reminder of His abiding presence, security, and love.

Deuteronomy 31:6 says, "Be strong and of a good courage, fear not, nor be afraid of them: for the Lord thy God, he it is that doth go with thee; he will not fail thee, nor forsake thee." God has never left us alone or without divine protection.

From the beginning of time, God has had ways and means to stay connected to His prized creation–man. God has given us special access to him, through different portals, modes, and channels. These pathways of communication to God include, but not limited to, dreams, visions, angels, our hearts, His Word, and the Holy Spirit.

Dreams convey meanings. Dreams are like parables whose origin is from a spiritual dimension. Although the Old Testament is filled with men whom God communicated with through dreams and visions, dreams and visions are not limited to the Old Testament.

On a roof top while waiting for food to be prepared, Peter became hungry. While praying, he fell into a trance. He saw the sky open and something like a large linen sheet was lowered by its four corners to the ground. In the sheet were all kinds of four-footed animals, reptiles, and birds. God spoke to him and said get up kill and eat. Peter answered and said he could not do that, for he had never eaten anything that is impure or unclean. God's response to him was what He has cleansed do not call unclean (Acts 10:9-15).

God spoke to Peter in a [trance-like] vision. A trance is a half-conscious state. Peter had a vision in which God commanded and instructed him to share the gospel with all people regardless of their nationality or ethnicity.

God speaks to us often through a myriad of channels. Many individuals have often complained that God never speaks to them. Not realizing how many times, in a single day, God has attempted to communicate and gain their attention.

Communication is designed to build relationships. God desires to know us and for us to know Him in a personal and direct way. We have been given much at our disposal as it relates to communicating with God and He with us. God uses different modes of communication to shows us who He is, His nature, and character.

Oftentimes, God uses His angels. Angels are servants of God, not man. Angels act and are motivated based on the Word of God. Angels do not take orders from man's word, only God's Word.

Angels are God's messengers. He uses angels to communicate with us. They are the main navigators of the fourth dimension to the third dimension. Angels transport messages and communicate to men on the earth the instructions of God.

Furthermore, angels are our personal bodyguards, employed of God to protect and escort us everywhere we go. Psalms 91:11 says, "For he [God] shall give his angels charge over thee, to keep thee in all thy ways."

Angels also transport and accompany our prayers from the third dimension to the fourth dimension in heaven. Even our prayers are protected. Angels are the "taxi drivers" who travel back and forth from the heavenly realm to the earthly dimension, carrying special cargo of the prayers of the saints.

Prayers of the saints are one of the most powerful and precious gifts we can give God on the earth. Prayers are more than petitions and request of man.

Many all ready know that our requests are granted through prayers. The Bible clearly states, "Don't worry about anything; instead, pray about everything. Tell God what you need, and thank him for all he has done" (Philippians 4:6, NLT). The Apostle James tells us further that, "...The effectual fervent prayer of a righteous man availeth much."

However, not only are prayers beneficial to man, but God honors our prayers. To God, prayers are eternal gifts which are presented to God in heaven. Prayers are illustrated in the Bible as "golden vials" of incense (Revelation 5:8). Our prayers ascend up before the throne of God as sweet-smelling incense. When we get to heaven, every prayer we ever prayed will be revealed in golden vials of incense. No prayer is ever wasted.

The fourth dimension is our MOD, Mode of Operation. Jesus is our prime example of the way we must live. Jesus lived and operated outside the confines of the third dimension, in the fourth dimension. Jesus walked on water, calmed raging storms, healed all infirmities, fed thousands of people, and raised the dead. He refused to be governed by the laws of the third dimension.

God is calling us to leave the third dimension of the senses and dwell in the "Promised Land" of faith. The third dimension is the world of the senses: taste, touch, sight, hearing, and smell. The senses limit your capabilities to the third dimensional world. The fourth dimension is not governed by the senses; it is governed by faith.

Faith represents the "gravity" of the fourth dimension. In the third dimension, gravity is the prevailing force that makes the earth and its surroundings viable and suitable for life. Likewise, faith is the fundamental attribute that sustains the fourth dimensional world.

Faith in God is the "life force" which makes operating and functioning in the fourth dimension possible. Hebrews 11:6 (NIV) says, "And without faith it is impossible to please God, because anyone who comes to him must believe that he exists and that he rewards those who earnestly seek him."

Many of us have been living in a maze all our lives. We travel only so far and hit a dead end because we are being governed by our senses instead of our faith. It is like we are living in a maze. We continuously turn left, right, or go back to where we started, only to hit another dead end. However, God wants us to step out of the third dimensional maze and enter into the fourth dimension of breakthrough and deliverance.

Furthermore, we have an adversary who does not want us to know and understand that we can operate on a higher dimension than what we can physically see. He constantly opposes our faith in God.

In fact, satan will not allow us to enter the fourth dimension, the place of supernatural miracles, without resistance. When you desire to enter the fourth dimension, you will experience turbulence; the enemy will fight you all the way to the door step of the fourth dimension to keep you from reaching your destiny.

Many have given up at the threshold of entering the fourth dimension. However, if they would have taken another step of faith in their pursuance of God, unprecedented victory would have been achieved. They would have entered the fourth dimension, a realm which would have far exceeded their wildest expectations.

Imagine traveling 340 miles per second, the speed of sound. To break the sound barrier, you will have to go beyond 340 miles per second. When a pilot in an aircraft reaches the sound barrier, there is a great turbulence and shaking of the aircraft. Many pilots have recorded that the plane's glass instrument panels have broken due to such turbulence.

However, when the pilot reaches over 340 miles per second, the turbulence ceases. This is referred to as supersonic flight. When the aircraft accelerates beyond the speed of sound, the aircraft will level out and become serene. All turbulence and resistance which was imposed on the aircraft ceases. In other words, the aircraft has broken the sound barrier and has moved into another dimension.

Before reaching the fourth dimension, you will experience turbulence. In other words, satan will violently oppose and attempt to keep you from leaving the world of the senses to the world of the spirit. However, once you step across the barrier from the third dimension to the fourth dimension, you will reach a level of supernatural dimensions never experienced before.

All believers in Christ are now traveling down the road to the fourth dimension. When you reach the level of the fourth dimension, you would have reached a level beyond the natural into the supernatural. You shall experience calmness, peace, and tranquility never experienced. This is the place God has for you. You are in the fourth dimension zone. The Bible says in Job 3:17, "There the wicked cease from troubling; and there the weary be at rest."

Trouble and turmoil can't affect you in the fourth dimension. You are about to break the "natural" barrier and enter into the "supernatural" realm of the fourth dimension where supernatural provision and prosperity await you!

It is God's desire that we prosper. Righteousness and obedience put us in line to receive prosperity. The Word of God says in Job 36:11-12, "If they obey and serve him [God], they shall spend their days in prosperity, and their years in pleasure. But if they obey not, they shall perish by the sword, and they shall die without knowledge."

It is God's will to prosper every believer. The Bible says in Psalms 35:27, "Let them shout for joy, and be glad, that favour my righteous cause: yea, let them say continually, Let the Lord be magnified, which hath pleasure in the prosperity of his servant." God takes great pleasure in your prosperity. He wants you to know how much He wants you blessed and whole.

God has given many channels, modes, and passageways to travel to the fourth dimension. Some day soon, we will see God face to face. 1 John 3:2 says, "Beloved, now are we the sons of God, and it doth not yet appear what we shall be: but we know that, when he shall appear, we shall be like him; for we shall see him as he is."

Take a leap of faith from the third dimension to the fourth dimension. You will never be the same again. The Holy Spirit, the chief communicator of God, is inviting you to allow Him to come into your heart. God uses the heart of man as a dimensional portal so that He can enter and dwell with us.

Moreover, the Holy Spirit wants to give you a heart replacement. Before real change can occur, the old heart must be replaced. God said, "I will give you a new heart and put a new spirit in you; I will remove from you your heart of stone and give you a heart of flesh" (Ezekiel 36:26, NIV).

Become a new heart recipient today. David prayed that God would create a new heart in him. He cried unto God saying, "Create in me a clean heart, O God; and renew a right spirit within me" (Psalms 51:10).

Only with a new heart can we clearly hear from God. God is ready and wants to speak with you. Surrender and let the Holy Spirit take you where only angels tread, the place called the fourth dimension.

Holy Spirit

Holy Spirit, through dreams and visions we now see Him,

Holy Spirit, loved ones gone on before we see them;

Holy Spirit, but one day we shall behold His face,

Holy Spirit, when Christ returns to take His rightful place;

Holy Spirit, never to leave His presence again,

Holy Spirit, for in the fourth dimension You already knew when;

Holy Spirit, living with Jehovah, 100 is our score,

Holy Spirit, by closing the book of life, time will be no more.

About the Author

Dr. Leslie Gamble Jr., a man who lives a "Faith Proven" life, has been ordained by God. His heart, mind, and soul are focused on winning more and more souls to the Kingdom of God through Christ. Dr. Gamble welcomes the invitation of the Holy Spirit and His Word of knowledge flows from the heart of God. He has lived a life from faith to faith and from glory to glory. His life proves every faithful Word of God is true.

The Life of Joseph in the Bible has been the life of Dr. Gamble. God made Joseph a promise, and God made Dr. Gamble a promise. Now he writes, preaches, teaches, speaks the faith of God and lives in the abundance of Christ.

Dr. Leslie Gamble Jr. is a graduate of Georgia Southern University with a Doctorate in Education Administration. Dr. Gamble is the emeritus pastor of Scurry Spring Baptist Church in Chappells, South Carolina. He is a spiritual mentor, advisor, and leader to World-Awakening Ministry. You may find many of his sermons, messages, prayers, and poems @ www.World-Awakening.com.

Dr. Gamble has taught for seven years in the public schools in the state of Georgia with additional years in the state of Alabama. He has been an elementary school teacher, middle school teacher, and high school teacher. Dr. Gamble has also been an assistant administrator at L.B.C Middle School in Warrenville, South Carolina. He is a former assistant principal, associate principal, and principal of Emerald High School in South Carolina. He is the son of Mr. and Mrs. Leslie Gamble Sr. of Mobile, Alabama. If you would like Dr. Les Gamble to speak at your church, seminar, convention, or convocation, you may e-mail him at Dr.LesGambleJR@yahoo.com.

OTHER BOOKS BY
DR. LESLIE GAMBLE, JR.

THE FOURTH DIMENSION SERIES
reveals the hidden mysteries of
the Kingdom of Heaven.

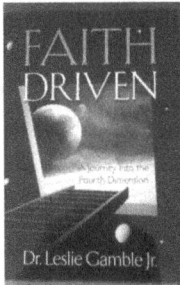

FAITH DRIVEN–A Journey Into the
Fourth Dimension

This book will challenge you to journey beyond the limitations of our three-dimensional world of time, space, and matter into the realm of the supernatural–the real where God dwells. It will set you free from the violence, anger, and strife of this world and usher you into God's peace, strength, courage, and fortitude–a life that is more real than anything you've ever experienced on planet Earth. $23.99, plus shipping. Hardback.

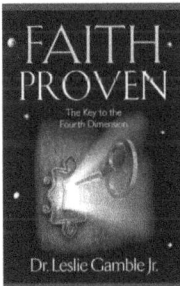

FAITH PROVEN–The Key to the Fourth
Dimension

This book is intended not only to encourage, inspire, and motivate the reader, but also to admonish that faith is stronger than fear. Faith opens the door to the supernatural. Miracles and supernatural breakthroughs only come through faith in God. You do not have to be afraid, stressed out or worried about tomorrow. $13.99, plus shipping. Trade paper.

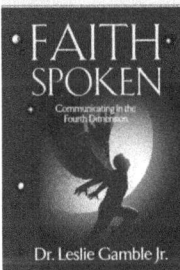

FAITH SPOKEN–Communicating in the
Fourth Dimension

Dr. Gamble expounds on communication in the Fourth Dimension–the supernatural realm of God. God uses many modes to communicate with His people. This book highlights those many modes which includes dreams, visions, and angels. You will experience an exciting adventure in learning to live the life of faith. $24.99, plus shipping. Hardback.

AVAILABLE AT YOUR LOCAL BOOKSTORE & ONLINE

www.ingramcontent.com/pod-product-compliance
Lightning Source LLC
Chambersburg PA
CBHW060656150426
42813CB00070B/3413/J